The Best Buddhist Writing 2004

THE BEST BUDDHIST WRITING 2004

Edited by Melvin McLeod
and the Editors of the *Shambhala Sun*

SHAMBHALA
Boston & London • 2004

Shambhala Publications, Inc.
Horticultural Hall
300 Massachusetts Avenue
Boston, Massachusetts 02115
www.shambhala.com

9 8 7 6 5 4 3 2 1

First Edition
Printed in the United States of America

♾ This edition is printed on acid-free paper that meets the American National Standards Institute z39.48 Standard.
Distributed in the United States by Random House, Inc., and in Canada by Random House of Canada Ltd

Library of Congress Cataloging-in-Publication Data
The best Buddhist writing 2004: edited by Melvin McLeod and the editors of the *Shambhala sun.*—1st ed.
p. cm.
ISBN 1-59030-189-7 (pbk.: alk. paper)
1. Buddhism. I. Title: Best Buddhist writing two thousand four.
II. McLeod, Melvin. III. Shambhala sun.
BQ4022.B49 2004
294.3—dc22
2004007934

Contents

Introduction

Here's how far Buddhism has come from just a few decades ago, when it had a relative handful of American adherents: Now there's a whole book of the best Buddhist writing—for just one year.

Of course, as far back as the Beat poets in the 1950s Buddhism has attracted some very talented people, people whose deeply questioning spirit made them cultural leaders. But today, Buddhism's insight, practices, and philosophy are having a wide impact on Western culture and thought. The range of issues touched on in this collection is proof of that—as well as that Buddhism continues to attract excellent writers and insightful thinkers.

Mind you, even today Buddhism's influence on North American culture far exceeds the number of actual practitioners. No one has a precise figure, but there are certainly no more than a few hundred thousand Western, or "convert," Buddhists in North America (as opposed to those whose roots are in traditionally Buddhist countries). Yet key Buddhist concepts and practices such as mindfulness, awareness, emptiness, and loving-kindness have become familiar to spiritual practitioners of all persuasions. His Holiness the Dalai Lama may be the most positively viewed religious leader in the world today. The Buddha is widely accepted, even by those who know little or nothing of Buddhism, as one of the greatest religious figures in world history and someone we would all do well to emulate.

Buddhism's influence in American society goes beyond the spiritual realm. In the cultural sphere, many important writers, artists, poets, actors, and directors have been influenced by

Buddhism or are serious practitioners. There are books and annual conferences considering the influence of Buddhism on Western psychology (for what, after all, is Buddhism but a twenty-five-hundred-year study of the nature of mind). In the hard sciences, physicists are exploring the common ground between Western science's most advanced theories and the way Buddhism has long described the nature of reality. In the helping professions, Buddhists are influencing the way we assist those in need and make peace among people who are in conflict. Buddhists are fundamentally changing the way we care for the sick and the dying.

These are all very good things—but they're not what Buddhism is finally about. Yes, Buddhism is the ultimate utilitarian religion, but it applies itself to the fundamental questions of existence: What is the cause of human suffering and its solution? What is the final nature of reality? What is the essence of mind? What happens to us after death? These are the mysteries Buddhism seeks to penetrate, the profound questions that make Buddhism a religion rather than a mere philosophy of life. It is no coincidence that two of the articles in this book have the word "radical" in their titles. These are radical questions Buddhism poses, and the answers it offers are equally radical—just consider its assertion that we do not really exist.

In this book, we find Buddhism itself—the religion and its practices—and also the many ways it has been utilized and adapted in modern life. We hear of the ways it has changed people's lives deeply—and how it could help change the world for the better.

Some of the selections in this book are Buddhist teachings delivered in the traditional style—as a teacher's discourse delivered to the students. For twenty-five hundred years Buddhist teachers have been offering the same great truths, but expressing them in many different styles and languages. Buddhism is renowned for the skill with which it adapts to the needs of each particular time and culture, and here we find teachings reflecting our place and time. They reflect the approaches of different Asian traditions—Theravada, Zen, and Vajrayana—blending with the emerging American style, proudly represented here by some of the outstanding Westerners who are now Buddhist teachers in their own right.

The irony, of course, is that all these words, no matter how skillful, merely aim us toward truths that are ungraspable by intellect. The essence of Buddhism is not in words but in lives lived. So, many of the most powerful selections in this anthology are personal stories. They are told by middle-aged people, punks, mothers, monks, cooks, and cancer patients. The stories are moving, funny, sharp, sweet, sad, insightful, and tender. They touch on how we relate to nature, illness, children, addictions, and enlightenment. They have a power beyond the best philosophy—the power of the heart—and the simple truthfulness of people talking honestly about what Buddhism has meant to their lives.

Because Buddhism aims not at heaven but at a transformed life here on earth, it has always been applicable to everyday life. In fact, it has never been separate from it. We find good counsel in this book, arising from wise people's Buddhist practice and applied to our real lives in this society. We discover that because Buddhism analyses the causes of our problems so accurately, it is very effective in offering specific techniques to make life better for ourselves and those around us.

Finally, Buddhism is compelled to address issues of politics, justice, and war and peace, because they are the cause of great suffering. To a politics based on anger, greed, and selfishness, Buddhism responds with a view of the world based on compassion, egolessness, and love. If we begin with these in our hearts and apply them with skill, we could end with a better world.

It's an odd conceit, this "best Buddhist writing." Certainly there is terrific writing in this book, pleasurable, well-crafted, and entertaining. But this isn't a book in which the emphasis is just on the quality of the writing. It's equally on the depth of insight being presented and how it can help us in our lives. Maybe that's always the definition of the best writing—yes, we enjoy and admire it, but more importantly, it changes the way we see the world and the way we live. Reading these articles, I have been moved and changed. I very much hope this book does the same for you.

To select the best Buddhist writing for this book, I have surveyed English-language books, magazines, journals, and Web sites published and widely available in North America during the calendar year 2003. In my job as editor-in-chief of the *Shambhala Sun* and of *Buddhadharma: The Practitioner's Quarterly*, I am familiar with most of the Buddhist writing being published, and I feel I have been generally successful in considering likely candidates for inclusion. If I have missed worthy material for this anthology I apologize, and I urge publishers and writers to contact me about books or articles which they would like considered for next year's anthology.

I would like to thank my good friend Peter Turner, president of Shambhala Publications, for conceiving this anthology and asking me to edit it. Shambhala's Beth Frankl has been a supportive and professional editor. The founder of Shambhala Publications, Sam Bercholz, has for a long time been a friend and guide. As much as anyone he is the founder of Buddhist publishing in North America, and the fine quality of writing in this book is in a real way his legacy. I would also like to thank the authors and publishers who have granted me permission to use their material in this anthology. The world of Buddhist publishing today—periodicals, specialty Buddhist publishers, and mainstream publishers with Buddhist titles—offers high-quality Buddhist writing for both the beginner and the serious practitioner.

I would like to thank all my colleagues at the *Shambhala Sun* and its sister publication, *Buddhadharma: The Practitioner's Quarterly*. In particular, the knowledge, insight, and experience of our excellent editorial department—Barry Boyce, Andrea McQuillin, Tynette Deveaux, Trish Deitch Rohrer, and Jeff Pardy—is reflected in the choices that make up this anthology. A special thanks to Jim Gimian, publisher of the *Shambhala Sun*, who is for me a friend, a partner, and a teacher. And finally, I thank my wife Pamela Rubin, and my young daughter Pearl, who provides the motive and inspiration for my work—the hope of contributing even a little so she can live in a saner and better world.

Melvin McLeod
Editor-in-chief
Shambhala Sun
Buddhadharma: The Practitioner's Quarterly

The Man Who Woke Up

Huston Smith and Philip Novak

Unique among the world's major religions, Buddhism started with a single person's path to awakening. Prince Siddhartha's journey is one any of us can take—seeing our suffering, analyzing its cause, discovering there is a way to end suffering, and following the path to enlightenment. Here Huston Smith, dean of comparative religion in America, and his collaborator Philip Novak offer us a wonderful narrative of the life of the Buddha.

Buddhism begins with a man. In his later years, when India was afire with Siddhartha Gautama's message and kings themselves were bowing before him, people came to him even as they were to come to Jesus asking what he was. How many people have provoked this question?—not "Who are you?" with respect to name, origin, or ancestry, but "*What* are you? What order of being do you belong to? What species do you represent?" Not Caesar, certainly. Not Napoleon, or even Socrates. Only two: Jesus and Buddha. When the people carried their puzzlement to the Buddha himself, the answer he gave provided an identity for his entire message:

"Are you a god?" they asked.
"No."
"An angel?"
"No,"
"A saint?"
"No."
"Then what are you?"
Buddha answered, "I am awake."

His answer became his title, for this is what "Buddha" means. The Sanskrit root *budh* denotes both "to wake up" and "to know." Buddha, then, means the "Enlightened One," or the "Awakened One." While the rest of the world was wrapped in the womb of sleep, dreaming a dream known as the waking state of human life, one of their number roused himself. Buddhism begins with a man who shook off the daze, the doze, the dreamlike vagaries of ordinary awareness. It begins with a man who woke up.

His life has become encased in loving legend. We are told that the worlds were flooded with light at his birth. The blind so longed to see his glory that they received their sight; the deaf and mute conversed in ecstasy of the things that were to come. Crooked became straight; the lame walked. Prisoners were freed from their chains, and the fires of hell were quenched. Even the cries of the beasts were hushed as peace encircled the earth. Only Mara, the Evil One, did not rejoice.

The historical facts of his life are roughly these: He was born around 563 B.C.E. in what is now Nepal, near the Indian border. His full name was Siddhartha Gautama of the Sakyas. Siddhartha was his given name, Gautama his surname, and Sakya the name of the clan to which his family belonged. His father was a king, but as there were then many kingdoms in the subcontinent of India, it would be more accurate to think of him as a feudal lord. By the standards of the day Siddhartha's upbringing was luxurious. "I was delicate, O monks, excessively delicate. I wore garments of silk and my attendants held a white umbrella over me. My unguents were always from Banaras." He appears to have been exceptionally handsome, for there are numerous scriptural references to "the perfection of his visible body." At sixteen he married a neighboring princess, Yasodhara, who bore a son whom they called Rahula.

He was, in short, a man who seemed to have everything: family, "the venerable Gautama is well born on both sides, of pure descent"; fine appearance, "handsome, inspiring trust, gifted with great beauty of complexion, fair in color, fine in presence, stately to behold"; wealth, "he had elephants and silver ornaments for his elephants." He had a model wife, "majestic as a queen of heaven, constant ever, cheerful night and day, full of dignity and exceeding grace," who bore him a beautiful son. In addition, as heir to his father's throne, he was destined for fame and power.

Despite all this there settled over him in his twenties a discontent that was to lead to a complete break with his worldly estate. The source of his discontent is impounded in the legend of the Four Passing Sights, one of the most celebrated calls to adventure in all world literature. When Siddhartha was born, so this story runs, his father summoned fortune-tellers to find out what the future held for his heir. All agreed that this was no usual child. His career, however, was crossed with one ambiguity. If he remained within the world, he would unify India and become its greatest conqueror, a *Chakravartin* ("Wheel-Turner"), or Universal King. If, on the other hand, he forsook the world, he would become not a world conqueror, but a world redeemer. Faced with this option, his father determined to steer his son toward the former destiny. No effort was spared to keep the prince attached to the world. Three palaces and forty thousand dancing girls were placed at his disposal; strict orders were given that no ugliness intrude upon the courtly pleasures. Specifically, the prince was to be shielded from contact with sickness, decrepitude, and death; even when he went riding, runners were to clear the roads of these sights.

One day, however, an old man was overlooked, or (as some versions have it) miraculously incarnated by the gods to effect the needed lesson: a man decrepit, broken-toothed, gray-haired, crooked and bent of body, leaning on a staff, and trembling. That day Siddhartha learned the fact of old age. Though the king extended his guard, on a second ride Siddhartha encountered a body racked with disease, lying by the roadside; and on a third journey, a corpse. Finally, on a fourth occasion he saw a monk with shaven head, ochre robe, and bowl, and on that day he learned of the life of withdrawal from the world in search of freedom. It is a legend, this story, but like all legends it embodies an important truth, for the teachings of the Buddha show unmistakably that it was the body's inescapable involvement with disease, decrepitude, and death that made him despair of finding fulfillment on the physical plane. "Life is subject to age and death. Where is the realm of life in which there is neither age nor death?"

Once he had perceived the inevitability of bodily pain and passage, fleshly pleasures lost their charm. The singsong of the dancing girls, the lilt of lutes and cymbals, the sumptuous feasts and processions, the elaborate celebration of festivals only mocked his brooding mind. Flowers nodding in the sunshine and snows melting on the Himalayas cried louder of the evanescence of worldly things. He determined to quit the snare of distractions his palace had become and follow the call of a truth-seeker. One night in his twenty-ninth year he made the break, his Great Going Forth. Making his way in the post-midnight hours to where his wife and son were locked in sleep, he bade them both a silent good-bye, and then ordered the gatekeeper to bridle his great white horse.

The two mounted and rode off toward the forest. Reaching its edge at daybreak, Gautama changed clothes with the attendant, who returned with the horse to break the news. "Tell my father," said Gautama,

> that there is no reason he should grieve. He will perhaps say it was too early for me to leave for the forest. But even if affection should prevent me from leaving my family just now of my own accord, in due course death would tear us apart, and in that we would have

> no say. Birds settle on a tree for a while, and then go their separate ways again. The meeting of all living beings must likewise inevitably end in their parting. This world passes away and disappoints the hopes of everlasting attachment. It is therefore unwise to have a sense of ownership for people who are united with us as in a dream—for a short while only and not in fact.

Then Gautama shaved his head and, "clothed in ragged raiment," plunged into the forest in search of enlightenment.

Six years followed, during which his full energies were concentrated toward this end. "How hard to live the life of the lonely forest dweller, to rejoice in solitude. Verily, the silent groves bear heavily upon the monk who has not yet won to fixity of mind!" The words bear poignant witness that his search was not easy. It appears to have moved through three phases, without record as to how long each lasted or how sharply the three were divided. His first act was to seek out two of the foremost Hindu masters of the day and pick their minds for the wisdom in their vast tradition. He learned a great deal—about *raja yoga,* the yoga of meditation, especially, but about Hindu philosophy as well; so much in fact that Hindus came to claim him as their own, holding that his criticisms of the religion of his day were in the order of reforms and were less important than his agreements. In time, however, having mastered the deepest mystical states his teachers knew, he concluded that these yogis could teach him nothing more.

His next step was to join a band of ascetics and give their way an honest try. Was it his body that was holding him back? He would break its power and crush its interference. A man of enormous willpower, the Buddha-to-be outdid his associates in every austerity they proposed. He ate so little—six grains of rice a day during one of his fasts—that "when I thought I would touch the skin of my stomach I actually took hold of my spine." He would clench his teeth and press his tongue to his palate until "sweat flowed from my armpits." He would hold his breath until it felt "as if a strap were being twisted around my head." In the end he grew so weak that he fell into a faint; and if a passing cowherdess had not stopped to feed him some warm rice gruel, he could easily have died.

This experience taught him the futility of asceticism. He had given this experiment all anyone could, and it had not succeeded—it had not brought enlightenment. But negative experiments carry their own lessons, and in this case asceticism's failure provided Gautama with the first constructive plank for his program: the principle of the Middle Way between the extremes of asceticism, on the one hand, and indulgence, on the other. It is the concept of the rationed life, in which the body is given what it needs to function optimally, but no more.

The experience also took his memory back to a day in his youth when, having wandered deep into the countryside, he sat down, quiet and alone, beneath an apple tree. The exertions of a farmer plowing a distant field bespoke the eternity of labor necessary to wrest sustenance from the earth. The sun's slow, ceaseless passage across the sky betokened the countless creatures in the air, on the earth, and under the ground that would soon perish. As he reflected steadily on life's impermanence, his mind opened onto a new state of lucid equanimity. It was now calm and pliable, and the clarity of its seeing was marred by neither elation nor sorrow. It was his first deep meditation—not an otherworldly trance, but a clear and steady seeing of the way things are. And more, it was accomplished in the normal conditions of life without needing to subject the body to starvation.

Having turned his back on mortification, Gautama now devoted the final phase of his quest to a combination of rigorous thought and deep concentration. One evening near Gaya in northeast India, south of the present city of Patna, he sat down under a peepul tree that has come to be known as the Bo Tree (short for *bodhi*, "enlightenment"). The place was later named the Immovable Spot, for tradition reports that the Buddha, sensing that a breakthrough was near, seated himself that epoch-making evening vowing not to arise until he was enlightened.

The records offer as the first event of the night a temptation scene reminiscent of Jesus' on the eve of his ministry. The Evil One, realizing that his antagonist's success was imminent, rushed to the spot to disrupt his concentrations. He attacked first in the form of Kama, the God of Desire, parading three voluptuous women with their tempting retinues. When the Buddha-to-be remained unmoved, the Tempter switched his guise to that of Mara, the Lord of Death. His powerful hosts assailed the aspirant with hurricanes, torrential rains, and showers of flaming rocks, but Gautama had so emptied himself of his finite self that the weapons found no target to strike and turned into flower petals as they entered his field of concentration. When, in final desperation, Mara challenged his right to do what he was doing, Gautama touched the earth with his right fingertip, whereupon the earth responded, "I bear you witness," with a hundred, a thousand, and a hundred thousand thunderous roars. Mara's army fled in rout, and the gods of heaven descended in rapture to tend the victor with garlands and perfumes.

Thereafter, while the Bo Tree rained red blossoms that full-mooned night, Gautama's meditation steadily deepened. During the first watch of the night, Gautama saw, one by one, his many thousands of previous lifetimes. During the second watch, his vision widened. It surveyed the death and rebirth of the whole universe of living beings and noted the ubiquitous sway of the law of karma—that good actions lead to happy rebirths, bad actions to miserable ones. During the third watch, Gautama saw what made the whole thing go: the universal law of causal interdependence. He called it *dependent arising*, and later identified it as the very heart of his message. Thus armed, he made quick work of the last shreds of ignorant clinging that bound him to the wheel of birth and death.

As the morning star glittered in the transparent sky of the east, his mind pierced at last the bubble of the universe and shattered it to naught, only, wonder of wonders, to find it miraculously restored with the effulgence of true being. The Great Awakening had occurred. Freedom was his. His being was transformed, and he emerged the Buddha. From the center of his joy came a song of spiritual victory:

> Through many a birth I wandered in this world,
> Seeking in vain the builder of this house.
> Unfulfilling it is to be born again and again!
>
> O housemaker! Now I have seen you!
> You shall build no more houses for me!
> Your beams are broken,
> Your ridgepole is shattered
> My mind is free from all past conditionings.

The event had cosmic import. All created things filled the morning air with their rejoicings, and the earth quaked six ways with wonder. Ten thousand galaxies shuddered in awe as lotuses bloomed on every tree, turning the entire universe into "a bouquet of flowers set whirling through the air." The bliss of this vast experience kept the Buddha rooted to the spot for seven entire days. On the eighth he tried to rise, but another wave of bliss broke over him. For a total of forty-nine days he was lost in rapture, after which his "glorious glance" opened onto the world.

Mara was waiting for him again with one last temptation. He appealed this time to what had always been Gautama's strong point, his reason. Mara did not argue the burden of reentering the world, with its banalities and obsessions. He posed a deeper challenge. Who could be expected to understand truth as profound as that which he, the Buddha, had laid hold of? How could speech-defying revelation be compressed into words, or visions that shatter definitions be caged in language? In short, how to show what can only be found; teach what can only be learned? Why bother to play the idiot before an uncomprehending audience? Why not wash one's hands of the whole hot world, be done with the body and slip at once into *nirvana,* the blissful state of liberation from the cycle of death and rebirth? The argument was so pervasive that it almost carried the day. At length, however, the Buddha answered, "There will be some whose eyes are only slightly dimmed by dust, and they will understand." With this, Mara was banished from his life forever.

Nearly half a century followed, during which the Buddha trudged the dusty paths of India preaching his ego-shattering, life-redeeming message until his hair was white, step infirm, and body nothing but a burst drum. He founded an order of monks and nuns—now the oldest historical institution on our planet—challenged the deadness of a society forged by the dominating *brahmins* (the Hindu priestly caste), and accepted in return the resentment, queries, and bewilderment his stance provoked. His daily routine was staggering. In addition to training monks and overseeing the affairs of his order, he maintained an interminable schedule of public preaching and private counseling, advising the perplexed, encouraging the faithful, and comforting the distressed. "To him people come right across the country from distant lands to ask questions, and he bids all welcome." Underlying his response to these pressures and enabling him to stand up under them was the pattern of withdrawal and return that is basic to all creativity. The Buddha withdrew for six years; then returned for forty-five. But each year was likewise divided: nine months in the world, followed by a three-month retreat with his monks during the rainy season. His daily cycle, too, was patterned to this mold. His public hours were long, but three times a day he withdrew, to return his attention (through meditation) to its sacred source.

After an arduous ministry of forty-five years, at the age of eighty and around the year 483 B.C.E., the Buddha died from dysentery after eating a meal of dried boar's flesh in the home of Cunda the Smith. Even on his deathbed his mind moved toward others. In the midst of his pain, it occurred to him that Cunda might feel responsible for his death. His last request, therefore, was that Cunda be informed that of all the meals he had eaten during his long life, only two stood out as having blessed him exceptionally. One was the meal whose strength had enabled him to reach enlightenment under the Bo Tree, and the other the one that was opening to him the final gates to nirvana. The many who approached his deathbed unable to contain their tears he chastised gently: "In the hour of joy, it is not proper to grieve." These are but two of the scenes that *The Book of the Great Decease* has preserved. Together they present a picture of a man who passed into the state in which "ideas and consciousness cease to be" without the slightest resistance. Two sentences from his valedictory have echoed through the ages: "All compounded things decay. Work out your own salvation with diligence."

This Is It

Aram Saroyan

Enlightenment is not especially a Buddhist experience. It can't be labeled at all. It's something that happens all the time, in small ways and sometimes big ways, to many kinds of people. Aram Saroyan wrote an essay on this ordinary experience that changes our lives, if only we pay attention. I think when you read it, you'll realize it's happened to you, too.

When I was in high school at Trinity in New York, and during the years I sporadically attended several colleges, I had a number of experiences that I recognize today were as important, as formative, as anything that occurred in the classroom, and probably more so. I came across a book by Alan Watts when I was going to Trinity called *This Is It*. In the title essay, Watts discusses moments, common to people all over the world and throughout recorded time, in which one perceives that one is a part of some larger whole. I found the book tonic for my own development, confirmation of experience I'd known but never discussed or heard discussed.

If a man or a woman, you or I, walks outside the house on a particular day and experiences a sense of this oneness—a very reassuring perception in the several instances I recall in my own life—this isn't something that will be the subject of a discussion on *Nightline* or Charlie Rose. Nor is it likely to be covered by any print media, not even *The Star* or *The Enquirer*. Watts quotes the following paragraph from *Sketch for a Self-Portrait* by Bernard Berenson, with the prefatory remark that it is "one of the simplest and 'cleanest' accounts of it I have ever seen":

> It was a morning in early summer. A silver haze shimmered and trembled over the lime trees. The air was laden with their fragrance. The temperature was like a caress. I remember—I need not recall—that I climbed up a tree stump and felt suddenly immersed in Itness. I did not call it by that name. I had no need for words. It and I were one.

An essentially nonverbal experience of this kind became the subject of one of my first poems, and an ongoing touchstone of my practice as a poet. I'm not sure what year this happened. I still may have been going to Trinity. That seems the most likely scenario because it takes place at the bus stop on the corner of Madison Avenue and 79th Street, where I used to wait in the late afternoon for the crosstown bus to take home to West End Avenue, after an hour or two of after-school revelry at Stark's coffee shop on 78th Street and Madison.

At a Bus Stop
I turned to
an accumulation of women

the instant
a break

the light was so clear
the forms

that instant
exceeded names

outsped
the words

which
follow

follow slowly
like thunder

its lights

Years later I came across a line in a book by Krishnamurti that seemed to refer to this experience: "Between apprehending and naming, is experiencing." If I understand correctly, Krishnamurti says here that in the interval between seeing something and putting a word to it inheres the true experience of what it is, or perhaps more accurately of *what is.* I remember trying to get this into a philosophy paper at NYU, and feeling pretty excited, only to be given an *F* on the grounds of it having nothing to do with the assignment. This sort of thing frustrated me. At the end of the term, one in which I was enthusiastically engaged in reading Plato and in writing the assigned papers, I received an *F*. The rest of my courses went no better, and after failing four out of five of them, with a *D* in English, an appointment with a staff psychiatrist was scheduled for me.

The psychiatrist turned out to be a dark-suited fellow with dirty fingernails, I noticed. He reviewed my academic record and then looked up at me.

"Well," he said summarily. "There are two possibilities here. One, you're mentally defective. Or, two, you have study inhibitions."

"I'll take number two," I said sheepishly. He didn't get the joke.

The philosophy paper may have been read by a student assistant. But the discouragement had the effect of helping to turn me away from the university system, a fateful occurrence in my life.

The judgment that my piece had nothing to do with the subject may even have been correct, on balance, because the state I was speaking about is nonverbal, an embodiment of what happens when words disappear for a moment. Poetry and certain prose works may be the paradoxical effort to portray the state in language. Here is a sentence from Gertrude Stein's *The Autobiography of Alice B. Toklas*, which was written late in Stein's career and became a bestseller. In it she adopts the more down-to-earth sensibility of her companion to tell the story of their life together. The eponymous Miss Toklas is describing an experience of Miss Stein's as a schoolgirl in Oakland (the city about which she famously said, "There's no there there"):

> She remembers a little school where she and her elder sister stayed and where there was a little girl in the corner of the school yard and the other little girls told her not to go near her, she scratched.

I'm not sure how it happens—partly at least a consequence of the cumulative effect of the sequence of thirty-eight words before the single punctuation mark, the comma that precedes the two final words—but "she scratched" occurs with a force and presence I find unparalleled. It reminds me of the brief parenthesis in *Lolita* that Tom Stoppard cites, in the profile of the playwright by Kenneth Tynan, as his favorite parenthesis in literature. Nabokov writes: "My very photogenic mother died in a freak accident (picnic, lightning) when I was three."

It occurs to me I'm writing another philosophy paper here, trying to redeem a failing grade of forty years ago. In another experience of my own, I was riding the 79th Street crosstown bus home. It was winter this time, already dark in New York at somewhere between four-thirty and five. I know I was at Trinity because I was worried about homework, lots of it, which I needed to do and hadn't a real will to do nor quite an adequate ability to do. I'm sixteen or seventeen, not a happy camper. I'm twisted with remorse and simultaneously a nervous system unlikely to bend to the required task of the moment, past a certain point. After we'd crossed Central Park, somewhere between Columbus and Amsterdam Avenues, the very stretch, it occurs to me now, where twenty years later my childhood friend Sandy Kirkland would jump to her death from an apartment building, an estranged wife and mother of two—somewhere along in this stretch it suddenly dawned on me that I was on a bus, that outside the bus, as it moved down the street, it had turned dark, night had come on, lights were on in the buildings that lined the street; and above the buildings was the night sky, and all was right with the world. In that moment, it would seem that my consciousness had switched from its microcosmic state of personal issues and problems, to a macrocosmic awareness that I inhabited a larger universe—that in fact my consciousness was but a single filament of this larger whole.

During the sixties, the poet Gary Snyder, an honorary elder of the hippies of my generation, said, "We must move from a preoccupation with material states to a preoccupation with states of being." Was it a Jungian synchronicity that a chemically synthesized form of this consciousness was widely distributed throughout my generation, like a sort of parting gesture of the industrial epoch itself? In his 1989 biography of Allen Ginsberg, Barry Miles records a meeting between Timothy Leary and Ginsberg during the early 1960s in which the two plan for the widespread dissemination of LSD to the new generation in order to accomplish a revolution in consciousness. I was appalled to read that.

During the summer of 1965, when I was twenty-one, I roomed with two actors in Woodstock, New York, where they were interning at the Woodstock Summer Theater, and I remember an evening when one of the roommates, Chris, came back to our place and told us that a waitress at the Expresso Coffee House, the local hangout, had LSD, and it cost five dollars. Five dollars—at that time a little more than the going rate for a first-run movie. So we had to weigh this—had it been twenty-five dollars it would have been easier to dismiss. Would we ante up five dollars to try this new thing? Some people said it produced the equivalent of Buddhist enlightenment, and that the state of mind lasted for eight hours or more. A bargain, no less.

I was, then, so I would learn a few decades later from Miles's biography, one of Allen Ginsberg and Timothy Leary's guinea pigs. Another aspect of this story is that the historic meeting between Ginsberg and Leary is not widely discussed. Here were these two leaders of the counterculture taking a meeting and deciding to accomplish a revolution in consciousness. Again there's been no significant coverage. I don't recall even a review of the Ginsberg biography that mentioned this meeting, and yet it seems to me perhaps one of the most historically significant occurrences of the second half of the twentieth century.

What did acid do? It rendered a variation on what I've already described, and quoted from Bernard Berenson, all of which occurred without chemical help. Indeed, I believe that most of us have these experiences but, as they are not the subject of public forums, what is one to do with them, finally, except perhaps to forget them?

In the late sixties, just after I'd gotten married, I remember staying briefly at the Chelsea Hotel. It was summertime, and one night there was a terrific thunderstorm. I was woken up and got out of bed and went over to the window and watched the lightning strike, spreading sudden, silent illumination over the city. Then would come the late-breaking thunder, the noise of the lightning, which traveled so much more slowly than the light. I got back into bed and listened to the thunder, entirely unpredictable and yet inarguable, inevitable, and hence as perfect as music—and again there was the sense of being part of something much larger than the self.

When something catches the attention so completely, our thought process gives way to a perceptual level that doesn't involve the mind's insistent duality of good and bad, yes and no. It's snowing! one suddenly sees, and in that moment exists all the wonder of the world without the imposition of any idea of right or wrong, good or bad. T. S. Eliot's famous remark about Henry James, that he had a mind so fine it was unviolated by an idea, seems to me to reflect such a state as the ideal for an artist, or perhaps for anyone. Not that James's—or Nabokov's or Gertrude Stein's—characters don't have many and frequent ideas, but their creator regards them with the same open perceptual gaze and equanimity with which he would notice a blossoming plum tree. The Hindus have a saying: "When the mind empties, the heart fills it."

With that in mind, I want to include one more variation, this one through the auspices of a holy man, Swami Muktananda. Having gone through the sixties and had my moderate share of psychedelic experiences, as well as having had those of the non-chemical kind I've noted, I wasn't particularly interested in the varieties of religious experience that proliferated in Marin County, California, where I lived with Gailyn and our three children during the 1970s. But one afternoon in 1976, in the Campolindo health food store in Fairfax, I passed a poster of Muktananda I'd seen dozens of times before. It featured a color photograph of the guru, a head shot in which he looked straight at the camera, and as I glanced at it this time—slightly depressed, I should say, as I happened to be that year—I was surprised to see something I'd never noticed before. With a multitude of planets in Leo, I wasn't a natural subject for a guru, but this time I thought I saw in Muktananda's expression not the ego I'd previously assumed, but rather that he seemed to be radiating reverence for the precious passing substance of life, moment by moment. How nice, I thought, and in that moment my heart experienced a pleasurable melting.

I went home, went to bed that night, and woke up early, as I often did, and lay in our sleeping loft in the dark with my mind going on its usual mental errands. Then I happened to remember the poster and the nice feeling I'd had about it. The poster was a familiar one in Marin County at the time because Muktananda himself was in residence at his Oakland ashram just then. "Be with Baba" were the words that accompanied the photograph, and the details of the Oakland ashram's address and phone were listed. I learned later that around the same time of the morning as I lay awake in the sleeping loft, Muktananda and his devotees were beginning their morning chanting in Oakland.

The moment I remembered the experience I'd had with the photograph, the third-eye area of my forehead seemed to open with violent suddenness, and a bolt of radiant energy flooded my body through the third-eye aperture. After this forced entry, I lay, as it seemed to me, bathed in the radiance. This has got to be healthy, I remember thinking. It was like each and every cell of my body was being rinsed in a divine, cleansing light. I'll insist that these words, however inadequate, are not a space-cadet's hyperbole but simply the best I can do. Another image that occurred to me was that I felt like a flower on a hillside in sunlight. I had a sense of being alone in the universe and at the same time in a sublime relationship to a providential infinity. I lay in the darkness for an hour or more in this state of light and warmth.

When I got up that morning, I went about my tasks but with a sense that I was "looking with the third eye." I'm no longer sure what I meant by that, except that the radiance lingered in everything. When I described to Gailyn what had happened, she told me, "I get that out of gardening." Is it any wonder I'm married to this person?

I called a friend, Tom Veitch, a writer of underground comics, and described what had happened and asked whether he had any information about it. Tom was a sort of Catholic mystic who had spent some time in a monastery in Vermont. He didn't say yes and didn't say no, which wasn't bad as things went, but it was less than I was hoping for in the way of an answer. Eventually I ended up doing some research of my own by reading Muktananda's autobiography, *Play of Consciousness*, which answered virtually all the questions I had.

What had happened to me was called *shaktipat*, the transmission of divine energy from the guru to a subject, and it hinged on an opening in the heart chakra, rather than an intellectual understanding. It could be done by the guru in person and it also could be transmitted through a photograph. What was essential, apparently, was the little melting I'd known in the Campolindo health food store. That had broken me open, as it were, for the *shakti* transmission.

Gailyn was pregnant that spring with our third and last child, our son, Armenak, and as the birth grew nearer, I took up the Hindu meditation practice recommended by Muktananda in *Play of Consciousness.* Any man, he says in the book, could make his home a palace of shakti, whether he believed or not, by following the simple procedure Muktananda lays out. The cover of the book was the same photograph that had catalyzed the shaktipat I received. Muktananda instructed the reader to use the cover photograph as the focus of a regular meditation and the house would fill up with shakti. I began to meditate each night and Gailyn told me she felt a palpable energy accumulating in the house. As she grew to term, she herself was as radiant as any guru. And there was also Strawberry, six years old, and her sister, Cream, who was three. It was quite a household.

Having thought about Muktananda's precept that shakti transmission hinged on an opening in the heart, I eventually replaced his photograph, as the object of my meditation, with Strawberry's first-grade school photograph, without any diminution in results as far as I could tell.

What is one to make of these experiences? What actual relevance to one's life can they have? In the rough-and-tumble of the years, with their inevitable dark surprises, I sometimes all but forgot about them. When the going gets tough, one would naturally like to be one of the tough who gets going. Only a year or two after the episode with Muktananda, when our son was still a baby, I was struggling to get the manuscript of *Genesis Angels: The Saga of Lew*

Welch and the Beat Generation published. Editors and agents were sympathetic or not, but no real connection happened. Meanwhile, all appreciation of ordinary life had gone from me. My book needed to be published and then I would resume my life. I was a sort of human bullet—and like a bullet, blind, deaf and dumb.

One afternoon during this time, after a dentist appointment in Larkspur, I was driving home on the two-lane Olema-Bolinas road. It was Memorial Day Friday. (The universe, I think, can be quite a wit.) I drove up a grade and discovered, at the top of it, that a motorcyclist was coming directly at me—passing a VW van in the oncoming lane—about the length of a car away from me when I first saw him. "Oh," I thought, "I may be saying goodbye to the world."

The van went by in the oncoming lane and I edged my car—a newly-bought yellow Pinto—across that lane to avoid a head-on collision with the motorcyclist. The bike glanced off the side of my car, and I braced my left foot against the floorboard—not a good move, I learned a moment later, when the front of the car smashed into a grassy embankment beside the road. I knew right away that my left ankle was broken. Though there was no skin puncture, it hung like jelly in my sock. Slowly I began to gather my wits to get out of the car.

I noticed it was a nice day—sunny with a gentle little breeze on the air. Birds were chirping in the bushes close by. And I was breathing in and breathing out, with pleasure in the act itself. For the first time in months, it occurred to me, I was alive in the moment. The moment, likewise, was alive in my consciousness of it. Apparently I'd almost had to get killed to restore that awareness.

The motorcyclist, a big man who might have been high, was striding up the grade from the side of the road where he'd totaled his bike, shaking his arms at the sky and yelling, "Oh, shit! Oh, shit!" He came over to where I lay stretched out on the pavement beside my car. "Are you OK, man?" he asked. I told him I was all right.

We both were taken in an ambulance to Kaiser Hospital in San Rafael, and the motorcyclist was released later that day. That night I had surgery for my fractured ankle.

Several days later I walked in the front door of our house on crutches. The afternoon light in the living room when I came through the door looked beautiful. I lay down on the bed in our back bedroom, physically at a low ebb but feeling glad to be home and mending.

At some point over the next day or two, I remembered the moment, twenty years earlier, when I rode the crosstown bus as night fell in New York, heading home with my heavy homework assignments from Trinity. Sitting up in bed writing a poem about it, I sensed that I was renewing my commitment to a life that had happened in part because of that moment's intimations.

During those first several days at home, I also remembered an agent I'd known years ago in New York, and called him and then sent the manuscript. Within a week after he received it, he sold it.

As the years went by, I began to view the accident as a sort of parable: I'd turned myself into a human bullet in pursuit of my goal. On that Friday afternoon, however, it happened that a motorcyclist I didn't know was playing Russian roulette, passing on a blind hill. As it turned out, I was *his* bullet.

Since the accident, I seem to have a built-in, interior warning system that issues an alert when things get so important that they start to preempt the daily gift each of us gets, just breathing in and out. If I go too far afield, I know from experience that that gift could be in jeopardy, and I try to take responsibility and knock off. The moments I've described here seem to have modeled for me in my youth, in an involuntary and heightened form, what today is a more routinely restorative process: one way or another of letting go. For instance, there's a place not too far from where we live in Los Angeles that serves a nice variation on an English tea, and once or twice a month I'll ask Gailyn if she'd like to drive up there. More often it's time to take a walk.

Paying disinterested attention paradoxically renews the self. There is no arguing, after all, with a fresh morning, a beautiful voice, or a sip of good tea. And the self that registers one or another seems to simultaneously surrender its baggage—ephemeral positions, opinions, attitudes—and, in effect, to grow young again.

Mama Raccoon

Barbara Gates

Two paradoxes: First, the journey of life is one we take alone, yet its heart is our connection to others. Second, it's when we see life's fragility that we feel its preciousness most. Barbara Gates was the mother of a five-year-old daughter when she was diagnosed with breast cancer. Looking back through her cancer journals, she reflects on the lessons of illness and the healing that comes from a sense of connection to the earth and all the beings around us.

Through the gate between our yard and what was once Carmen's, our young neighbor Berto trundles a wheelbarrow of leaves and vegetable peelings in various stages of decay. It's hot today, and the air still. I breathe in a faint scent of rot as load after load is carried to our compost heap by the willow from the compost heap in the yard next door. We are hoping to protect the new owner of Carmen's house, Cathy, whose immune system has been destroyed by leukemia. Cathy has no way to fight the bacteria that feed on this decomposing life.

As Berto hauls, the pile of refuse mounts. Restless, I watch his progress as I try to make myself a comfortable place to sit on the ground. Frayed blue notebooks are spread around me. These are my cancer journals. It was five years ago—twenty-two years after I had fled to California—that I was diagnosed with breast cancer.

Panicked, I descended into dread. Would I die young, be shut out from life, leave behind a motherless five-year-old?

Beneath the dawn redwood, the needles darkening now in late spring, I'm mustering stamina this morning to read through these journals, to decipher a scrawl I've never reread. I hate to think about that scary time. But I am convinced: terror of death sent me into the broad terrain. I've got to understand how that happened.

Pasted inside the cardboard cover of the first cancer journal is a photograph of my daughter Katy. In thirty years of keeping journals, this is the only picture I have pasted in. It's an Easter photo of her at five, embracing a basket of colorful eggs. All revolved around her. To take care of my babe, I had to survive.

I study this picture, quintessential Katy: shiny brown hair like her father's, tilted head, teasing eyes, crooked grin, blood glowing in her cheeks. On her dress of striped pastels is a polka-dot palm tree; over her heart, a yellow sun. With arms encircling the brightly painted eggs, she looks like an Easter egg herself, bursting its shell.

Reading through my thoughts on life at this scary time brings back many memories.

Exhausted and drained one morning, I had descended into the backyard and thrown myself onto the grass. As my breast, pelvis, and thighs sank into the contour of the land, for the first time in many weeks, I felt as if my body might be able to relax; the toxins in my chest, in my limbs, even in my mind, might drain into the ground. In those difficult months, this became a practice to which I return sometimes even today: "lying on the earth."

After I tried it once, I did it again the next day. Each day, after a walk, I sank gratefully into a bed of clover and dandelions. Hauling my work out into the sunshine, I set up an outdoor office and did my editing right here in the yard. And belly to belly with the earth—knowing its heat, its breadth—I rested.

Driven by my imperative as Katy's mom, I was making an all-out effort to survive. I followed all recommendations, Western and Eastern: surgery, radiation, visualization, acupuncture, Chinese herbs, walking, resting, meditation. After a biopsy and diagnosis, I turned to my husband Patrick as he drove me home from the hospital and said, "Whatever comes, I want to keep my eyes wide open." In the ensuing months, I groped to remember anything I had ever learned about how to live. And how to die.

Twenty years earlier, when I had begun to explore Buddhist meditation, it was to learn exactly this. Now, with urgency, I turned to what I had gleaned. Finding myself unable to sit on a cushion with any regularity, I began vigorous daily walking to complement the practice of lying on the earth.

Craving green, quiet, and solitude, I began to walk in the Berkeley Hills. Early each morning, I drove up, leaving behind the noisy city streets by my house, and hiked along the borders of Tilden Regional Park, our Bay Area patch of wilderness, 2,065 acres of meadows and forests in the upper valley of Wildcat Creek. But wary of wildcats and coyotes, mountain lions and rattlesnakes, and most of all, the human predators known on occasion to make their attacks on remote trails, I chose the manicured streets beyond the gates of the park. Wary as well of my own poor sense of direction, of my tendency to distrust my instincts and end up lost and disoriented, I chose familiar streets, well labeled and neatly ordered. Here I could catch glimpses of scrubby hills and wooded ravines. I could watch deer foraging in the gardens of the well-to-do and reflect in silence. And safety.

Along with this walking practice, I met with both Western and Eastern doctors. A local genius of a healer—an acupuncturist and herbalist—told me, "Cancer is a chronic disease; it cannot be cured. But it can be contained." Sensing my resistance, he coolly invited me to open to this uncertainty. After several hours of questions from me, he took my pulses. He described the imbalances in the flow of energy through my body. "Here's the prescription." He paused, meeting my eye. "Take more risks!"

Oh, sure! "Do you say this to everyone?"

"No," he said. "I read your pulses. I'm saying it to you."

"What do you mean, 'risks'? Bungee jumping? Camping I can

imagine; backpacking, maybe. But if you mean rock climbing or spelunking, no way!"

"More risks in your actions and in your thinking. You'll have to figure out what is appropriate for you. But," he laughed, "once you've gotten used to something, then it won't qualify as a risk anymore, and you'll have to find something else. Once you begin to call that home, you'll have to dive deeper into the unknown. At some point in camping there may be nothing left to do but to try scaling a cliff . . . or exploring a cave."

Scared, confused, even outraged by this prescription I didn't understand, I rebelled. Who did he think he was, challenging me in this way? Yet something resonated. Wasn't this the task I was taking on in Buddhist practice? The risk of meeting each moment as a surprise, without expectations, and letting it go, without holding on to it or pushing it away. I scoured my everyday activities, my relations with Katy and Patrick, for ways that I clung to the expected, to habits and safety. And I continued to remind myself of this dictum: Take more risks.

One morning, I turned off the predictable streets and, with a reckless energy, risked a wandering path into the wildness of the wood. Heart knocking, I kept right on walking through the dry grasses and sharp-toothed blackberry brambles, plunging through fears about my safety (What or who might be around the bend? Would I know how to get back?). I stepped out into the unknown.

As I struggled over my first treatment decision—whether to have the breast removed or excise the tumor—I felt stumped. Alarmed that an early death would bar me from everything I knew—as a mother, a wife, a friend—I yearned to tap into my own deepest intuition.

From inside myself, from someplace deeper than my intellect, deeper than my heritage as agnostic Jew or Unitarian, I heard the strict and bold voice of a nun: "Who needs hair? Who needs breasts?" This ascetic voice had influenced many decisions over the years—to keep my now-white hair undyed, my clothes and possessions simple. Here, the verdict was absolute. On some vast and fundamental scale, it doesn't matter whether I have two breasts or one or none, or even whether I live in this earthly form or not.

I'd planned to tell the surgeon, "Cut the damn thing off!" But all the experts, and even the acupuncturist, urged me to simply cut out the tumor and follow that with radiation. I searched my mind and heart for an internal reason to do the more limited surgery. My thoughts ricocheted back and forth over this decision: breast or no breast. I wrestled with the whole question of what it means to be embodied. What is this body? If I am not my body, can I simply let the body go and take to the mind as refuge?

As I took my morning walks, my mind contracted in fear. It was hard to pay more than cursory attention to the green and brown world I walked through. But I urged myself to keep my eyes wide open, my senses keen.

Eucalyptus pods crunched underfoot. Lupine sent out its sweet scent. Startling blue flowers burst through the spiky crowns of wild artichokes. Sticky stems of monkey flower and manzanita branches with their tiny apples brushed my bare arms. If a scary scenario took over my thoughts—of dying, of Patrick trying to care for Katy all by himself—I wrenched my attention back to flowers, trees, and nests. High in an oak hid a wood-rat nest where generations of diverse creatures had made their homes. By the creek waved frothy horsetail—ancient plants, four hundred million years old, reproduced by spores ever since plants first invaded land. With a sense of continuing life, with primeval presence so tangible here, many of my terrors dissolved.

Back at the house, when tangled thoughts closed my mind, I opened the kitchen door, as I do now, and from our second-floor landing, looked out over the garden. Carmen, weeding in her yard, waved; so did Sheryl, putting out bowls for the cats. The dawn redwood, our resident elder, rose high, proclaiming an ancient lineage, vast spans of space and time. I felt somehow more permeable, expanded.

A day before the appointed surgery, still undecided as to whether I would keep the breast or not, I spent a few feverish hours digging narcissus and anemone bulbs into the hard February soil by the cherry tree in the backyard and the princess in the front. Then I laid my body down on the ground in my favorite napping place beneath the dawn redwood. The breath of soil in my nostrils, dirt under my nails, and mud on my bare feet, the basic elements—air, water, earth—moved through me. From deep inside, a more gentle voice urged, "Through gardening you honor the body, the body of ground. Appreciate the human body too." So, cradled by earth flesh, I pledged to honor my own. The next day, I finally confronted the cancer and made my decision. I told the surgeon that unless he saw signs that the cancer was spreading, he should save the breast.

And instead of having the breast cut out—of body, sight, mind—I took another risk, to feel what I might lose. So I remembered: delicate nipples of adolescence like tender pink stars, new breasts, velvet to my touch under my nightie; erotic breasts caressed by Patrick and past lovers over these many years; milk-filled mother's breasts that suckled Katy. I felt through the history of this embodiment, always changing.

How much easier for me to be absolute and drastic ("Cut it off!" "Forget the breast!") than to look fully, to allow myself to love this changing form of flesh, bones, and blood in an open and uncertain way—not to hold on to it. Katy's plea came to mind: "Mommy, you can hug me, but don't grip." All of my habits pulled the opposite way, to clasp tight and resist change. Could I live fully in this body without insisting that it stay young and healthy and never die? The task seemed almost impossible.

On a morning walk weeks after the surgery, I took another risk. I turned off the ranger-made trail onto one beaten into the earth by hoof and paw. Braving this high trail, I wound my way up toward the crest of a hill. At a sudden twist in the path, two mule deer, a doe and her fawn, loped down past me as I climbed up. The doe was so close that I could see the quivering of her nostrils and the pink glow where the sun shone through her cocked ears. Was she heading for the gardens in the city below? What reciprocity. I hiked up from the city into the hills to be nourished, and the deer descended from the hills into the city to feast in the backyards. We crisscrossed and exchanged.

Up a steep incline and around a turn, I unexpectedly arrived at the summit. Winded, I staggered around the small circular crest of the hill. Then I lost my bearings. Which path had I followed? On all sides, narrow trails descended the downward slopes, passing through anonymous groves of trees. Below me shimmered several lakes and what looked like the Bay on both sides. From far below what sounded like a train whistled. I couldn't tell from which direction it called. Where was I? What time was it? Dizzy, I looked up to the sun high in the sky. Lightheaded, unhooked for a moment from time or place, I rested in exhilaration.

Suddenly, I felt a surge of fear. Would the cancer recur? Would I die young? Concentrating all of my effort, I drew the landscape into my awareness, risked to see myself in this land. Welcoming the hills of dry summer grasses, the glimmer of the Bay and sky, I opened the field of who or what I perceived myself to be. I saw the vast exchange.

For hundreds of years, a wood-rat nest has offered a home to frogs, salamanders, scorpions, and mice. The stems and leaves of monkey flower have offered healing poultices to generations of Ohlone people, while the manzanita apples have provided cider. With bumblebees, the lupine exchanges nectar for pollen; and with soil, nitrogen for other nutrients.

I ran my palms along my own arms and thighs. Isn't this narrow self within this particular package of mortal flesh an expression of ongoing exchange? Resting my full attention on this possibility, I felt, for a moment, more fully alive and also not so afraid to die.

* * *

While recovering from treatments, I tried to find at least a few minutes each day to relax into the wide hug of the yard, to continue the practice of lying on the earth. One morning, Sheryl called through the fence, "Barbara, come quick. You'll never believe this!" When I looked through the gate in the fence, I could see the usual line of cats at their bowls in front of the garage and then, at the far end in broad daylight, a raccoon feeding at the farthest bowl. Sheryl whispered, "It's a female."

Indeed, this mama raccoon, her teats distended and red, clearly ravenous after days of nursing her babies, had the audacity to forage side by side with the cats in view of us people. I imagined her exhausted, starving. Challenged to survive, she had felt compelled to leave her cubs in their nest in the shed of some overgrown yard and, without the protection of night, to brave this territory. Now, seemingly oblivious to the cats, she moved from bowl to bowl. Suddenly, one cat, defending his food, humped and hissed. The mama raccoon reared, bared her teeth, and flattened her ears. Darting at her, Sheryl shouted, "Git!" And the raccoon fled. Watching this exchange, I felt a kinship with this raccoon that I didn't understand.

When I submitted to the technology of radiation, I felt disowned by life. I sat in the narrow hallway in a "lineup" with other green-gowned patients avoiding each other's eyes and watching unlucky fellows roll through on gurneys. In the treatment room, technicians carried on conversations over and through me, arranging my limbs as if they belonged to a corpse or were some extension of the equipment. The door clicked shut and I was left alone with the Star Wars equipment gliding over the breast and the high-pitched yammer of the machine.

To counterbalance the touch of the radiation, the machines, and the technicians (this touch without contact), I decided to get some massage. Surprised when the masseuse introduced herself as a beginner, I commented on her strong hands, her sure sense in rooting for knots. She told me that before she worked on humans, for many years she had massaged horses. As her fingers worked the braided muscles of my back, I daydreamed of the tight flank of a mare contracted from hours of work in the ring. I felt my own back as "flank." Through the touch of the horse masseuse and her story, I took further risks of imagination, risks in the very way I saw who or what I was. I knew my animal body; I felt sister to the mare; I remembered the raccoon.

Through rounds of radiation, I continued to take naps on the earth, to peek through the slats in the fence, and to spy on that mama raccoon. As I watched her, I was shaken by opposing feelings. Sometimes I delighted in her, my heroine. How brazen she was. What courage she had in full daylight to claim her place among the cats. Other times, I disparaged her as thief. In her black mask, she stole from bowls set up for the cats. Did the ferocity of her hunger serve her? No! She scared Sheryl, who, instead of offering her food, chased her away. Distraught, I saw myself in this persona. I recognized the pain of the "intruder."

That pain felt familiar, a challenge to overturn. Old habits came to mind. After my parents were divorced, I saw myself as intruder in both my father's and my mother's homes; now in Berkeley, I often felt like a gate-crashing New Yorker, and in New York, like an infiltrating Californian. I wept into the grass for the mama raccoon, driven by her ravenousness to break in, and for myself, driven by my hunger to belong.

Calling me from my reading under the dawn redwood, Suzanna, with her dog, Radio, at her heels, comes into the garden. I put down my cancer journals to join her, to continue our work in the composting corner. The willow is now in full leaf, and purple clematis climbs over the fence from Sheryl and Roy's. Suzanna and I are making a compost hill, drawing ingredients from our sorted piles. Suzanna plans to grow pumpkins on this hill despite my pessimistic warnings. As far as I'm concerned, in this yard pumpkins will never survive.

We lay down branches and dry sticks to let in air, then dried hay and grass clippings, then some already-composted dirt. Suzanna fluffs the layers to allow earthworms and bacteria to pass through and break down the vegetable matter into humus. For two weeks, Suzanna will water the hill to help the compost cook, thus preparing for planting. We plan to meet at the compost hill when it is thoroughly soaked to plant the pumpkin seeds together.

During these weeks, I lie on the earth each day and peruse old journals. As I listen to the sprinkler watering our compost hill, more memories from my time recovering from cancer return to me.

As treatments continued, mothers at Katy's preschool offered to provide my family with dinners. The nourishment I experienced went far beyond the meals themselves. A woman who made one of the first dinners said, "I thought about you as I was cooking this and imagined what foods would make you strong." Later that evening, as I ate the lentils and chickpeas, the tomatoes and carrots, I remembered this mother remembering me. Each evening, Katy, Patrick, and I ate lasagnas, corn soups, and chiles rellenos—grandmothers' formulas and favorite recipes passed from friend to friend—passed from these families to ours.

And I continued to be nurtured each morning by the ground itself. One morning, during an earth-nap, I heard Andy from down the street making plans with Sheryl. I listened to them talking through the back fence. Andy would be gone for a week, so could Sheryl be sure to put out extra food for the cats whose care they shared? Sheryl could be counted on to care for cats (and as they got used to the raccoons, for the raccoons, too, despite efforts of some neighbors to eliminate them). My imagination stirred. People had put out bowls for feral cats in backyards throughout this neighborhood, throughout Berkeley, Oakland, Albany, Richmond, and beyond. Who knew how far? When she fed at the cat bowls, this mama raccoon tapped into a great network that was already there. Was I tapping into such a network as well? Could I continue to rest in this vast net of connectedness, always there, needing only to be recognized?

An image of the many bowls offered me a certain romantic solace, but it didn't translate for me as a mother. During those months of treatments, I was consumed with fears for Katy—my tender five-year-old, vulnerable, dependent on me. Often, I came to my nap worrying. Is Katy sturdy? Am I passing on my upset, my fragility? If I die, what motherly soul will help Patrick protect and nurture her? Will Katy know to look for the bowls that may be out there?

In daydreams about the mama raccoon, I saw her returning to her nest. Strengthened after feeding, she nursed her cubs. As they grew older, she perhaps led them on foraging expeditions, showing them the yards of the neighborhood almsgivers. But on her rounds, she might be trapped in a broken fence, hit by a car. What if this mama didn't make it back?

At the end of one day of worry, my friend Marie said to me, "I have to believe that if I weren't there, the universe would take care of my children." This seemed inconceivable. Such a risk to trust in this. Yet just positing the thought was briefly comforting at that scary time.

Over these weeks, as Suzanna waters the compost hill, the days are heating up. From the compost corner, I catch the whiff of decay. Eggshells, apple cores, matted hair from the brush, nail parings—all decompose, their scent heavy in the air. As a welcome breeze shakes Bob's cherry tree, tender white and pink blossoms flutter down and sift through the yard.

This morning, as I sit beneath the dawn redwood, I steel myself against a sense of loss. The ambulances came last night for Grandma Darlene, who is almost eighty and has had a stroke. Her family, including Dee—cold sober for once—is gathering. And after a period of arduous and ultimately failed leukemia treatments, my neighbor Cathy has come home to die. Just my age. I palpate my breast, uneasily feeling the scar. Is there anything steady on which I can rely? I think of uncontrollable forces—sickness, epidemics, extinctions, the collision of tectonic plates or even whole galaxies. Now, years since the cancer, I feel pressed to look after myself and my family. And I'm not sure who is looking after us. I think of the raccoons. Sometimes people put out bowls for their fellow creatures, but it can't be assured. Sometimes they put out rat poison.

A sudden shout. Suzanna strides out from the compost corner. "Why didn't you tell me you were doing a planting?" she demands. When I look confused, she insists, "The pumpkins! They're sprouting! You didn't wait for me!"

"But I didn't plant anything!" I say, exasperated. "I thought we were planning to do it together." But indeed, when I follow her, I see tiny sprouts all over the compost hill, their yellowgreen leaves and ovate seeds visible just below the green shoots. These seedlings certainly do look like pumpkins. I study them closely to see the new roots pushing out from the seeds as they begin to germinate.

Suzanna and I look at one another awkwardly. This seems weird. Were these seeds still intact, left over from years of failed plantings? Or did last year's market-bought Halloween pumpkin, cast out by the fence to rot, disperse seeds that found their way into the compost hill? Or what? I don't know whether this feels more unsettling or miraculous.

These mysteriously appearing pumpkins—carrying on against the odds—bring me back to visions of the mama raccoon. Even now, as I sit down in my old napping spot, the mama raccoon calls up heat in my belly. Suddenly I see it. Mammal to mammal, I feel the pull toward this impassioned mother fighting for food so she can convert it into milk. What is the key to mammalness? Mammaries. A mammal mother is able to protect her babies in their nest. They thrive only because she can nurse.

With breast cancer, I confronted a crisis in my very mammalness, a sickness in my mammary. When I was in treatment, Katy and I continued a favorite pastime, sharing baths together. Scooping the soap dish into the water, Katy poured a cooling balm over my raw radiated breast, over the hard contour of the hematoma left from surgery. How I loved these bathtub blessings. As I recall them now, floods of other memories return to me.

So many worries of this city gal, feeling outside the cycles of life. When I was about to give birth, I did not trust my breasts. Although they were larger than I had imagined was possible, the nipples dark and swollen, I didn't believe that these breasts of mine could ever produce milk. When Katy was first born, vigorous and rosy, how amazed I was that she could so naturally root for and find my breasts. How relieved, how proud I was—a slipping into grace—when she suckled and the milk flowed.

This lack of trust is so familiar. As a teenager, I was afraid my body wouldn't know how to menstruate, that it wouldn't know how to kiss, that it wouldn't know how to make love. At forty, when for the first time I focused all my effort on having a baby, I didn't trust that I'd be able to conceive (despite Patrick's lively sperm, which, after a year of failed attempts, we witnessed in all their exuberant activity on a slide under the microscope). Once pregnant, I worried. Could I grow a baby and carry her to term? Would my body know how to give birth, how to suckle?

Distrust following distrust (it seems absurd and sad as I look back), I doubted that this woman's body would know how to live out its nature as mammal, as animal. Now, five years after I first recognized myself in the mama raccoon and wept here for my craving, I cleave to this same soil. Many times I have felt barred from the primal cycles.

Yet even now, just feeling these distrusts, I sense a shift. Lying on the earth beneath the dawn redwood, there's a welling up of precisely what I mourn. I see a lineage of mammal mothers to which the raccoon belongs, to which I too belong. Through this raccoon mama, I knew the pain of being excluded; now I glimpse a sense of belonging—to this yard, to this my home terrain where, through the millennia, life has germinated, suckled, foraged, died, and reseeded.

Butterfly Kiss for the Buddha

Anne Cushman

One of the special features of Buddhism in the West is how many serious meditators are also committed family people. That's not the way it is in Asia, where most of the serious meditators are monastics and the laity often doesn't meditate. That means Westerners are creating a new model of Buddhism, one in which family life is not only compatible with spiritual practice but is one of its highest expressions. Here's Anne Cushman on her own discovery that there's no separation between her practice and her life as the mother of a two-year-old.

So there I was, speeding down a winding country road on a glorious day last fall, running through yellow lights, completely stressed out, trying to get to the meditation hall on time.

I was teaching daily yoga classes at a women's meditation retreat at Spirit Rock, a Buddhist center in a rural valley north of San Francisco. But my beloved babysitter, Megan—a twenty-something Zen student with beads and small electronic parts woven into her turquoise-and-blonde dreadlocks—had gotten caught in a traffic jam and arrived at my house an hour late, and then I had gotten stuck in the same freeway snarl myself. As I barreled along, I kept imagining a cop pulling me over: "But officer, it's a dharma emergency!" I burned rubber into the Spirit Rock parking lot, walked to the meditation hall as fast as possible while still appearing mindful and serene, and got there with seconds to spare, just as the bell was ringing to end the last sitting period.

It was two days into the retreat, and I was exhausted. I would have loved to have participated in the entire schedule of this five-day silent intensive, whose title—"Reclaiming the Sacred Feminine"—hinted that it might explore some territory that wasn't exactly mainstream Buddhist orthodoxy. But as the mother of a two-year-old, sitting a full retreat wasn't possible. So I was flip-flopping identities: a mom all night and all morning, a yogini all afternoon and evening.

Unfortunately, Skye was cutting two molars. The previous night he had awakened me six times between 11:00 p.m. and 4:00 a.m., when I finally brought him into my bed—where he thrashed around for another two hours, whimpering and talking in his sleep. ("What's that down there? It's . . . it's the gas pedal!" he cried out in delight; then half woke up and began rooting at my chest, mumbling, "More gas pedal!" in what appeared to be an archetypal male conflation of the car and the breast.)

And by day, he had been in classic two-year-old mode, exploring the limits of his personal power. All was harmonious as long as I let him indulge his current obsession: sniffing and identifying every jar in my spice drawer. That morning we had sat and smelled them together for over an hour—"nutmeg! cardamom! rosemary! turmeric!"—until my nose hummed and tingled, in what felt like a practice dreamed up by a Zen master on LSD.

But when I tried to pry him away to meet another mom and child at a nearby park, all hell broke loose. All Skye wanted to do was sit in his car seat listening to Al Green's "Love and Happiness" nineteen times in a row, while taking periodic whiffs of his cinnamon bottle. I was starved for adult company, even if it was just comparing teething notes. The outing ended with the absurd spectacle of me grimly hauling a screaming, flailing child toward a playground, while he shrieked like I was carrying him off to the electric chair: "No slide! No swing! Just more 'Yove and Happiness'!"

So as I drove off to the retreat that afternoon, let's just say I did not feel like the Divine Mother. But arriving at Spirit Rock felt like diving into a pool of peace. The center is tucked in a valley of burnt-gold hills; the autumn air was a musky, minty blend of sage and pennyroyal. After teaching two gentle yoga classes, I sat the rest of the afternoon in the meditation hall, dipping thirstily into a vast well of silence.

In two years of motherhood, my body had forgotten the exquisite and excruciating sensations of a meditation retreat. It was astonishing to find myself, even for a few hours, in the midst of a hundred silent women, all of them moving slowly, as if underwater—sometimes smiling, sometimes sobbing as they sat down in the middle of their hundred lives, each as vivid and complicated as my own. I sank into the luxury of having nothing to do but swim into the depths of my body and heart, breath by breath.

As I walked from my silent dinner toward the meditation hall—pausing to savor the crimson sunset and the wild turkeys rustling through the long grass—I found myself asking the perennial question of lay practitioners: How can I make my life feel more like a meditation retreat? How do I bridge the apparent gap between yogini and mom?

In a dharma talk that evening, Vipassana teacher and psychotherapist Debra Chamberlin-Taylor spoke about the qualities of the "sacred feminine"—a psychological term for an archetypal dimension that exists in both men and women. The feminine principle, she said, is nonlinear and receptive. It's about being, rather than doing; feeling, rather than analyzing. It moves in spirals and circles, rather than lines and angles. It intuitively perceives all of life as an interconnected whole. It values the world, the body, the emotions, the relationships, the connections of the heart. And in our daily life—and even in our spiritual practice—it is often paved over by the more masculine attributes of action, analysis, and achievement.

In Buddhist practice, this powerful energy is symbolically represented by images such as Kuan-yin, the graceful female bodhisattva, with arms extended to ease the suffering of the world, or the compassionate goddess Tara, in her myriad forms and colors. In other spiritual traditions, it takes the form of a Divine Mother or consort such as Parvati or Mother Mary. Invoking such images, says Chamberlin-Taylor, can help us relax and expand our meditation practice to embrace the chaos of our ordinary lives, rather than trying to escape it.

"For women to come together and honor the sacred feminine can be powerful, liberating—and a new doorway into the Buddhist practice," Chamberlin-Taylor says.

Whether shaped by biology or by culture, women's deep involvement with relationships, family, children, and home has traditionally been viewed primarily as an impediment to spiritual practice. "On a women's retreat with women teachers, they will come into dharma interviews talking about their divorces, their hot flashes, the pain of leaving their children for the first time to go on retreat—things they say they have never dared to talk about on a meditation retreat.

"And when these things are seen as part of the sacred journey—rather than as something to be passed over en route to something more 'spiritual'—the whole field of awareness opens up, and they can go deeper into their meditative practice than they have ever gone before."

That night, Skye was restless again, waking and calling me over and over. He didn't want to come to my bed, but he didn't want to be alone in his crib. Finally, at three in the morning, I lay down on the floor of his bedroom, wrapped in a quilt, to keep him company as he drifted off.

The floor was too hard for me to sleep. So I lay there and felt my breath go in and out. I was trying to rest with exactly what was: the exhaustion. The aching bones. My beloved child lying in his crib, clutching his blue blankie and his stuffed lion. His earthy, yeasty smell, like a cross between fresh-cut grass and baking bread.

Tara, I remembered, does not hide from the world. She embraces it like a mother holding a child. I could find the sacred in the teething pains, the relationship struggles, the mound of dirty dishes, the guitar riffs of "Love and Happiness," the smells of cardamom, nutmeg, and ginger. I could remember that rebirth is possible in every moment, and indeed, is only possible in this moment, in this life.

The next morning, still dressed in his polar-bear pajamas, Skye pointed to the beautiful sandalwood Buddha on my mantelpiece. "There's the Buddha! Let's go see him," he suggested.

I handed him the statue. "Eskimo kiss for the Buddha!" he said, and rubbed his nose against the Buddha's. "And now a butterfly kiss for the Buddha!" And he fluttered his eyelashes, intimately, against the Buddha's cheek.

The Wordless Proclamation

Jakusho Kwong

Of all its teachings, Buddhism is most renowned for the profound doctrine of emptiness. There are many ways to point to emptiness, many different levels at which it can be understood. But none tells the whole story, since the way things really are is beyond (empty of) all concepts. Here, as only a teacher of Zen can do, Jakusho (Bill) Kwong, a teacher in the lineage of Suzuki-roshi, alludes to the indescribable.

Someone once asked a Zen master, "How old is Buddha?" The Zen master replied, "How old are you?" This is good Dharma. To help us to remember and to realize this, every year in April we have a celebration for the birth of the Buddha. The Dharma, or truth, expressed by this ceremony is very profound. As the entire community and all of our guests intone a primordial chant, one by one we approach the shrine where a small figurine of the Buddha is standing in wordless proclamation with one hand pointing toward the earth and the other hand pointing toward heaven. This sign of the Buddha's birth is asking that the vastness of heaven and earth recognize and acknowledge the very vastness within each of us since the original minds of human beings and buddhas are exactly the same. Then, with acknowledgment and reverence, we bathe the baby Buddha by pouring a portion of sweet tea over its crown. This sweet tea is reminiscent of the sweet, misty fragrance of gentle rain that descended upon the garden of Lumbini where the Buddha was born, and each person has an opportunity to offer it in his or her own way. But we should ask ourselves, Who is being bathed by this act? Who is being acknowledged? It is certainly not something outside ourselves. Again, the vastness of the Buddha's birth is our very own vastness, and so the Buddha's wordless proclamation is that you yourself, standing between heaven and earth, are Buddha, and the physical gesture of pouring sweet tea recognizes and reminds us of this truth.

The significance of the small Buddha standing there alone under the shrine canopy, receiving the offering of sweet tea from each person, is very important for us to understand because it points to another fact: that ultimately there is nothing we can rely on. Remember, it is said that Shakyamuni Buddha's last words were: "You are the light." We want to rely on something or somebody—our family, our car, our computer. But just like the Buddha's birth, each of us stands alone, and as you must remember, the body we have is with us for only a limited period of time. It's on loan, a kind of rental body. In our everyday life it's pretty common for someone to ask, "Do you rent, do you lease, or do you own?" When it comes to these bodies, these minds, and these lives, we don't do any of the three. But when we really know that we don't, then we realize that we do and that the time we have with this body is very limited; so life becomes very precious.

It's an established fact in the Buddhadharma that this body is not ourselves. In Dharma teachings all human beings are made up of five clusters or groups, known by the Sanskrit word *skandhas.* These skandhas include form, sensation, perception, discriminating thought or activity of the mind, and consciousness. In the *Heart Sutra* we chant that the five skandhas that compose human beings are all empty. The word *emptiness* is very important for those who practice the Dharma or simply seek the truth. When you first hear this word, it may sound negative, but it truly describes the fullness of your mind whose spacious nature is ready to receive. Emptiness is the same as no-mind, but when you use the phrase *no-mind*, it can be misunderstood quite easily because we do have a mind. But both *no-mind* and *empty mind* could refer to something like an empty bottle. We say that the bottle is empty of any content, and yet there is the bottle before us. Only when it is empty can it receive and be filled.

As we continue to live our lives, it's very difficult to receive something because more and more we fill ourselves with everything else, often searching to find something, anything, to rely on. But first we must return to zero so we can receive. Emptiness in this sense is very important. We especially need to be empty of our idea of ourselves, of who we think we are. Who we think we are is not who we are. This practice, and zazen, is the vehicle that helps us to express this inconceivable, wondrous fact. Once we do realize it, we also realize the other side: Who else could this wondrous condition be but ourselves? This self is filled with awareness and wisdom-knowing, accompanied by compassion.

I find it interesting that in Europe and America scientists have been using atom smashers to discover what is behind even the most infinitesimal elements of matter. What is behind, behind, behind? This is the big question that has inspired religion, philosophy, and science alike. Basically, when the scientists complete their exploration, their conclusion will be what the Buddha also realized almost twenty-six hundred years ago: emptiness.

Empty of the self, yet filled with bright awareness. I suppose the difference may be that the scientists will then have the theory and recipe, but they may not be interested in eating the meal.

There is a cathedral that was built in the eleventh century in Krakow, the ancient capital of Poland, called the Wawel Cathedral. I had heard about the Wawel many times because it is supposed to be one of the powerful energy spots or *chakras* of the earth. We had a rare opportunity to visit, and when we got there, we were allowed to go below the altar underneath the cathedral. I don't know exactly what I was expecting to encounter, but when I arrived, there was a deep quiet and calm presence, a truly pervasive sense of peace. It was so calm and peaceful that I felt as if I were being embraced.

This is the same with your mind. We say we are a cerebral brain or mind, but that mind is not us by far. Your body is not yours; your mind is not yours; therefore you may not be who you think you are. This is the exact opposite of what we are told everyday in our society. But in the Dharma, instead of looking outside for everything, you look inside through practice, while you begin to trace and return sights and sounds back to their origin. When you try to locate this mind, you'll discover that there is nothing there. Eventually you will arrive within yourself at the same pervasive peacefulness that I encountered at the Wawel Cathedral. There is a term Zen master Bankei used to describe this place that I like very much: *the unborn.* When you become aware of this unborn, you will see that Bankei's great compassion in leaving this term is the same original mind as yours.

Living words like *the unborn* help us to see things we've studied over and over again but from another angle. It's like seeing Sonoma Mountain from a different view; it is the same mountain you've seen many times, but you see it from its many perspectives. I recall first seeing Mount Fuji in Japan. From the tourist side it looks perfect, the mountain is very symmetrical with the snowcap on top, but one time I was behind the mountain, and it was quite different. It was not the "postcard Fuji" but asymmetrical and somehow more alive, with its own unique beauty. At the time I thought I was looking at Mount Fuji, but now I realize I was actually looking at myself.

When words are living words, like *the unborn* and *standing alone*, they can act just like this view from the other side and provide many insights for us. For instance, Buddha's second noble truth is that we suffer in life because we think everything is fixed and permanent. But the truth of life is that everything is in constant change, impermanent, full of the energy of life, and, ultimately we face it alone. We can't rely on anything. But actually this is our saving grace.

One time when Zen master Seung Sahn asked his student a question, the student answered, "One." Seung Sahn said to the student, "Where does this 'One' return to?" Even the One has to return somewhere. The student replied, "I don't know." Seung Sahn smiled at her and said, "Only don't know—wonderful!" It's the same with the unborn; you can't define it, you can't grasp it, but it is to be realized. We long for this.

The birth of the Buddha is about the proclamation of the unborn. If it's unborn, it means it can't die, because it never was created. When the temporal body of a great teacher dies, there is still this eternal life that continues aeon after aeon, beyond space and time. Realized or not, this is the case because there is no beginning and no end. It is the same when ordinary people die; there is the same eternal life because eternal life is the no-mind, or unborn, this infinite spaciousness and great peace that we cannot define because it is not limited by any conditions. Some of you may have experienced this by being with those who have died. It is neither here nor there, big nor small, female nor male, neither living nor dead. It's beyond words. That's what it means to be a wordless proclamation. We can't say anything about it. But that's also why it's great. (*Great* means "no beginning, no end.") We should know that we are inherently endowed with this greatness. This is what the proclamation of the birth of Buddha is all about. Real practice is the realization of this. That's our celebration.

When you bathe the Buddha during the ceremony, you are really bathing yourself as an acknowledgment of the unborn within and without you. The unborn is your original self nature, your original mind. Only in this way is there eternal life. From the unborn there is the birth of the Buddha. And the Buddha's birth is the celebration of your unbornness. No creation, no destruction, no process of realization, no Zen, no Buddha. Just complete affirmation. And as I've said earlier, the fact that not one word can be said about it is what makes it great.

It takes some kind of attention or focus, which we call *samadhi*, for a person to turn their light inward so that they may enter the space of the unborn. Samadhi's function is the light or soft focus on this unborn space. And just as at Wawel, your experience of being there may also be this pervasive sense of peace. This spaciousness is the origin from which all energy emerges and to which it returns. Awareness of the unborn is the characteristic of *prajna.* Prajna is your intrinsic wisdom, innately bright. We say that in samadhi there is prajna and in prajna there is samadhi. They go together like two wings of a bird that know the essence of soaring through and through. Samadhi is the focus on the essence of original mind. Prajna is the active awareness of that pervasiveness. Samadhi is the unwavering attention needed to touch the unborn, and prajna is the awareness of that essence. Samadhi is calm and quiet yet aware. Prajna is aware yet calm and quiet. Samadhi is samadhi and prajna is prajna. The essence of meditation practice is both samadhi and prajna. We are two very good, longtime friends.

Even though you may practice and cultivate samadhi and love sitting in samadhi so much that you do not want to leave it, you cannot just remain there. Sticking in samadhi is being stuck. You have to activate the samadhi, and this is the functioning of prajna. The spaciousness that characterizes samadhi is not a matter of conscious knowing; it is the equanimity of the "don't know" mind. As you become more and more able to return to this "don't know" mind (which is another name for the unborn, or emptiness, or self-nature, or original mind) during zazen, you will find that you can begin functioning with it in your nonmeditation hours as well. For example, you will discover that you are not in the kind of hurry you've been used to, and there will be a spaciousness in your work. There will be energy, curiosity, zest, humor, and joy. And there will also be a certain newness to everything because your living is an expression of the unborn. Even if it appears that what you are doing is the same old thing, you will find that it is new; you can see and appreciate the flowers on the roadside even as you just drive by. With spacious awareness as its foundation, this is the way that prajna functions in your daily life.

Remember, the center of a moving cyclone is still. You are not in a hurry, but things still get accomplished. It's not like you will suddenly start walking slowly or thinking slowly, but you will find that things are actually being accomplished and that they are getting done right on time by themselves. "We" are doing less. *Nondoing* is a good word for this. In this way absolute time is relative time. There's no need to be in a hurry, though if you are in a hurry, you should be aware that you're in a hurry, and you should hurry one hundred percent. When you "only hurry," it's no hurry at all. It's the same as "only sit." Only sit, only hurry. It's quite different and not at all the struggle of the dualistic hurry. It's only hurry *as it is.* Real practice enables us to live in this way.

When you become familiar with returning your radiance inward to your pervasive awareness and cultivate just this as your life force, you can return and cultivate it anywhere. No matter where you are or what is going on, you can "fix" or "turn on" your mind. This phrase comes directly from my own experience with my teacher. In the early days Suzuki-roshi urged me to "fix my mind." That's what he said. After all these seasons I am now understanding that what he was urging me to do was to maintain my focus on this pervasive awareness everywhere, not only during zazen. He was encouraging me to regain the imperturbable composure in whatever I did so that I could be free.

This is one of the reasons I encourage you to maintain practice. You will discover from your personal experience there is great joy and gratitude—when your practice has foundation. Little by little you will begin to realize the teachings are actually true; that the precious Dharma manifested and expressed is always with you. Of course, it's paradoxical that in Zen you can't say what this unborn is, and yet there are a multitude of Zen texts written about it. In all the sutras and Dharmas, each and every volume upon volume is directly pointing to "you." But eventually you will realize the truth behind the living words. You will come to know without doubt that it is the unborn because it was never created. And since it was never created, it's beyond any conditions; it does not change. We can say, in a way, it is permanent and real. Therefore this is the only *stuff* we all can rely on.

Canyons in a Cup

Steve Hagen

Here's another approach to the emptiness question. Because Buddhism says that reality is beyond conceptualization, it seeks to disprove all assertions. So Buddhist philosophy makes heavy use of negation. (If you were wondering, it also negates negations.) See what Zen teacher Steve Hagen does with the simple statement, "This is a cup."

Zen practice is about being awake, being aware. But if the point is to be awake, what do we do about it? How do we wake up? And what does it mean to be awake? Aren't we awake now?

Huang Po, a Chinese Zen master of the ninth century C.E., said,

> If you students of the Way do not awake to this Mind, you will overlay Mind with conceptual thought. You will seek Buddha outside yourselves, and you will remain attached to forms, pious practices, and so on—all of which are harmful and not at all the way to supreme knowledge.

This is precisely what we do. We overlay our direct experience of Reality with our *ideas* of what is real. And because our ability to do this is so subtle and so highly developed, we don't even know we're doing it. Thus we become chronically confused.

Take any object—a mountain, the sky, or an everyday object like a teacup. Our usual way to think is, "It's just a cup." Often we know the object so well, and we size it up so quickly, that we ignore it almost entirely. We make ourselves a pot of tea and blindly fill the cup with no thought and barely any awareness of what we're actually doing. We do this because we "know"—we believe—it's just a cup and nothing more.

But if we really pay attention to what's actually experienced, it's not just a cup. If we look, we can see the whole universe right here, as this cup. Inside this cup, as the Sufi poet Kabir would say, "are canyons and pine mountains."

The cup doesn't appear by itself. Someone took clay and fashioned it. And someone made that potter's wheel. And there's the tree that fueled the fire for the kiln. And the sun and the rain and the soil that grew the tree.

When we see that all this has gone into the picture, we can then actually experience a cup. We can *see* the cup for what it is—which is to say that it really isn't anything in particular.

Try to nail down what anything is. You can't. It's like trying to answer the question, "Is that you in your baby picture?" What can you say? You may say, "Yes, that's me." But obviously it is not. You're not a baby. But can you say, "No"? Who is it in the picture, then?

And if you say, "That *was* me," how could you still be you if you're six times bigger and far more articulate? Indeed what does "you" refer to? And if you say, "It's both me and not me," what can this mean? Have you ever seen anything that both is and isn't what it is? And if it's neither you nor not you, what are we even talking about? If we really look carefully, such simple, everyday questions as these can set our minds spinning.

There's nothing absolute about our objects, ever, even though we usually think there is. We quietly assume a cup is a cup is a cup. But where can we draw the line between the cup and everything else? If you pay very close attention, you'll see that you can't.

Anything you can package in your mind, anything you can frame and divide from other things, is a concept. And confusing our concepts with Reality is what gets us into so much trouble.

Once again the question becomes, how do we wake up?

First of all, you have to want to wake up. But wanting to wake up is not like wanting a new car or a new job or respect or love. If you really want to wake up, these other things are irrelevant. To want in this way is not ordinary wanting. If you want to wake up to how the world really is, you must be totally open to *this*—the reality of *this moment*—even while knowing full well that you can't conceive of how it really is. Waking up can only come about through seeing, not through coercion or the application of will. It requires a willingness to let go of all your cherished opinions.

To seek enlightenment as though we expect some kind of payback is only to frustrate ourselves. If you really want to wake up, then just wake up.

Start paying attention to your objects. Notice what you're thinking, believing, conceiving—what you're constructing in your mind. And start to notice how baffling and contradictory and pervasive the constructions of your mind really are.

Once we really understand what's going on, we're less likely to hang on to our cherished opinions because we can now see that everything we pick up is like water trickling out between our fingers. We know we're not going to get too far with our mental constructions before they all fall apart and no longer work.

The universe is not mysterious. Reality is clearly displayed at all times. Nothing is hidden. But for our thoughts we would *see* it.

The True Path is meeting your eyes even now. Just attend to what is actually going on—but keep it simple and keep it clear. Just open your wisdom eye and *see*.

Everything Confirmed in an Instant

Brad Warner

Here's one of the rare younger voices in American Buddhism, which remains dominated by baby boomers. Brad Warner is sharp and funny, but most importantly his story rings true. Working on a sci-fi TV show in Tokyo, plodding along in his Zen practice, he is unexpectedly struck by a kensho *experience—a sudden hit of enlightened mind. Rarely will you find a more credible description of this experience, and I think the great Zen masters of the past would have given their approval.*

While living in Tokyo and working on selling the Ultraman TV series to the world, I kept attending the Zen monk Gudo Nishijima's weekly zazen sittings, finding them alternately stimulating and exasperating. The nice little Zen books on the shelves these days don't give you much of a sense of how truly grating Zen masters can be. They're the ultimate in know-it-alls. You can't tell them anything. And Nishijima may be the very worst of the lot. He seems to delight in throwing lines into his talks that are guaranteed to put everyone in the room on edge. The image of the gentle Zen master soothing his audience with tranquil words of serenity and peace is a Hollywood invention that far too many wannabes spend far too much energy learning to imitate. Nishijima's talks are never stilling—they're downright irritating.

In addition to his weekly sittings and lectures, Nishijima also hosts several zazen retreats at a temple near the city of Shizuoka, in the foothills of Mount Fuji about two hours south of Tokyo by bullet train. It's a beautiful old Zen temple surrounded by tea fields, miles from the nearest convenience store and not a McDonald's® or Starbucks® in sight. Still, if you desperately need a sugar-laden soft drink, you can take a five minute walk down the hill to the vending machine out in front of the little noodle shop that caters to tourists who stop by the temple and folks who come around to arrange funerals.

As far as I could tell during my first visit the main activities of the monks at the temple seemed to be hanging out in the kitchen watching vapid TV chat shows, drinking beer, and brushing up on the chants used in funeral services. Over the next few years I discovered I was pretty off base with that assessment. The guy I'd seen drinking all the beer turned out not to be one of the monks (though he did have a shaved head and lived in a temple—sue me for getting that one wrong) and managed to give up the booze by the following summer—no small feat in Japan where you can get plastered seven nights a week and still not be considered an alcoholic. The monks are in fact all hard-working guys who perform an important service for their community. Still, apart from the head of the temple who usually joins us for at least one sitting, the only other monk there I've ever seen doing zazen—which is the central practice of Zen Buddhism, mind you—was a Sri Lankan guy from the Theravada school of Buddhism who was there as part of some Buddhist exchange program. Unfortunately, this is pretty typical of Buddhist temples all over Japan.

Nishijima's retreats are pretty lightweight as Zen retreats go. While many such retreats have their students wake up at three o'clock in the morning, Nishijima lets his students get up at a very leisurely 4:30. There are four zazen periods each day, two of which are forty-five minutes while the other two are an hour and a half each (that's forty-five minutes of zazen, fifteen minutes of walking meditation, and another forty-five minutes of zazen). This is about half, if that, of what the really rigorous temples make their students do. The retreats are just three days long, rather than the week-long or even month-long affairs elsewhere. Still, if you've never done that kind of thing before, even this can be a major jolt to the system.

By the time I went to my first formal retreat, I'd already been doing zazen for eleven years and going to Nishijima's lectures for two. But my first retreat with Nishijima was my first experience in an actual temple with an actual Japanese Zen priest running the show.

I hated it.

For starters I was completely confused about the arrangements. Bonehead that I am, rather than signing on for the annual English-language retreat for foreigners, I signed on for the one Nishijima holds for new members of the cosmetics company he works for. The company president is enamored of zazen and requires all new employees to attend one of these. A bunch of spotty-faced new college grads who've just entered the fabulously exciting cosmetics industry are herded up to the mountains to sit still for three tedious days. There's no beer, no dried-fish snacks, no karaoke or party games—just peace and solitude and sitting up straight facing a wall all weekend long. Needless to say these kids are not happy campers.

I ended up being one of three of Nishijima's special guests that weekend, along with Jeremy Pearson, one of his long-time students, and a strange Korean man who was apparently some kind of philosophy professor somewhere. The four of us shared a room on the temple's second floor.

I didn't know Jeremy very well at the time, but he had a shaved head, knew every chant and mealtime ritual, and wore a set of monk's robes all weekend. Clearly he was a very serious Zen guy. I never could work out exactly why the Korean guy was there. He spoke fluent English and could get by moderately in Japanese, and he had obviously studied a lot of Buddhist literature and considered himself quite the expert in the field. For all I knew he might have been one of Korea's most renowned Buddhist scholars. He certainly carried himself like Korea's most renowned *something*. Maybe he had come to get a bit of hands-on experience with Japanese Zen, no doubt so that he could go back to Korea and legitimately claim to have been through some real Japanese-style Zen training.

But my main impression of him was this: He farted a lot.

Now don't get me wrong, of course passing gas is fine and normal and natural. But this man seemed to have no idea that doing so loudly and odiferously in the middle of a polite conversation was potentially a bit off-putting. He'd just be chattering away then lift a cheek and let one rip without the slightest pause in his speech. I'd heard about some Asian countries where nose-picking in public is not considered odd or rude, but I don't think there's any part of the world where farting is considered an ordinary part of polite social intercourse—and Japan *certainly* is not such place. The man had a lot of the qualities of the autistic people I used to work with when I'd been an instructor at the Summit County Board of Mental Retardation. He seemed unaware that there were other people in the world. He spoke only in monologues as if he'd created his own mental images of people and reacted to those images rather than the people themselves. Before he asked you a question, he already had your answer worked out in his mind and no matter what answer you actually gave, he responded to the one he'd heard in his mind. It made for some very odd conversations. Something like this:

> Farting man: What's your favorite color?
> Me: Blue.

Farting man: You know red is a symbol of . . .
(blah-blah-blah about red for an hour)

Okay, I'm exaggerating a little—but not much.

Anyhow, I arrived at this particular retreat with a chip on my shoulder. I'd been doing zazen for over a decade by then and I was pretty miffed that I had yet to reach enlightenment. I'd read all the major Buddhist sutras and had made a thorough study of most of the major Indian holy books. I had shelves full of dog-eared books by big-wig spiritual teachers like Krishnamurti, Ramana Maharshi, Shunryu Suzuki, and anybody else who'd written on the subject of being enlightened. I'd even been to Christian churches to check out their ideas about "born-again experiences," which I figured might have been a kind of Christian version of enlightenment. (They weren't, FYI.) Buddy, if anyone shoulda been enlightened it was me!

One evening, I was upstairs with Nishijima, Jeremy, and Farting Man, and I steeled up my nerves enough to ask Nishijima about enlightenment.

Let me give you a bit of background. In a nutshell there are two major schools of Zen in Japan: Soto, to which Nishijima belonged and in which my teacher Tim McCarthy had studied and taught; and the Rinzai school, Soto's main competitor, as it were. The difference between them is this: the Rinzai school believes in enlightenment and the Soto school doesn't.

All right, admittedly it's a good bit more complex and interesting than that. But for now, that's all you need to know to follow the story.

Knowing that Nishijima was a Soto guy, I was trying to be cool about the whole enlightenment thing. I didn't actually use the e-word, I just kinda hinted around, saying stuff like "I've been studying for ten years and I still haven't *got it*, you know? I mean I don't, like, y'know, *understand anything* . . ."—everything short of nudging and winking to show him I was in on the big secret.

So at this point Farting Man piped in, in a fatherly tone, like a learned Oxford don: "Don't worry, it will come . . . ," he said, smiling broadly, "*with enlightenment!*" I'm sure he would have patted me on the knee if I hadn't sat myself a safe distance away to avoid being gassed.

"Don't say that!" Jeremy snapped. "That's not it at all!"

This reprimand made absolutely no impression on Farting Man, who continued to smile beatifically. I'm not sure he even heard it. Judging by the smug, satisfied smile on his face, what he'd heard must have been something like, "Yea brother, verily you speak the truth which this young one has yet to meet."

Nishijima himself ignored all this and tried his best to explain the problem to me. I don't recall what he said but it didn't clear anything up for me. I listened respectfully and asked a few questions but he seemed to be talking in circles.

Enlightenment is probably the single most written-about subject in all of Buddhism. But it's a damn tricky subject. In Philip Kapleau's famous book *The Three Pillars of Zen* there are several descriptions of people's "enlightenment experiences." This was a bold move on Kapleau's part, since such experiences are generally considered "secret" and not appropriate for talking about, and had rarely been published up until then. In that book there were stories of guys watching the sky open up and start laughing with them, and there were tears and shouts and drama all over the damn place. This was one of the first books I read about Zen, so I walked around for the first year or two of practicing zazen waiting for the moment when something like that would happen to me. Once, while strolling around the campus of Kent State University, I thought I'd got it. I just suddenly got all giddy and laughed like an imbecile at everything. Later I talked to Tim, my Zen teacher at the time, saying stuff like, "Y'know, was that, like, um . . . *it?*"—again carefully avoiding the e-word. Nope, he'd said, laughing like an idiot was just something that beginners in Zen sometimes did. *Beginner?!* I'd been practicing for almost two whole years, dammit!

By the time I ended up at Nishijima's retreat, though, I'd had eight more years of practice. For the year or so prior to that retreat I'd even been pretty good about practicing. I was starting to believe in it again for some reason. But zazen is a pretty hard thing to believe in since the results appear so slowly. In fact, I'd be inclined to tell you these days that the results never appear at all. Well, it isn't that there aren't any results. Not exactly. The problem is in the concept of what constitutes a "result." But let's not go there just now.

I've met people who've fallen ass-over-teakettle in love with zazen after only a day or two, maybe even one lecture. Those people always strike me as airheads, the kind of goofballs who could just as easily go for crystal healing or angels. Enthusiasm is fine but too much is never a good thing. Folks who get too hot on zazen right at the beginning rarely stick with it long. Pretty soon the fervor cools, the crush passes, and they lose interest. Me, I hated zazen from the start and still do sometimes. I did it the way people go on diets or give up smoking. It sucked, but I could tell it was somehow good for me. Hating zazen, on the other hand, is no impediment to coming to real understanding. In fact it's a time-proven method.

In my years of zazen nothing like what was written in Kapleau's book had ever happened to me. I kept waiting and waiting, but no dice. There's an old Zen tale about a monk who got enlightened when he heard the sound of a pebble hitting a tile. So every time I heard a sharp little sound like that I'd think, "Okay! Maybe I'll get it right now. Wait for it, wait for it. . . . Nope. Nuthin'. *Crap!*"

I went through the rest of the retreat remaining thoroughly unenlightened. Farting Man remained oblivious. And Jeremy remained, well, bald and Buddhist-looking. But I was pleased when once, after Farting Man left the room, Nishijima whispered to me and Jeremy, "You know, he is a very strange man."

It would take several more years of struggle and frustration before I got any glimmer as to what the answer to the whole enlightenment question might be, or to even properly understand the question itself. I'd formed a pretty clear image of what enlightenment ought to feel like and I kept waiting for that image to become reality. Unsurprisingly, it never did. Now I'm sure it never will.

D. T. Suzuki, the first really popular Zen Buddhist writer in the Western world, was a Rinzai man all the way. His books are chock full of references to *satori*, the Japanese word for enlightenment. Rinzai teachings stress the importance of enlightenment experiences and students in the Rinzai school strive very hard to achieve them. The Soto school has a completely different view of the subject.

A lot of Soto school Zen teachers refuse to even talk about "enlightenment." It's pointless, they'll tell you. All it does is muddle the issue. The Soto view is that these so-called enlightenment experiences just aren't really all that and a bag o' chips. And yet Soto teachers do acknowledge there is something, a kind of experience that eventually occurs and that has been mistakenly and misleadingly called "enlightenment." Nishijima likes to call it "solving the philosophical problems." Sometimes, if you catch him in a good mood, he'll call it "*second* enlightenment." The first enlightenment is, of course, zazen.

The experience that Nishijima calls solving the philosophical problems is undeniably real—but it should not be overemphasized or overvalued. A lot of people have the idea that enlightenment will be a kind of retirement from life. They figure that once they get it, everything will just flow easily and they'll never have to make any more effort. They look at the Zen life like a kind of marathon race. You have to run real hard for a real long time but once you cross the finish line, you're done. You win. You can sit back and sip lemonade for the rest of your life. It really isn't like that at all. If anything, the opposite is true. Once you've solved those philosophical problems it's your duty to put those solutions into effect. It doesn't get easier, it gets harder.

The good news is that one of the biggest philosophical problems you clear up is the confused belief that being lazy is somehow better than working hard. Being saddled with the whole universe to take care of is better than winning the lottery or having Miss November or Mister Universe knock on your bedroom door one morning and flash you their goods when you open it. Solving those philosophical problems does mean you've won—but nothing so piddling as the marathon race of life. You've won all creation. It's yours to do with as you please—and you discover what pleases you most is doing the right thing for all creation in moment after moment.

As I've said, talking about enlightenment is risky—and leaving it to people's imaginations is equally risky. So nonetheless, leaving the e-word aside, I'll tell you about my own experience of solving the philosophical problems.

I guess it was early fall, maybe five years after my encounter with Farting Man. I was walking to work alongside the Sengawa River, just like I did every day, when in an instant everything changed. In old Buddhist stories there's always some catalyst, like that guy who heard the pebble strike the piece of bamboo, or else someone reading a certain verse, or getting whacked by some teacher's stick. But I really can't recall anything unusual. I was just walking to work.

About a week earlier I'd finished yet another summer zazen retreat, so my brain was maybe a bit quieter than usual. Although I can't recall what I was thinking about at the time, I'm sure I *was* thinking, and probably about what I needed to do at the office that day or some similarly banal thing. I wasn't worrying or mulling over anything very deeply—just the usual stream of images bouncing around up in my head.

What I do recall very clearly is the geographical spot where it started to happen. There's a narrow road along the Sengawa River and in order to get to where I work I need to cross the river on one of the many small bridges built over it. The shortcut I like to take has me crossing one particular little bridge every morning. I was walking along the road and just about to cross that bridge when all my problems, all my complaints, all my confusions and misunderstandings just kind of untwisted themselves from each other and went plop on the ground. I'm not talking some of my problems, I'm talking about *all* of them, every last one. *Plop!*

Every damned thing I'd ever read in the Buddhist sutras was confirmed in a single instant. The universe was me and I was it. I looked up at the sky and that experience was exactly like looking at a mirror. I don't mean that metaphorically either. You know the feeling of recognition you get when you look in a mirror? "That's me," you think to yourself, "My hair needs to be combed and, hey, there's a pimple on my nose!" Well I got that same feeling no matter where I looked. I looked at the asphalt road and it was my face. I looked at the bridge and the bridge was me staring back at myself. It was a physical sensation, as if the sky had my eyes and could see me staring up at it. There was no doubt that this state was "true." It was far more true than the state I had considered to be normal up until then. I had no need to confirm it with anyone.

It's all me.

Even if I want to put this realization down I can't. Sometimes it's excruciating. You know those morons that rammed those planes into the World Trade Center? That was me. The people that died in the collapse. Me again. Every single person who ever paid money for a Pet Rock? Me. I don't mean I identify with them or sympathize with them. I mean I am them. It's impossible to explain any more clearly than that, but this isn't a figure of speech or bad poetry. I mean it absolutely literally.

But the universe is sooooo much bigger than any of that.

The sky is me, and the stars too, and the chirping crickets and the songs they make; sparkling rivers, snow and rain, distant solar systems and whatever beings may live there: it's all me. And it's you, too.

Was this the same state that Gautama Buddha experienced

that early December morning twenty-five hundred years ago? Yes it was. It is. Absolutely.

Is there anything special about me? Not a damned thing.

Has it changed my life? Yup.

Was it a big deal? Buddy, everything's a big deal, but yes, this was a big deal.

I'd been driving through a dark tunnel for countless years when all at once I emerged into the sunlight along the shore of a lush tropical island. Yet there were no bells, no whistles, no gongs; no thunder, no earthquakes; no peals of laughter, no tears, no drama.

And then I went to work and did my job.

It was all very ordinary and normal. But in that very normality and ordinariness was something more wonderful than anything special I could ever have imagined. All imagination pales into nothing compared to what your real life is right here and right now. There's not a single dream you can have, no matter how pure or beautiful, that's better than what you're living through right now no matter how lousy you think right now is.

Why should you believe in any of this? Why should you care? No reason. No reason at all.

There's nothing I can possibly tell you that could communicate this state to you. Because human language by its very nature just isn't up to the task. If I say "kumquat" or "droopy granny boobs" or "Johnny Ramone on stage at CBGB's circa 1975," you have an idea what I mean. But there's nothing I can say that can communicate the reality of that experience.

Do a lot of zazen though and you'll see it for yourself. I can promise that, without doubt and without reservation.

But what happened to me won't happen to you. At all. And yet it will. Exactly.

Sounds like nonsense doesn't it? I empathize.

Here's as clear as I can be about this stuff: The only enlightenment that really matters is right here and right now. You have it right in the palm of your hand. It shines from your eyes and illuminates everything you see.

Oh, and one last thing: People imagine enlightenment will make them incredibly powerful. And it does. It makes you the most powerful being in all the universe—but usually no one else notices.

Spacing Out

Diana Winston

Buddhism's basic practice is coming back from our thoughts to what's happening on the spot. When we try this, the first thing we notice is how much time we actually spend lost in thought, a discovery many people find shocking when they first start meditating. Here, in her book on Buddhism for teens, Diana Winston describes the wandering mind we all suffer from and how much of life it causes us to miss.

Where was your mind most of the day today? Can you even remember how you got from where you were a few hours ago to where you are right now reading this book? Probably not.

Why is it that something so recent should be completely lost to our memory? Because most of us, most of the time, are spacing out.

What we call "spacing out" is a trancelike operating mode. Our focus is internal rather than external and it can seem as though we are not focused on anything at all; we are in a complete stupor. This happens in classes that we find boring or irrelevant, or in the midst of habitual activity—brushing our teeth, eating lunch, or cleaning our room; it can even happen when we are listening to our friend's problems! We simply stop following the action in the scene around us and withdraw our consciousness until someone or something snaps us out of it, bringing our awareness back to the present moment.

This spacing out is often like watching TV in our mind. When we space out, our minds tend to go to one of two places: the past or the future. That is, we spend our present moment either "reliving" or "preliving." When we relive stories and past events we replay wonderful memories—that fantastic party from last weekend, or our first (or fiftieth!) kiss. But sometimes we spend hours lost in painful memories, reexperiencing how we had felt, or imagining different outcomes or how we might have done things differently, like seventeen-year-old Graham's experience after a breakup:

> The other day in math class, all I could think about was Anna breaking up with me. She called me up and said, "Yo, it's over." I said, "Wait, can we talk about this?" And she said no. So my mind kept obsessing how I should have treated her . . . if things could have been different . . . I completely forgot about algebra till my teacher called on me.

Our minds also hang out in the future. Fifteen-year-old Jia's recollection illustrates how we can spend hours designing a future that is not present, yet seems so vivid:

> I wanted to get on the volleyball team and I thought for sure I'd make it. Then my mind imagined I would be chosen captain, then MVP, then that our team would win the tournament, especially against the school that always beats us, and then . . . I hadn't actually even made the team yet. It was weird. I do that all the time.

Worry is another kind of "preliving" way of spacing out. Spacing out isn't always pleasant. Many of us are all too familiar with anxiety about the future. *What if my parents find out about . . . ? I should have studied harder. Will I finish high school? Will I get into the college I want? What if I'm pregnant?* And so on endlessly, until we have tied ourselves up in knots. Worry can cause a lot of suffering—ironically over things that have not yet, and may never happen!

Spacing out is a protective ability that we probably learned when we were very young. When humans experience too much pain—physical or emotional—one natural reaction of the mind is to dissociate, that is, to let our mind separate from the body, from this place and time, the present moment. In truth, this capacity is very helpful as it prevents us from hurting too badly. The problem is, however, that spacing out has become habitual, overused. We space out not only in extreme situations to avoid pain, but virtually any time that our attention is not absolutely grabbed. It has become more like our normal way of being.

So what? If our life is boring or painful at times, then why not space out? Why not go to sleep and wait for the next amazing experience or the next movie that will entertain us? What is the big deal with spacing out? Well, the big deal is that we are missing the now, when truly, now is all there is. The bottom line is we are missing our lives.

Turning the Mind into an Ally

Sakyong Mipham

Once we discover the wildness of our mind, we seek a way to tame it. This is done through the meditation practice called peaceful abiding, *or* mindfulness. *In this teaching, Sakyong Mipham Rinpoche presents the essential points of this practice that makes the mind our friend rather than the source of our suffering.*

Even though the bewildered mind is untrained, it is already meditating, whether we know it or not. Meditation is the natural process of becoming familiar with an object by repeatedly placing our minds upon it. Whatever we're doing, we always have a view; we're always placing our mind on one object or another. For example, when we get up in the morning and we're anxious about something, anxiety becomes our view for the day: "What about me? When will I get what I want?" The object of our meditation is "me."

In peaceful abiding, we ground our mind in the present moment. We place our mind on the breath and practice keeping it there. We notice when thoughts and emotions distract us, and train in continually returning our mind to the breath. This is how we shift our allegiance from the bewildered mind that causes its own suffering to the mind that is stable, clear, and strong. We proclaim our desire to discover this mind of stability, clarity, and strength by learning to rest in our own peace.

Turning the mind into an ally is a matter of learning to see ourselves as we are. Ordinarily we just can't handle the natural joy of our mind, so we end up churning up intense emotions. These emotions keep us trapped in suffering. In peaceful abiding we begin to see how the mind works.

"Peaceful abiding" describes the mind as it naturally is. The word *peace* tells the whole story. The human mind is by nature joyous, calm, and very clear. In peaceful abiding, or *shamatha*, meditation we aren't creating a peaceful state—we're letting our mind be as it is to begin with. This doesn't mean that we're peacefully ignoring things. It means that the mind is able to be in itself without constantly leaving.

From a Buddhist point of view, human beings aren't intrinsically aggressive; we are inherently peaceful. This is sometimes hard to believe. When we're angry or upset, our untrained mind becomes belligerent and we routinely strike out at others. We imagine that reacting aggressively to the object of our emotion will resolve our pain. Throughout history we have used this approach over and over again. Striking out when we're in pain is clearly one way we perpetuate misery.

With a trained mind, a stable mind, a mind with a larger motivation than its own comfort, we find another way to work with the difficulties of daily life. When we're in a difficult situation, we maintain our seat. Instead of perpetuating misery by acting out aggression, we learn to use the rough spots to spark the courage to proceed on our journey. Eventually we may actually be able to turn the mind of anger into the energy of love and compassion.

But first we learn how to abide peacefully. If we can remember what the word *shamatha* means, we can always use it as a reference point. We can say, "What is this meditation that I'm doing? It is calm, peaceful abiding." At the same time we'll begin to see that our mind is always abiding somewhere—not necessarily in its peaceful natural state. Perhaps it's abiding in irritation, anger, jealousy. Seeing all of this is how we begin to untangle our bewilderment.

We're accustomed to living a life based on running after our wild mind, a mind that is continually giving birth to thoughts and emotions. It's not that there's anything inherently wrong with thoughts and emotions—in fact, the point of making our mind an ally is that we can begin to direct them for benefit. Through peacefully abiding we begin to see our emotions at work. We begin to see that we have to work with these intense emotions because if we don't, they'll grow. Once they grow, we act on them. When we act on them, they create our environment.

Meditation shows how discursive thoughts lead to emotion—irritation, anxiety, passion, aggression, jealousy, pride, greed—which lead to suffering. For example, the person sitting next to you on the bus has a really fancy CD player. First you're intrigued by all the bells and whistles. Then, before you know it, you want one just like it, even though your own player was perfectly adequate two minutes ago. You were sitting there peacefully, and now you're a volcano of desire. On top of that, you're jealous of this total stranger for having something you want. You were enjoying the ride, and now, a few thoughts later, you're miserable.

Reacting to emotion creates further reactions later. We're planning a vacation with a friend and disagree about what day to leave. Our friend is angry, which makes us angry, which makes him angrier, and before we know it, our trip is down the drain. Being discursive might feel good, just as food we're allergic to tastes good, but after we eat it, we suffer.

Meditation is a very personal journey. Simply by being conscious of the present moment so we can ground ourselves in it, we relax our sense of self and begin to tune in to reality as it is. We begin to realize what we don't know, and we become curious: "What is truly valid? What is the truth of my experience?" If we lived in the wilderness, we'd observe nature's patterns around us: the activity of the birds and animals, the behavior of the weather, and changes in the plant life. After a while, we'd be intimate with the environment. We might be able to predict when winter is coming and whether it would be long or short. Similarly, in peaceful abiding we can begin to observe and understand our thought patterns. We can watch how our mind weaves from one idea to another, one emotion to another. We can see how it fabricates a comfort zone. We can see how it wants to take action. We can begin to understand its course without judging it. We just notice the internal environment and become familiar with it.

After we've spent some time watching thoughts and emotions come and go we begin to see them clearly. They no longer have the power to destabilize us, because we see how ephemeral they are. Then we can actually begin to change our patterns, and in doing so, change our whole environment. But to reap this benefit requires consistent practice.

Once we establish a regular practice, our life can feel like it's undergoing a major upheaval. Meditating is a new way of looking at things. We have to be willing to change. When we begin to tame the movement of our mind, it affects everything else. It's like renovating: once you start, it's hard to stop. For example, at Shambhala Mountain Center, where I teach every summer, our meditation hall was getting old and funky, so we built a new one. Then by contrast, the kitchen looked small and old, so we needed to build a new kitchen, too.

In beginning to meditate, you might see things about yourself that you don't like, so it's important to ask yourself if you're willing to change. Before you consider entering a spiritual path, you have to begin by looking at the basic ground. Before you even sit down, ask yourself these questions: Do I actually want to become a better person? Do I really want to work with my mind? We're not talking about becoming a goody-goody. We're saying that we can choose to become stronger, kinder, wiser, and more focused. We can become more in tune with how things are. Do we really want to do that?

The notion of meditation is very simple. We slow down and begin to look at the pattern of our life. We have to start with the mind, then the body follows. This is not to say that once we start meditating, everything will work out and we'll have no problems. We'll still have disagreements with friends and family, we'll still get parking tickets, we'll still miss flights, we'll still burn the toast on occasion. Meditation doesn't take us to the end of the rainbow—it opens the possibility of completely embodying our enlightened qualities by making our mind an ally. When we meditate, we're training ourselves to see our weak points and strengthen our positive ones. We're altering our basic perception. We're beginning to change how we relate to the world—but not forcefully.

Once we start really looking at the mind, we see some elements of how it works. For one, the mind is always placing itself on something. It has to do this in order to know what's going on. Generally we ingrain the tendency to follow distractions—which is the opposite of stabilizing the mind. Maybe the mind places itself on the idea of dinner. Then we think about what's in the refrigerator. Then we think about a restaurant. Then we think about what we'd wear to the restaurant. Then we think about buying new clothes. The mind is continually placing itself, usually for only a few seconds at a time. That is the case even when we're thinking systematically about something, such as a plan.

For instance, if I'm going from New York to Paris, I think about how I am going to do that. "What day will I fly, at what time? Will I get frequent-flier miles? How long will it take? Then where will I go? And who will I see when I get there?" If we look at our mind as it's planning, we'll see that between all those planning thoughts, other thoughts are arising. Although it may seem as if we're having a stream of thoughts about our vacation, if we look closely, we'll see that the mind is continuously bouncing back and forth between many thoughts—"It feels warm in here; shall I open a window? I wonder what's for lunch. Is there time to pick something up at the grocery store before the meeting this afternoon?"

But since most of the thoughts are about the trip, we say, "Oh, I am planning my vacation."

Something else we'll see when we begin to look at our mind carefully is that we don't really perceive several things at once; we can only perceive one thing at a time. Try it out. It feels as if we hear the bird and see the sunshine at the same time, but in terms of the actual experience, the mind is moving from one perception to another. If we're thinking about what we are cooking for dinner, we'll have consecutive thoughts about it; in between, our mind places itself on other things many times over. The memory of a pleasant telephone encounter earlier in the day pops up; we notice that someone has washed the breakfast dishes; we like this track on the CD and we wonder who's singing. If we look closely at our mind, we see that it always behaves this way.

If we have enough similar thoughts, we call it a stream of consciousness, a stream of thought. However, the current of the mind is always fluctuating. The mind weaves an illusion of solidity by putting things together; it's actually going back and forth. At the beginning of peaceful abiding we discover what the mind is by drawing it in. We do this by sitting still and training in holding it to something for more than a few seconds. Repeatedly bringing it back to the breath may feel unnatural at the beginning, like having to hold a child to keep him from squirming. But if we keep doing it, at some point we begin to see that underneath the distraction and bewilderment, something else is going on. We begin to see the mind's underlying stillness. There is intelligence; there's some kind of stability; there's some kind of strength. We begin to see how the discursiveness of thoughts and emotions keeps us from experiencing these natural qualities of the mind.

In peaceful abiding we use the present moment as a reference point for relating to our mind and overcoming its wildness and discursiveness. When we sit down to meditate, there's so much going on in our mind that it's easy to get lost. We wander around in this dense jungle, not knowing where we are going. The present moment and the breath are like a hilltop in the distance. We keep our eyes on it as we walk toward it. We need to get to the hilltop, climb it, and look around so that we can figure out where we are.

Returning our mind to the breath is how we learn to be mindful and aware. It's like giving a child a pet: caring for a living creature teaches us responsibility and loving-kindness. When we grow up, we can express what we have learned to others. In the same way, we are using the breath as a vehicle to bring us into the present moment.

When I was young, I trained falcons. I would use tiny pieces of meat as a reference point. After a while, whenever I blew a whistle the bird would fly over to take the meat from my hand. It was challenging work, since the birds' natural tendency is not to trust a human. Training them for many months in captivity taught me the value of accepting small improvements day by day. After the trust was there, I could release the bird into the wild. That was the moment of truth: when I blew the whistle, would the bird return to my hand? This is very much like how we train our minds to return to the breath in peaceful abiding. It takes patience.

When we experience a moment of peacefully abiding, it seems so far-out. Our mind is no longer drifting, thinking about a million things. The sun comes up or a beautiful breeze comes along—and all of a sudden we feel the breeze and we are completely in tune. We think, "That's a very spiritual experience. It's a religious experience. At least worth a poem, or a letter home." But all that's happening is that for a moment we're in tune with our mind. Our mind is present and harmonious. Before, we were so busy and bewildered that we didn't even notice the breeze. Our mind couldn't even stay put long enough to watch the sun come up, which takes two and a half minutes. Now we can keep it in one place long enough to acknowledge and appreciate our surroundings. Now we are really here. In fact, being in the present moment is ordinary; it's the point of being human.

Learning to be present for the moment is the beginning of the spiritual path. By sitting still and training our mind to be with the breath, we begin to relax our discursiveness. We see how the mind creates our solid sense of self and begin to discover the mind's natural state of being. With this experience, we can cultivate our garden. The flowers of love, compassion, and wisdom gradually take over, and the weeds of anger, jealousy, and self-involvement have less and less room to grow. In peaceful abiding we become familiar with the ground of basic goodness. This is how we turn the mind into an ally.

The Lama in the Lab

Daniel Goleman

For centuries science has been skeptical of religious experience because it couldn't be seen or measured. That's changing now as advances in neurotechnology allow scientists to "see" how the brain reflects what the meditator is experiencing. Daniel Goleman is a Buddhist, a psychologist, and the author of Emotional Intelligence, *and he's participated in a series of dialogues between scientists and meditators led by His Holiness the Dalai Lama. Here's Goleman's report on what some leading scientists see when they watch the brain of a seasoned meditator.*

Lama Öser strikes most anyone who meets him as resplendent—not because of his maroon and gold Tibetan monk's robes, but because of his radiant smile. Öser, a European-born convert to Buddhism, has trained as a Tibetan monk in the Himalayas for more than three decades, including many years at the side of one of Tibet's greatest spiritual masters. But today Öser (whose name has been changed here to protect his privacy) is about to take a revolutionary step in the history of the spiritual lineages he has become a part of. He will engage in meditation while having his brain scanned by state-of-the-art brain imaging devices.

To be sure, there have been sporadic attempts to study brain activity in meditators, and decades of tests with monks and yogis in Western labs, some revealing remarkable abilities to control respiration, brain waves, or core body temperature. But this—the first experiment with someone at Öser's level of training, using such sophisticated measures—will take that research to an entirely new level. It can take scientists deeper than they have ever been into charting the specific links between highly disciplined mental strategies and their impact on brain function. And this research agenda has a pragmatic focus: to assess meditation as mind training, a practical answer to the perennial human conundrum of how we can better handle our destructive emotions.

This issue had been addressed over the course of a remarkable five-day dialogue held the year before between the Dalai Lama and a small group of scientists at his private quarters in Dharamsala, India. The research with Öser marked one culmination of several lines of scientific inquiry set in motion during the dialogue. There the Dalai Lama had been a prime mover in inspiring this research; he was an active collaborator in turning the lens of science on the practices of his own spiritual tradition.

It was at the invitation of Richard Davidson, one of the scientists who participated in the Dharamsala dialogues, that Öser had come to the E. M. Keck Laboratory for Functional Brain Imaging and Behavior, on the Madison campus of the University of Wisconsin. The laboratory was founded by Davidson, a leading pioneer in the field of affective neuroscience, which studies the interplay of the brain and emotions. Davidson had wanted Öser—a particularly intriguing subject—to be studied intensively with state-of-the-art brain measures.

Öser has spent several months at a stretch in intensive, solitary retreat. All told, those retreats add up to about two and a half years. But beyond that, during several years as the personal attendant to a Tibetan master, the reminders to practice even in the midst of his busy daily activities were almost constant. Now, here at the laboratory, the question was what difference any of that training had made.

The collaboration began before Öser even went near the MRI, with a meeting to design the research protocol. As the eight-person research team briefed Öser, everyone in the room was acutely aware that they were in a bit of a race against time. The Dalai Lama himself would visit the lab the very next day, and they hoped by then to have harvested at least some preliminary results to share with him.

Tibetan Buddhism may well offer the widest menu of meditation methods of any contemplative tradition, and it was from this rich offering that the team in Madison began to choose what to study. The initial suggestions from the research team were for three meditative states: a visualization, one-pointed concentration, and generating compassion. The three methods involved distinct enough mental strategies that the team was fairly sure they would reveal different underlying configurations of brain activity. Indeed, Öser was able to give precise descriptions of each.

One of the methods chosen, one-pointedness—a fully focused concentration on a single object of attention—may be the most basic and universal of all practices, found in one form or another in every spiritual tradition that employs meditation. Focusing on one point requires letting go of the ten thousand other thoughts and desires that flit through the mind as distractions; as the Danish philosopher Kierkegaard put it, "Purity of heart is to want one thing only."

In the Tibetan system (as in many others) cultivating concentration is a beginner's method, a prerequisite for moving on to more intricate approaches. In a sense, concentration is the most generic form of mind training, with many non-spiritual applications as well. Indeed, for this test, Öser simply picked a spot (a small bolt above him on the MRI, it turned out) to focus his gaze on, and held it there, bringing his focus back whenever his mind wandered off.

Öser proposed three more approaches that he thought would

usefully expand the data yield: meditations on devotion and on fearlessness, and what he called the "open state." The last refers to a thought-free wakefulness where the mind, as Öser described it, "is open, vast, and aware, with no intentional mental activity. The mind is not focused on anything, yet totally present—not in a focused way, just very open and undistracted. Thoughts may start to arise weakly, but they don't chain into longer thoughts—they just fade away."

Perhaps as intriguing was Öser's explanation of the meditation on fearlessness, which involves "bringing to mind a fearless certainty, a deep confidence that nothing can unsettle—decisive and firm, without hesitating, where you're not averse to anything. You enter into a state where you feel, no matter what happens, 'I have nothing to gain, nothing to lose.' "

Focusing on his teachers plays a key role in the meditation on devotion, he said, in which he holds in mind a deep appreciation of and gratitude toward his teachers and, most especially, the spiritual qualities they embody. That strategy also operates in the meditation on compassion, with his teachers' kindness offering a model.

The final meditation technique, visualization, entailed constructing in the mind's eye an image of the elaborately intricate details of a Tibetan Buddhist deity. As Öser described the process, "You start with the details and build the whole picture from top to bottom. Ideally, you should be able to keep in mind a clear and complete picture." As those familiar with Tibetan *thangkas* (the wall hangings that depict such deities) will know, such images are highly complex patterns.

Öser confidently assumed that each of these six meditation practices should show distinct brain configurations. The scientists have seen clear distinctions in cognitive activity between, say, visualization and one-pointedness. But the meditations on compassion, devotion, and fearlessness have not seemed that different in the mental processes involved, though they differ clearly in content. From a scientific point of view, if Öser could demonstrate sharp, consistent brain signatures for any of these meditative states, it would be a first.

Öser's testing started with the "functional MRI," the current gold standard of research on the brain's role in behavior. The standard MRI, in wide use in hospitals, offers a graphically detailed snapshot of the structure of the brain. But the fMRI offers all that in video—an ongoing record of how zones of the brain dynamically change their level of activity from moment to moment. The conventional MRI lays bare the brain's structures, while fMRI reveals how those structures interact as they function.

The fMRI would give Davidson a crystal-clear set of images of Öser's brain, cross-cutting slices at one millimeter—slimmer than a fingernail. These images could then be analyzed in any dimension to track precisely what happens during a mental act, tracing paths of activity through the brain.

Öser, lying peacefully on a hospital gurney with his head constrained in the maw of the fMRI, looked like a human pencil inserted into a huge cubic beige sharpener. Instead of the lone monk in a mountaintop cave, it's the monk in the brain scanner.

Wearing earphones so he could listen to the control room, Öser sounded unperturbed as the technicians led him through a lengthy series of checks to ensure the MRI images were tracking. Finally, as Davidson was about to begin the protocol, he asked, "Öser, how are you doing?"

"Just fine," Öser assured him via a small microphone inside the machine.

"Your brain looks beautiful," Davidson said. "Let's start with five repetitions of the open state." A computerized voice then took over, to ensure precise timing for the protocol. The prompt "on" was the signal for Öser to meditate, followed by silence for sixty seconds while Öser complied. Then "neutral," another sixty seconds of silence, and the cycle started once again with "on."

The same routine guided Öser through the other five meditative states, with pauses between as the technicians worked out various glitches. Finally, when the full round was complete, Davidson asked if Öser felt the need to repeat any, and the answer came: "I'd like to repeat the open state, compassion, devotion, and one-pointedness"—the ones he felt were the most important to study.

So the whole process started again. As he was about to begin the run on the open state, Öser said he wanted to remain in the state longer. He was able to evoke the state but wanted more time to deepen it. Once the computers have been programmed for the protocol, though, the technology drives the procedure; the timing has been fixed. Still, the technicians went into a huddle, quickly figuring how to reprogram on the spot to increase the "on" period by fifty percent and shorten the neutral period accordingly. The rounds began again.

With all the time taken up by reprogramming and ironing out technical hitches, the whole run took more than three hours. Subjects rarely emerge from the MRI—particularly after having been in there for so long—with anything but an expression of weary relief. But Davidson was pleasantly astonished to see Öser come out from his grueling routine in the MRI beaming broadly and proclaiming, "It's like a mini-retreat!"

Without taking more than a brief break, Öser headed down the hall for the next set of tests, this time using an electroencephalogram, the brain wave measure better known as an EEG. Most EEG studies use only thirty-two sensors on the scalp to pick up electrical activity in the brain, and many use just six.

But Öser's brain would be monitored twice, using two different EEG caps, first one with 128 sensors, the next with 256. The first cap would capture valuable data while he again went through the same paces in the meditative states. The second, with 256 sensors, would be used synergistically with the earlier MRI data.

This time, instead of lying in the maw of the MRI, he sat on a comfortable chair and wore a Medusa-like helmet—something like a shower cap extruding a spaghetti of thin wires. The EEG sessions took another two hours.

It seemed from the preliminary analysis that Öser's mental strategies were accompanied by strong, demonstrable shifts in the MRI signals. These signals suggested that large networks in the brain changed with each distinct mental state he generated. Ordinarily, such a clear shift in brain activity between states of mind is the exception, except for the grossest shifts in consciousness—from waking to sleep, for instance. But Öser's brain showed clear distinctions among each of the six meditations.

The EEG analysis bore particularly rich fruit in the comparison between Öser at rest and while meditating on compassion. Most striking was a dramatic increase in key electrical activity known as gamma in the left middle frontal gyrus, a zone of the brain Davidson's previous research had pinpointed as a locus for positive emotions. In research with close to two hundred people, Davidson's lab had found that when people have high levels of such brain activity in that specific site of the left prefrontal cortex, they simultaneously report feelings such as happiness, enthusiasm, joy, high energy, and alertness.

On the other hand, Davidson's research has also found that high levels of activity in a parallel site on the other side of the brain—in the right prefrontal area—correlate with reports of distressing emotions. People with a higher level of activity in the right prefrontal site and a lower level in the left are more prone to feelings such as sadness, anxiety, and worry. Indeed, an extreme rightward tilt in the ratio of the activity in these prefrontal areas predicts a high likelihood that a person will succumb to clinical depression or an anxiety disorder at some point in his or her life. People in the grip of depression who also report intense anxiety have the highest levels of activation in those right prefrontal areas.

The implications of these findings for our emotional balance are profound: we each have a characteristic ratio of right-to-left activation in the prefrontal areas that offers a barometer of the moods we are likely to feel day to day. That ratio represents what amounts to an emotional set point, the mean around which our daily moods swing.

Each of us has the capacity to shift our moods, at least a bit, and thus change this ratio. The further to the left that ratio tilts, the better our frame of mind tends to be, and experiences that lift our mood cause such a leftward tilt, at least temporarily. For instance, most people show small positive changes in this ratio when they are asked to recall pleasant memories of events from their past, or when they watch amusing or heartwarming film clips.

Usually such changes from the baseline set point are modest. But when Öser was generating a state of compassion during meditation, he showed a remarkable leftward shift in this parameter of prefrontal function, one that was extraordinarily unlikely to occur by chance alone.

In short, Öser's brain shift during compassion seemed to reflect an extremely pleasant mood. The very act of concern for others' well-being, it seems, creates a greater state of well-being within oneself. The finding lends scientific support to an observation often made by the Dalai Lama: that the person doing a meditation on compassion for all beings is the immediate beneficiary.

The data from Öser was remarkable in another way, as these were also most likely the first data ever gathered on brain activity during the systematic generation of compassion—an emotional state for the most part utterly ignored by modern psychological research. Research in psychology over the decades has focused far more on what goes wrong with us—depression, anxiety, and the like—than on what goes right with us. The positive side of experience and human goodness have been largely ignored in research; indeed, there is virtually no research anywhere in the annals of psychology on compassion per se.

While Davidson's data on compassion were surprising in themselves, still more remarkable results were about to be reported by Paul Ekman, one of the world's most eminent experts on the science of emotion, who heads the Human Interaction Laboratory at the University of California at San Francisco. Ekman was among the handful of scientists who had attended the Dharamsala meeting, and he had studied Öser a few months earlier in his own laboratory. The net result was four studies, three of which are described here.

The first test used a measure that represents a culmination of Ekman's life's work as the world's leading expert on the facial expression of emotions. The test consists of a videotape in which a series of faces show a variety of expressions very briefly. The challenge is to identify whether you've just seen the facial signs, for instance, of contempt or anger or fear. Each expression stays on the screen for just one-fifth of a second in one version, and for one thirtieth of a second in another—so fast that you would miss it if you blinked. Each time the person must select which of seven emotions he or she has just seen.

The ability to recognize fleeting expressions signals an unusual capacity for accurate empathy. Such expressions of emotion—called micro-expressions—happen outside the awareness of both the person who displays them and the person observing. Because they occur unwittingly, these ultra-rapid displays of emotion are completely uncensored, and so reveal—if only for a short moment—how the person truly feels.

From studies with thousands of people, Ekman knew that people who do better at recognizing these subtle emotions are more open to new experience, more interested and more curious about things in general. They are also conscientious—reliable and efficient. "So I had expected that many years of meditative experience"—which requires both openness and conscientiousness—"might make them do better on this ability," Ekman explains. Thus he had wondered if Öser might be better able to identify these ultra-fast emotions than other people are.

Then Ekman announced his results: both Öser and another advanced Western meditator Ekman had been able to test were two standard deviations above the norm in recognizing these super-quick facial signals of emotion, albeit the two subjects differed in the emotions they were best at perceiving. They both scored far higher than any of the five thousand other people tested.

"They do better than policemen, lawyers, psychiatrists, customs officials, judges—even Secret Service agents," the group that had previously distinguished itself as most accurate.

"It appears that one benefit of some part of the life paths these two have followed is becoming more aware of these subtle signs of how other people feel," Ekman notes. Öser had super-acuity for the fleeting signs of fear, contempt, and anger. The other meditator—a Westerner who, like Öser, had done a total of two to three years in solitary retreats in the Tibetan tradition—was similarly outstanding, though on a different range of emotions: happiness, sadness, disgust and, like Öser, anger.

One of the most primitive responses in the human repertoire, the startle reflex, involves a cascade of very quick muscle spasms in response to a loud, surprising sound or sudden, jarring sight. For everyone, the same five facial muscles instantaneously contract during a startle, particularly around the eyes. The startle reflex starts about two-tenths of a second after hearing the sound and ends around a half second after the sound. From beginning to end, it takes approximately a third of a second. The time course is always the same; that's the way we're wired.

Like all reflexes, the startle reflects activity of the brain stem, the most primitive, reptilian part of the brain. Like other brain stem responses—and unlike those of the autonomic nervous system, such as the rate at which the heart beats—the startle reflex lies beyond the range of voluntary regulation. So far as brain science understands, the mechanisms that control the startle reflex cannot be modified by any intentional act.

Ekman became interested in testing the startle reflex because its intensity predicts the magnitude of the negative emotions a person feels—particularly fear, anger, sadness, and disgust. The bigger a person's startle, the more strongly that individual tends to experience negative emotions—though there's no relationship between the startle and positive feelings such as joy.

For a test of the magnitude of Öser's startle reflex, Ekman

took him across San Francisco Bay to the psychophysiological laboratory of his colleague Robert Levenson at the University of California at Berkeley. There they wired Öser to capture his heart rate and sweat response and videotaped his facial expressions—all to record his physiological reactions to a startling sound. To eliminate any differences due to the noise level of the sound, they chose the top of the threshold for human tolerance to huge sound, like a pistol being fired or a large firecracker going off near one's ear.

They gave Öser the standard instruction, telling him that they would count down from ten to one, at which point he would hear a loud noise. They asked that he try to suppress the inevitable flinch, so that someone looking at him would not know he felt it. Some people can do better than others, but no one can come remotely close to completely suppressing it. A classic study in the 1940s showed that it's impossible to prevent the startle reflex, despite the most intense, purposeful efforts to suppress the muscle spasms. No one Ekman and Robert Levenson had ever tested could do it. Earlier researchers found that even police marksmen, who fire guns routinely, are unable to keep themselves from startling.

But Öser did. Ekman explains, "When Öser tries to suppress the startle, it almost disappears. We've never found anyone who can do that. Nor have any other researchers." Öser practiced two types of meditation while having the startle tested: one-pointed concentration and the open state. As Öser experienced it, the biggest effect was from the open state: "When I went into the open state, the explosive sound seemed to me softer, as if I was distanced from the sensations, hearing the sound from afar." Ekman reported that although Öser's physiology showed some slight changes, not a muscle of his face moved, which Öser related to his mind not being shaken by the bang. Indeed, as Öser later elaborated, "If you can remain properly in this state, the bang seems neutral, like a bird crossing the sky."

Although Öser showed not a ripple of movement in any facial muscles while in the open state, his physiological measures, (including heart rate, sweating, and blood pressure) showed the increase typical of the startle reflex. From Ekman's perspective, the strongest overall muting came during the intense focus of the one-pointedness meditation. During the one-pointedness meditation, instead of the inevitable jump, there was a decrease in Öser's heart rate, blood pressure, and so on. On the other hand, his facial muscles did reflect a bit of the typical startle pattern; the movements "were very small, but they were present," Ekman observed. "And he did one unusual thing. In all others we've tested, the eyebrows go down. In Öser they go up."

In sum, Öser's one-pointed concentration seemed to close him off to external stimuli—even to the startling noise of a gunshot. Given that the larger someone's startle, the more intensely that person tends to experience upsetting emotions, Öser's performance had tantalizing implications, suggesting a remarkable level of emotional equanimity.

Finally, in the last experiment, Ekman and Robert Levenson showed Öser two medical training films that have been used for more than three decades in emotion research simply because they are so upsetting. In one a surgeon seems to amputate a limb with a scalpel and saw—actually preparing an arm stump to be fitted with a prosthesis—and there is lots of gore and blood. But the camera focuses only on the limb, so you never see the person getting the surgery. In the other, you see the pain of a severely burned patient, who stands as doctors strip skin off his body. The main emotion evoked in the scores of research subjects who have viewed both these films during experiments is highly reliable: disgust.

When Öser viewed the amputation film, the emotion he reported feeling most strongly was the usual disgust. He commented that the movie reminded him of Buddhist teachings about impermanence and the unsavory aspects of the human body that lie beneath an attractive exterior. But his reaction to the burn film was quite different. "Where he sees the whole person," Ekman reported, "Öser feels compassion." His thoughts were about human suffering and how to relieve it; his feelings were a sense of caring and concern, mixed with a not unpleasant strong sadness.

The physiology of Öser's disgust reaction during the amputation film was unremarkable, the standard changes indicating the physiological arousal seen during that emotion. But when he spontaneously felt compassion during the burn film, his physiological signs reflected relaxation even more strongly than they had when the signs had been measured during a resting state.

Ekman ended his report of the results by noting that each of the studies with Öser had "produced findings that in thirty-five years of research I have never seen before." In short, Öser's data are extraordinary.

From the perspective of neuroscience, the point of all this research has nothing to do with demonstrating that Öser or any other extraordinary person may be remarkable in him- or herself, but rather to stretch the field's assumptions about human possibility.

A decade ago the dogma in neuroscience was that the brain contained all of its neurons at birth and it was unchanged by life's experiences. The only changes that occurred over the course of life were minor alterations in synaptic contacts—the connections among neurons—and cell death with aging. But the new watchword in brain science is neuroplasticity, the notion that the brain continually changes as a result of our experiences—whether through fresh connections between neurons or through the generation of utterly new neurons. Musical training, where a musician practices an instrument every day for years, offers an apt model for neuroplasticity. MRI studies find that in a violinist, for example, the areas of the brain that control finger movements in the hand that does the fingering grow in size. Those who start their training earlier in life and practice longer show bigger changes in the brain. Still, neuroscientists do not know with certainty what accounts for this change—whether the change is in the synaptic weights as added connections bulk out neurons, or whether an uptick in the number of neurons may also be playing a role.

A related issue revolves around the amount of practice that it might take in order for the brain to show such a change, particularly in something as subtle as meditation. There is an undeniable impact on the brain, mind, and body from extensive practice. Studies of champion performers in a range of abilities—from chess masters and concert violinists to Olympic athletes—find pronounced changes in the pertinent muscle fibers and cognitive abilities that set those at the top of a skill apart from all others.

The more total hours of practice the champions have done, the stronger the changes. For instance, among violinists at the topmost level, all had practiced a lifetime total of about ten thousand hours by the time they entered a music academy. Those at the next rung had practiced an average of about seventy-five-hundred hours. Presumably a similar effect from practice occurs in meditation, which can be seen, from the perspective of cognitive science, as the systematic effort to retrain attention and related mental and emotional skills.

Öser, as it turned out, far exceeded the ten-thousand-hour level in meditation practice. Much of that practice came during the time he spent in intensive meditation retreats, along with the four years living in a hermitage during the early period of his training as a monk, as well as occasional long retreats over the subsequent years.

While Öser may be a virtuoso of meditation, even raw novices start to show some of the same shifts. This was clear from other data Davidson had gathered on similar brain changes in people just beginning to practice a variety of meditation called mindfulness. These studies had given Davidson convincing data that meditation can shift the brain as well as the body. While Öser's results suggested just how far that shift could go with years of sustained practice, even beginners displayed evidence of biological shifts in the same direction. So the next question for Davidson to tackle was this: can specific types of meditation be used to change circuitry in the brain associated with different aspects of emotion?

Davidson may be one of the few neuroscientists anywhere who

can dare to ask this, because his lab is using a new imaging technique—diffusion tensor imaging—to help answer this question. The method shows connections among different regions in the nervous system. Until now, diffusion tensor imaging has mostly been used to study patients with neurological diseases. Davidson's lab is among a select group that use the technique for basic neuroscience research, and the only one to be using it for research on how methods that transform emotion may be changing the connectivity of the brain.

Perhaps most exciting, the images created by diffusion tensor imaging can actually track the subtle reshaping of the brain at the heart of neuroplasticity. With the method, scientists can now identify the changes in the human brain as repeated experiences remodel specific connections or add new neurons. This marks a brave new frontier for neuroscience: it was only in 1998 that neuroscientists discovered that new neurons are continually being generated in the adult brain.

For Davidson, one immediate application will be searching for new connections in the circuitry crucial for regulating distressing emotions. Davidson hopes to see if there actually are new connections associated with a person's increased ability to manage anxiety, fear, or anger more effectively.

From the scientific perspective, what does any of this matter? Davidson sums it up by referring to *The Art of Happiness*, a book the Dalai Lama wrote with psychiatrist Howard Cutler, in which the Dalai Lama said that happiness is not a fixed characteristic, a biological set point that will never change. Instead, the brain is plastic, and our quota of happiness can be enhanced through mental training.

"It can be trained because the very structure of our brain can be modified," Davidson said. "And the results of modern neuroscience inspire us now to go on and look at other practiced subjects so that we can examine these changes with more detail. We now have the methods to show how the brain changes with these kinds of practices, and how our mental and physical health may improve as a consequence."

Öser, reflecting on the data gathered in Madison, put it this way: "Such results of training point to the possibility that one could continue much further in such a transformation process, and, as some great contemplatives have repeatedly claimed, eventually free one's mind from afflictive emotions."

When I asked the Dalai Lama what he made of the data on Öser—such as being able to mute the startle reflex—he replied, "It's very good he managed to show some signs of yogic ability." Here he used the term yogic not in the garden-variety sense of a few hours a week practicing postures in a yoga studio but in its classic sense—referring to one who dedicates his or her life to the cultivation of spiritual qualities.

The Dalai Lama added, "But there is a saying, 'The true mark of being learned is humility and mental discipline; the true mark of a meditator is that he has disciplined his mind by freeing it from negative emotions.' We think along those lines—not in terms of performing some feats or miracles." In other words, the real measure of spiritual development lies in how well a person manages disturbing emotions such as anger and jealousy—not in attaining rarified states during meditation or exhibiting feats of physical self-control such as muting the startle reaction.

One payoff for this scientific agenda would be in inspiring people to better handle their destructive emotions through trying some of the same methods for training the mind. When I asked the Dalai Lama what greater benefit he hoped for from this line of research, he replied: "Through training the mind people can become more calm—especially those who suffer from too many ups and downs. That's the conclusion from these studies of Buddhist mind training. And that's my main end: I'm not thinking how to further Buddhism, but how the Buddhist tradition can make some contribution to the benefit of society. Of course, as Buddhists, we always pray for all sentient beings. But we're only human beings; the main thing you can do is train your own mind."

The Test of Truth

Larry Rosenberg

Another way to test the Buddhist teachings is against our own reason and experience. The Buddhist teachings shouldn't be taken on faith, says Larry Rosenberg, but that doesn't mean we chose among them according to our personal preference—that would be ego's game. It means that the way to know the dharma intimately is to test it against the reality of our own lives—to feel the "ouch" of it, as Rosenberg says.

The practice of the dharma is learning how to live, and this is both hard and joyful work. Practice makes extraordinary demands of us. It requires that we take nothing for granted, that we accept nothing on faith alone. If we practice with diligence and honesty, then we must question everything about ourselves; we must challenge our most basic beliefs and convictions, even those we may have about the dharma itself. Of all the teachings of the Buddha, the *Kalama Sutta* is one of my favorites precisely because it encourages such rigorous inquiry into our beliefs. Indeed, if Buddhism were not infused with the spirit of this *sutta*—a spirit of questioning, of critical examination—I'm quite sure I would not have a meditative practice today.

I was raised in what you might call a tradition of skepticism. My father was the first to teach me the importance of asking questions. He came from a line of fourteen rabbis but, like his own ex-rabbi father, he rejected that heritage—although "rejected," actually, is too weak a term. He frequently expressed contempt not only for Orthodox Judaism, but for all religions. I remember that before Hebrew school, my father would pull me aside and say things like, "Ask the rabbi just how Moses got that river to split." Well, I would go along with it, but as you can imagine, that never went over very well. Rabbi Minkowitz was not particularly pleased to be questioned in this way. I think my father was the first in recorded history actually to pay a rabbi *not* to give a talk at his son's bar mitzvah. My father said, "Please. Here's the money. *Don't* give a talk." But the rabbi gave the talk anyway. And my father was fuming.

So my father believed in the necessity of thinking critically, and he instilled this in me. His way of parenting was very similar to the scientific approach. If I got into trouble—I was usually very good at home, but I got into a lot of mischief at school and in the neighborhood—I'd be put on trial when my father came home from work. He had always wanted to be a lawyer or a judge, but he drove a cab, so he had to settle for a court made up of my mother and me. His court was very sensitive and reasonable: He would hear the accused out, and sometimes, after listening to all sides, he would drop the charges. Of course, my mother would smile, and they were both happy that I got off. But my father always explained to me *why* I should have acted differently: "When you did that, your Aunt Clara got aggravated, then she called up your mother, and now I have to listen to it. Next time, just pick up the rye bread and bagels and come home. It's simple." He'd always explain to me that my actions had consequences. And, most important, he taught me that we have the right to ask questions about anything and everything. But with that right comes a responsibility: If we're going to question the actions of others, we also have to be willing to question our own.

The Kalamas of the *Kalama Sutta* were, like my father, a skeptical but responsible bunch. They were quite alive to spiritual matters, but they were overrun with teachers and teachings, each teacher competing for an audience, each propounding a different philosophy or path. Their situation was not very different from ours now. We're inundated with possibilities: "You're interested in religion? Well, what kind? Buddhism? What flavor would you like? Tibetan? Okay, we have about ten flavors there. Theravada? Oh, you've tried that? A little too dry for you? Too much talk about suffering and impermanence? Perhaps you'd prefer Dzogchen, the innate perfection of the mind. That sounds much better, doesn't it? And they have more colorful outfits. Most Vipassana teachers aren't Asian and aren't even monks; they just wear sweatpants. At least the Tibetan teachers *look* like teachers, you know? And then you get to Zen: beautiful—those great stories that teach you and make you laugh. Theravada teachings go on and on, but Zen is just hilarious one-liners."

So we have this great swirling spiritual marketplace, with lots of claims being made. It's no wonder that many of us find it confusing. Well, like us, the Kalamas were confused. They went to the Buddha to hear his perspective:

> So the Kalamas of Kesaputta approached the Buddha. On arrival, some of them bowed down to him and sat to one side. Some of them exchanged courteous greetings with him and sat to one side. Some, raising their joined palms, sat down to one side. Some, announcing their name and clan, sat to one side. Some of them sat to one side in silence. As they were sitting there, they said to the Buddha: "Lord, some teachers come to Kesaputta, expounding and glorifying their own doctrines. But as for the doctrines of others, they abuse them, disparage them, deprecate them, and pull them to pieces. Other teachers, on coming to Kesaputta, do the same thing. When we listen to them, we feel doubt and uncertainty as to which of these teachers are speaking truth and which are lying."

The Kalamas were overwhelmed by all these claims to exclusive truth. And when the Buddha arrived, despite his reputation as a great sage, they were concerned that he might be just one more teacher with a competing point of view. Actually, I think their skepticism is very admirable, and rather unusual. The history of the world reveals that people are drawn to those who provide a strong, uncompromising teaching. We're drawn to those who say, "This is it, and everyone else is wrong." Certainly we see this pattern in contemporary politics, but we also see abuse of this sort within spiritual circles. It makes you wonder: Do we really want freedom? Can we handle the responsibility? Or would we just prefer to have an impressive teacher, someone who can give us the answers and do the hard work for us?

Of course, foolishness exists within Buddhist circles as well. After all the problems that have come up in dharma centers in the past twenty years, I still see Westerners who check their intelligence at the door, who grovel at the feet of a teacher, saying, "Just tell me how to live." Well, I've been taken a few times myself. I don't know if you have. But I deserved it. I just wanted to have my special teacher, someone with special access to the truth. It felt fantastic to be their student. My spiritual life was taken care of. I didn't have to worry anymore. I was absolved of the responsibility that comes with exercising the right to ask questions. But, of course, I wasn't free.

After hearing the concerns of the Kalamas, the Buddha replied:

> "Come, Kalamas. Don't go by reports, by legends, by traditions, by scripture, by logical conjecture, by inference, by analogies, by consistency with your own views, by probability, or by the thought, 'This contemplative is our teacher.' When you know for yourselves that 'these mental qualities are unskillful; these mental qualities are blameworthy; these mental qualities are criti-

> cized by the wise; these mental qualities when acted on lead to harm and suffering' then abandon them. When you know for yourselves that 'these mental qualities are skillful; these mental qualities are blameless; these mental qualities are praised by the wise; these mental qualities when acted on lead to well-being and happiness' then keep following them."

There's a teaching story from China: People came from far and wide to hear the dharma talks of a young teacher. Apparently he had some depth. And one day, an old master came to hear him. He sat in the back of the meditation hall while the young teacher was giving a dharma talk. But the young teacher saw him, and out of respect, knowing that he was a renowned teacher and also much older, said, "Please, come up here, sit next to me while I give my talk." So the old master rose and sat next to him. The young teacher resumed his talk, and every other word was a quotation from a different sutra or Zen master. The old master started to nod off in front of everyone. And the young teacher could see this out of the corner of his eye, but he just continued. The more authorities he cited, the sleepier the old master became. Finally, the young teacher couldn't stand it anymore, so he asked, "What's wrong? Is my teaching so boring, so awful, so totally off?" At that point, the old master leaned over and gave him a very hard pinch and the young teacher screamed, "Ouch!" The old master said, "Ah! That's what I've come all this way for. This pure teaching. This 'ouch' teaching."

Like the old master in this story, the Buddha, in his response to the Kalamas, is trying to emphasize the importance of direct experience. He acknowledges that people rely upon many different modes of authority, sometimes internal, sometimes external. Some of them are reliable and others are way off the mark. The question is, how do we tell which is which? How do we balance internal authority with external authority? As the Buddha says, just because something is ancient doesn't mean it's true. Just because it's new doesn't mean it's true. Just because it's in the scriptures doesn't mean it's true. Just because it seems reasonable, or you like the person teaching it, doesn't mean it's right.

What's left, then? Where do we turn for authority in terms of knowing how to act? In the *Kalama Sutta*, the Buddha is not saying that ancient teachings are irrelevant, or that you have to reinvent the dharma wheel every time you think. He's not saying *not* to accept the guidance of teachers or *not* to read the scriptures. After all, how else are you going to find out what's criticized and praised by the wise? No, what he's saying is: Don't give final authority to these things. Don't give final authority to your own ideas. You have to test the teachings, and your ideas, in the laboratory of your actions.

When you put something to the test, really to the test, don't you find that it challenges, that it stretches you, too? This has certainly been my experience. Some of these wonderful teachings are inspiring. It can be intellectually satisfying and emotionally nourishing just to hear them. But you can't stop there. If you want to gain any real benefit from them, you have to let them stretch your own lived experience. For the dharma to become firsthand knowledge—to feel the "ouch" of it—you have to live intimately with it, hold it up to scrutiny, and let it hold you up to scrutiny. In the end, the ball is always thrown back to you: "Be a lamp unto yourself," says the Buddha. In other words, you must ultimately find the way on your own, by putting your ideas of the truth to the test. Your questions light the way.

So what is the test of truth? The Buddha offers a simple formula: Test things in terms of cause and effect. Whatever is unskillful, leading to harm and ill, should be abandoned; whatever is skillful, leading to happiness and peace, should be pursued. Apply the test of skillfulness to all teachings in all your actions. Where is this teaching taking you? Is it moving you in a direction that is wise and kind? One quick test isn't enough, you know. You have to keep at it, so that your sensitivity to the results of your actions grows more and more refined with practice. When you've done the hard work of asking these questions, then you can decide for yourself whether a teaching, or a teacher, is worth following. And at the same time, you've also taught yourself how to live—a learning that can bring with it joy and the energy to go even deeper.

A Path of Radical Sobriety

Daizui MacPhillamy

Our desire knows no limit, and therefore we can never find real satisfaction. We feel the pleasure of one thing and immediately we hunger for the next. So because the nature of our desire never allows us to experience rest or contentment, says Rev. Daizui MacPhillamy, Buddhism recommends a path of radical sobriety.

I once heard a country and western song called "Faster Horses." It was one of those partly humorous, partly philosophical songs about the meaning of life. An idealistic young man meets an old cowboy sitting in a bar, his face weather-beaten, his hands gnarled; the youngster just knows that this guy has the secret of life. So he asks him all sorts of deep questions about what makes life worth living, and no matter what the young man asks, the old timer comes back with the same answer, "Faster horses; younger women; older whiskey; more money!" Well, I thought, that may not say much about the true meaning of life, but it sure does sum up the problem of human existence: we're never satisfied.

If we don't have it, we want some; if we have some, we want more; if we have lots, we're afraid of losing it. Now, the "it" can be anything, but mostly the song had it right: it's either "faster horses" (power, excitement, fame, things which others envy), "younger women" (which works in the song but strikes me as being a little one-sided—it could just as easily be "wilder guys"), "older whiskey" (better sensual experiences of all sorts, and especially ones that make us forget our problems), or, of course, "more money." This business of never being satisfied may not seem like all that big a problem, but it goes right to the heart of some of the most difficult things in life. If we're never satisfied, it guarantees that we can never really be completely at peace within ourselves and also that we never get a chance to fully enjoy the simple pleasures that actually do make life worthwhile. How can you be fully present, watching a sunset beside your partner, when half of you is itching to be with someone else, wishing you had your camera, or thinking about how to beat the competition at work? How can you fully enjoy the satisfaction of a job well done when part of you knows that you succeeded at the expense of someone else or have made a product that doesn't really help anybody? Sure, there is pleasure in a new car, a wild romance, a great new piece of music, a promotion; but how long does it last? And are those the things that actually stand out as having given life meaning, when you look back over your life?

By never being satisfied, it seems that we are destined to rob ourselves of the very things we value most: a peaceful heart, true and lasting love, real friendship, the satisfaction of doing something worthwhile in this world. Instead, we seem to propel ourselves in exactly the opposite direction: into fear, anger, worry, and discontent. Why do we do this to ourselves? How did we get into this mess?

No one really knows for sure, but the answer might be as simple as basic biology. Inside our complicated human brain lies the same simple sort of brain that all the other animals have, and that brain is wired to seek pleasure and avoid pain. Now, that works just fine if you're a dog or a cat. Except for those times of the day when you're on the prowl for the next meal or mate, if you're reasonably well fed, warm, and dry, then you're happy;

you're satisfied, you're at peace. But there's more to our human brain than just the basic animal bits, and these extra parts allow us to think, plan ahead, fantasize, and the like. This gives us the ability to apply our basic animal tendencies of pleasure seeking and pain avoiding to all sorts of things where it doesn't work so well. Instead of just hunting for the next meal when we're hungry, like a dog or cat does, we are capable of scheming on how to get more and finer tasting food, how to store it for later, how to add to the pleasure with drink and music, and on and on. And, because we are able to engage in this sort of thinking and fantasizing, and because it works—it gets us more and better food than we would have otherwise—we tend to go ahead and do it. All of this is fine, and it certainly has value for the preservation of our species. But it comes at a price: since there is no end to how much food we might have nor to how good it might be, we become so lost in pursuing it that we never allow ourselves to be at rest, and we often miss the opportunity to actually taste, and be grateful for, the food right on our plate. And we apply this way of doing things not just to food but to everything in life.

Whatever its reason for being, this complicated human form of the basic animal drives to seek pleasure and avoid pain is part of who we are, and it's part of what led us to create art and science and all of the things we call "civilization," so it's by no means bad. It simply has a cost: vague unhappiness, chronic dissatisfaction, constant dis-ease. Need it have such a cost? I'm afraid so. The reason is that, no matter what goals we set for ourselves using this approach to life, there will always be the possibility of "faster, wilder, tastier, more . . ." And, since we are wired as we are, it is very hard not to grab onto those possibilities. Furthermore, our complex brains also realize that at any moment it all can be taken away from us. As a matter of fact, we all know that, if it hasn't been taken away before, in the end it will all be taken away by death. We yearn for something permanent, something we can have, hold, or be . . . forever. And since somewhere inside ourselves we know that this cannot be, at least this side of heaven, this desire makes it even more difficult to be completely at peace. So, here we sit: "cowboys at the bar of life," right in the middle of a world full of simple satisfactions that really matter, drowning our sorrows in older whiskey and dreaming of faster horses.

Nothing Stays Put

Now, why is it that "heaven on earth" cannot be? Why can't we be satisfied with one really fast horse? Why doesn't getting the things and experiences we want give us lasting peace and happiness? There is actually a very simple reason for this: in our universe everything is always changing, always in motion. Nothing stays put. And because nothing stays put, there's no keeping what we've got, and no end to what we might be able to get, if only . . .

What does it mean to say that everything is always changing? Consider material things, "stuff." Things are never quite the same the next time you look at them. That's easy to see with fast-changing objects like a burning log or a rotting tomato, but the same principle is true for things that change more slowly; you just have to look harder. The log will not last forever even if it doesn't burn: in the forest it will break down from the action of termites, molds, and the like, and even if you make it into lumber and put it in a nice dry building, it gradually loses strength and the wood worms and dry rot will get it in the end. You can put the tomato in the fridge, but that simply slows down the process. This book, as another example, is changing, too. The acids in the paper are gradually weakening it; the air and light are yellowing the paper. The chemicals in the ink and paper are moving around and some of them are even hopping off the pages into the air. You can tell that by sniffing the book; it smells like a book because your nose can detect some of those chemicals. And if you did just sniff it, some of what was the book a minute ago has just gone inside your lungs and become part of you!

Really slowly changing or far away stuff like rocks and metal and stars and galaxies change too, but you need special tools to be able to see it because the changes happen in ways we can't sense directly. The same is true for super-fast changing things like atoms and atomic particles: they are too small and their changes are too fast for us to sense directly, but change they do. And, so I am told, Dr. Einstein and his colleagues have discovered that even the things we use to measure how stuff changes, things like time and space, change too. The whole universe of what we call "things" is therefore really a flow: an ever-changing swirl of space/time/being.

In addition, what holds true for stuff is also true for you and me: we're always changing as well. You've got book chemicals in you now that weren't part of you a moment ago. You're growing older every moment, like it or not. The experience I had in typing the sentence above is now gone; it will never return. I can remember it, think about it, dream or have nightmares about it, but they are not the same as returning to that moment. That point in time and space is gone, and, having been through it, I am slightly different now than I was before. So, we too change: we change in body and we change in mind, and at the end of life there is a profound and mysterious change we call "death."

This fact of change is a fundamental principle of Buddhism. It is called the Law of Change; the ancient term for it is *anicca*, and it is regarded as a natural law, just like gravity. For a Buddhist, change simply is; no one makes it happen and no one can alter it; no one can escape from it; change is just the way the world works. Because there is always change, nothing that we have in this world is destined to remain ours. Knowing this, it is hard to be fully at peace. Furthermore, because there is always change, there is always one more thing tempting us to seek after it. And because we do chase after such things, we are never satisfied and never happy for long.

How Unhappiness Happens

Recognition of this state of affairs—of this chronic dissatisfaction or uneasiness which results from both our desire for faster horses and our wish to hold onto things in the face of a changing world—is actually the first principle of Buddhism. It is called the "First Noble Truth"; other terms for it are the "truth of suffering" or the "existence of unsatisfactoriness." Both of these expressions are translations of the term *dukkha* in the ancient Indian language of Pali, and no one English word quite captures the whole meaning. For instance, to say that the First Noble Truth is simply that "life is suffering" is misleading, since it implies that Buddhists are somehow obsessed with the painful aspects of life. Actually, the fact that life is sometimes painful is not the real problem. People can handle the occasional pain; it is the constant internal background state of vague unhappiness and nameless yearning that keeps us from being truly at peace. In other words, this First Noble Truth is the "faster horses problem," compounded by the law of change.

The "faster horses problem" and the law of change explain *why* our lives have a background of dissatisfaction and unpeacefulness, but they don't fully explain *how* that happens. What is the actual chain of events that leads to these feelings? Am I, for example, frustrated because I don't have more money, or does my frustration come from thinking that I deserve more money than I have? Do I feel unfulfilled because I'm not a star athlete, or is it because I dream of being one and don't seem to be able to do it? Do I actually fear getting older, or does the uneasiness come from the fact that getting older means giving up the things of my youth? It seems pretty clear that what actually distresses us is the second alternative in these sorts of circumstances. After all, there are lots of folks in the world who have less money than we, but who don't feel frustrated; most people are not famous athletes, and most of them frankly don't care; plenty of older folks are not dismayed by their situation, and they actually enjoy maturity. Of course, most of the individuals who are not dissatisfied by the things I've just mentioned are plenty unhappy about something else. It's not that they are not affected by life in the same basic way that you and I are, it's just that they don't happen to care about the particular things which bother us.

That "not caring" is an important clue to how the process of unhappiness works: we're only dissatisfied by those aspects of life where we feel a need, where we "have a stake," where we are attached to something. So it's not really the lack of a faster horse that's at the root of the problem; the real basis of the problem is believing that we won't be happy until we get one. In other words, it is craving for things which seems to be at the core of the problem, and it causes unhappiness in two different ways. First of all, craving (attachment, grasping, lusting, wanting, longing, desire, et cetera) hurts, in and of itself. To be constantly wanting things that we can never fully have, or never completely hold onto, leaves us permanently in a state of frustration, and that hurts. Lusting, longing, desire, and the like are, by their very nature, feelings of being unfulfilled, of being incomplete, discontented, unpeaceful. Because nothing stays put and everything is always changing, no matter how fast our horse is, we condemn ourselves to chronic unhappiness so long as we hold onto the desire for faster horses.

The second way in which attachments rob us of inner peace is by leading us to do things which cause harm to ourselves and others. Some of this damage is completely internal, such as developing a set of beliefs about how the world is unfair or doesn't care about us. Some of it is external, such as trying to get the raise we desire by unfairly competing with our coworkers, cutting corners on the job to make it look like we're more efficient, or browbeating our subordinates. The internal things tend to make us miserable in ways that we don't recognize easily. For example, now we're angry about unfairness instead of being aware of our simple frustration about lack of recognition and reward: we have created a whole new layer of misery for ourselves. And, we have given ourselves a whole new problem to solve: the unfairness of the world. Unfortunately, it is not the real problem, and so trying to solve it just produces even more frustration. The external things sometimes work to get to our short-term goal, but always at the cost of creating other forms of suffering in the long run. To use the example of getting that raise, we do things that cause us to lose friendship, lose trust, lose self respect, or have the nagging knowledge that we have harmed others.

This observation, that craving or attachment is at the core of how unhappiness happens, is another basic principle of Buddhism. It is known as the "Second Noble Truth," and a Buddhist would say that if one looks closely enough at any form of unhappiness or discontentment, a core of craving, longing, wanting, et cetera, will be found. The ancient Indian word for this core of attachment is *tanha,* which has the meaning of "inner thirst," a pretty good term for what we're referring to.

Is Peace Possible?

So far, I've been painting a rather grim picture of life: here we are in an ever-changing universe, trying to hold onto things that never stay put, always being tempted to try to get that faster horse, never really completely at peace with ourselves, and rarely even able to be fully present to experience the joys that do come our way. But this state of affairs is not inevitable, because there is one thing in the whole chain of events that we can do something about. We can't change the fact of change; we can't change the fact that our brains are wired to tell us that we always need "more" and "better"; but we can change what we *do* when our brains tell us this. We don't have to quite believe it. And we are not forced to act on it. We can simply watch our brain produce all of its urgent and tempting messages, and say to it, "No, actually I *don't* need a faster horse, thank you." It is possible, in other words, to do something about the attachment factor: the grasping after, the holding onto, the clutching at. And since that factor is at the very core of the process, changing this one thing can change the whole business.

The idea that we do not have to believe in and act upon everything our brain tells us (or, to put it another way, that we tell ourselves) is, in itself, revolutionary. That we actually do have this ability is easy to see if we use extreme examples. My brain can tell me that I am Napoleon or that the moon is made of green cheese, but that does not make it so; our brains can tell us that we'd like to have all the money behind the bank window, but most of us don't try to grab it. Yet, somehow, when it comes to everyday things, we just sort of assume that because we think something, especially something about ourselves, it's true. We assume that because we want something, we are supposed to try to get it. But when you stop to consider it, these thoughts and desires are no different than the extreme ones: they are simply thoughts, simply desires. We no more have to believe that we need a new car than we have to believe that the moon is made of green cheese; we no more have to seek a younger lover than we have to grab the money and run. *Thoughts are simply thoughts and desires are simply desires: you can believe them if you choose, you can act on them if you choose, or you can simply watch them rise and fall within your mind, if you choose.*

If a person does choose to just watch them go by after awhile something quite remarkable happens. The individual both starts to recognize them for what they are—just products of your brain—and begins to cease being controlled by them. And this suggests the possibility that there actually might be a way to true freedom and to peace of mind. Our complex human brains may have gotten us into this mess through their ability to take simple animal desires and turn them into never-ending thoughts of longing, but those same brains can get us out of the mess because they have the remarkable ability to step back and simply observe themselves in operation.

When we do this, the law of change starts to work in our favor. One of the things that often surprises people, when they watch their desires instead of acting upon them, is that those desires do not remain constant. We tend to assume that a thought or feeling which we do not act upon will stay with us and that it will pester or plague us until we fulfill it. But that is not what happens. If we simply observe those thoughts and feelings, without entering into them or otherwise feeding them, they rise and then fall away all by themselves. In other words, attachments, like everything else, don't last. Since change is a law of the universe, this can be relied upon. And because they do fall away when we refuse to feed them with either thought or action, this means that we have real freedom of choice about them. If we wish to follow along with an attachment we are free to do so, developing it with our mind and acting upon it with our body. But if we wish to give up an attachment, it can be done simply by using our mind to observe itself whenever that attachment arises, in the sure knowledge that the attachment will eventually pass away, just as a wave does in the ocean. There is even a reliable way to do this; it is called "meditation."

People who choose to simply watch their desires rise and fall start to discover another fascinating thing about them. The more we believe a particular craving or attachment, follow it with our thoughts, and act upon it, the stronger it gets. It arises more often and becomes more demanding of our attention. But desires that we simply observe going by like waves on the water do the opposite: they come up less often and are not quite so compelling. Over time, they weaken to the point that they stop being a major force in our mind. It is possible, in other words, to permanently give up or set aside attachments. And *that* breaks the whole chain that binds us to the "faster horses problem."

How to actually accomplish all of this is a whole other question. The point here is simply that it is possible. And this is the Third Noble Truth upon which Buddhism is founded: *there actually is a way to freedom from the chronic unhappiness and dissatisfaction of life, and that way is to give up the habit of attachment.* Put in other words, to set aside attachment is to find peace of mind; it is to live in harmony with how the universe works.

Radical Sobriety

A way of life of radical sobriety, which sets aside all attachments and all intoxicants, is Buddhism's surprising route to both personal fulfillment and religious truth. And there are specific guidelines for how to do this: there is a path that leads ordinary people like you and me directly to being one with the universal flow of space/time/being. The existence of this path is the Fourth Noble Truth of Buddhism. The path itself, because it has eight steps, is called the "Eightfold Path"; sometimes it is also called the "Middle Way," or simply the "Way." Although these eight steps run directly counter to "how we usually do things," they are quite practical and not all that difficult to describe. A practicing Buddhist tries to do all eight of them at once, and so they are more like aspects or factors rather than steps.

I do not want to push our comparison with addictions too far, but I think that speaking of this path as adopting a life of radical sobriety is a useful way of talking about it. There are even a few similarities between some of the aspects of the Eightfold Path and some of the twelve steps of the well-known approach to recovery from alcohol and drug abuse. While those similarities can be interesting to think about, I am not going to dwell on them because the differences are even more significant. I will just point out that what I see as the one really important similarity is that, in both cases, sobriety is a way of life free from the bonds of self-imposed obstacles, and it requires of people both that they fully accept themselves as they are and also that they undertake a completely new way of life. The most important difference is in the sheer scope of what is undertaken. The Eightfold Path does not simply lead to recovery from the addictions of daily life; its purpose is nothing less than to take people all the way to the heart of the problem of human existence and to put them in contact with basic spiritual truths. These eight aspects are, in other words, the Buddhist gateway to being fully present in the world in a way which leads to truth, peace, and real satisfaction. Therefore, one of the remarkable things about the Eightfold Path is that it is not only a way out of the addictions of "how we usually do things," it is also a solution to the "faster horses problem." This is because it provides a way not only to set aside the compound attachments of greed, anger, and delusion, but also to drop away the simple attachments which are basic to the human condition. While the normal sort of sobriety from drink and drugs is immensely valuable, this radical sobriety is total in both its scope and its effects.

Its scope is total because the Eightfold Path forms a complete way of life. Everything, from how Buddhists see the world to how they think, what they say, what they do, and even to how they earn their living, is involved. The path of radical sobriety has to be that comprehensive, because if any aspect of a person's life is held back as being a place where desires and delusions are clung to, then that part of the person's life will limit his or her understanding of truth and will be a source of continuing discontent.

The Way also offers the promise of being total in its effects. Yet there is no magic in this. The effects are proportionate to the commitment: total commitment yields total results, half-hearted commitment yields mediocre results. Now, human nature being what it is, there are Buddhists who do not take their religion fully seriously, just as there are people in all religions who are lukewarm about what they do. Buddhists can only be that way, however, by ignoring the major teachings of their faith, because it obviously invites its followers to practice a comprehensive Way that involves their entire being, every day. It invites this, but does not demand it: the responsibility of a person's religious development in Buddhism rests squarely upon their own shoulders.

The word that is used to describe the promised effect of this Path of radical sobriety is "enlightenment," and it is a word that is notoriously hard to define. Since it is the alternative to a life of attachment and intoxication, it obviously must have something to do with the complete cessation of all forms of grasping and delusion, and also with living in harmony with the truth of "things as they really are," including their changeable nature. But what is that actually like? Over the centuries, writers have tried various ways of describing it, but the one thing that they all agree upon is that no description is really adequate or accurate. That is because enlightenment is not a state or an experience; rather, it *is an entire way of being,* and it is a way of being that requires of people (among other things) that they give up the very thinking about things which is the basis of talking about anything. Nonetheless, if I don't even try to talk about it, there is not much point in mentioning the Eightfold Path at all. While enlightenment itself may be ultimately indescribable, words can at least point in its general direction, and that seems worth doing. Such words are sometimes described in Buddhism as "a finger pointing at the moon," with the moon being enlightenment itself. What follows are a bunch of such words; please don't mistake this "finger" for the "moon."

Enlightenment is said to be unborn and undying, eternal and changeless, simultaneously empty of all things and totally full, the ultimate happiness and at the same time calm and even-minded, filled with a love and compassion which are awe-full, wise within unknowing, consciousness unbounded and unfettered. It has been compared to awakening from a long dream, returning home, being released from prison, or becoming sober from a lifelong drunk. From these descriptions it is plain to see that, whatever enlightenment actually is, it involves both the end of dissatisfaction and the finding of ultimate truths. As such, it unites people who have come to Buddhism because of the "push" of suffering with those who have come out of the "pull" of love for truth.

The reason for this remarkable union is that, in the Buddhist way of doing things, the cessation of suffering and the finding of ultimate truths both happen to require the same thing: giving up all attachments, including all forms of intoxication. Enlightenment is another word for what happens when all of these are dropped away. The reason giving up all attachments is necessary in order to find freedom from suffering was explained in the Second and Third Noble Truths. The reason giving up all attachments is required for drawing near to ultimate truths is because attachment sets into motion complicated chains of cause and effect that distort our natural abilities to see and understand what is really there. How attachment does this, and how the chains of cause and effect work, is described in detail in a fascinating area of Buddhist teaching known as "dependent origination" or "conditioned coproduction" (*paticca samuppada* in the Pali language).

In view of how total the scope of enlightenment is, it is somewhat surprising that its outward signs are not all that spectacular. They are simple yet unbounded charity, tenderness, benevolence, and empathy. The person who dwells within enlightenment does not appear unusual, special, or different. Such people are, on the contrary, both ordinary and plain, yet there is something about them which makes a person want to be around them. This "dwelling within enlightenment" is not something which is all that uncommon.

Admittedly, it has always been rare to have enlightenment as one's permanent state of being, to have all attachments permanently given up, all illusions permanently dissolved. Such a person is said to have realized complete enlightenment (or "nirvana") and is sometimes called an *arahant*, a "fully awakened one." But many are those who have managed to set aside the bonds of desire and addiction long enough to experience a good, full taste of enlightenment. Such people are called "stream enterers," and one such taste is enough to revolutionize their lives. Continuing onward along the Path, such tastes become more frequent and deep, and so does a person's commitment to go even further. The fortunate side of this is that it means that the truly serious Buddhist is amply satisfied in his or her search for truth and peace, long before reaching the point of nirvana. The unfortunate side is that it also means that the word "enlightenment" gets used for all sorts of different things, ranging from the first brief taste to the complete enlightenment of nirvana, and this causes lots of confusion. But that is just the way things are, and a little verbal confusion is a small price to pay for recognizing the fact that enlightenment is not restricted to only the most advanced practitioners of the religion.

One might ask why different words are not used to refer to these different types of enlightenment. As a matter of fact, sometimes they are, but not generally. And with good reason, I think.

The problem with using various terms for enlightenment is that there actually aren't "different types of enlightenment." Whatever it may be, enlightenment is one and undivided: a little taste is as much enlightenment as the full and permanent thing. And, at another level, the confusion caused by using just one term for enlightenment is usually resolved by the course of ongoing Buddhist training. This is because *enlightenment is inseparable from the process of training itself:* even the arahant (or perhaps I should say "especially the arahant") continues to practice the eight aspects of the Way every moment of the day, every day of his or her life. Ultimately then, *enlightenment is the Path and the Path is enlightenment.* This explains why Buddhism places so much importance on the eight aspects of the Path of radical sobriety.

Pointing-Out Instruction

His Holiness the 17th Karmapa

The Vajrayana tradition of Tibet is vast and elaborate, but its essence comes down to a simple act, a single moment when the teacher shows the student the true nature of mind. This is called "pointing-out instruction," and it can take place in many different forms. Then it is up to the student to deepen the realization they have glimpsed because, as always in Buddhism, no one—even the Buddha himself—can do it for you. Here are two pithy instructions pointing out the true nature of mind by His Holiness the 17th Karmapa, the young head of the Kagyü school, with notes by translator Michele Martin.

Pointing Out Mahamudra

Like the illusory face of this appearing world,
It is not altered by action, freedom, or realization.
To remain in the depths of mind free of reference
Is known as mahamudra.

Notes

The Karmapa gave this verse to Lama Tenam to use in his meditation practice. Within the Kagyü lineage of Tibetan Buddhism, the practice of *mahamudra* is the deepest form of meditation. It is deceptively simple to describe and quite difficult to practice. Mahamudra practice could be described as remaining settled into the nature of mind, immersed in its nature that is awareness and emptiness inseparable, *not touched by artifice*, which means that there is no effort to do anything, and *free of reference*, which means that the mind is not grasping at anything at all.

If you were working with this verse, you would first memorize it and reflect on its meaning until it became very clear. Then, resting in meditation, you would float the verse in your mindstream, keeping a gentle focus, much as a *koan* is held. Then, after a while, you would let it go and rest in the space it has opened out, free of referent or mental activity. When thoughts arose again, you would fold them into the verse, which would become your referent again, and so you would continue, naturally shifting between resting in meditation and reflecting on the verse.

Equal Nature

From the space of the utterly pure extent of phenomena,
deep and clear wisdom expands.
Mind's primordial nature is forever free of elaboration.
Not deluded by habitual mind or samsara and nirvana as
they naturally arise,
To this expanse, the equal nature of all things, I bow.

Notes

This brief homage to the equal nature of all phenomena could also be used for meditation. The *pure extent of phenomena* is another way to signal emptiness. From this vast space, the wisdom intrinsic to it unfolds. *Habitual mind* is the collection of tendencies lodged in the all-basis consciousness; when the right conditions appear, the habits are activated into concepts that bring experience. This again leaves its traces in the all-basis consciousness, and so continues the cycle of samsara, understood here as the uninterrupted linking of one concept to another.

Mind's primordial nature, however, is *free of* such *elaboration* or concepts. As you rest in this nature, *samsara and nirvana naturally arise.* Appearance and emptiness are inseparable; seeing this, you know that all phenomena have the same or *equal nature.* To *bow* to this nature is to recognize and appreciate it and, through humility, perhaps to move the ego aside long enough to make a true connection with it. This verse is another that the Karmapa gave to Lama Tenam to use in his practice of meditation and which he has generously shared.

Elegy for Everything

Martha Beck

When her unborn son was diagnosed with Down syndrome, Martha Beck, author of The Joy Diet, *gave up all the conventional hopes a mother might have for her child. She gained so much more in return.*

I was a twenty-five-year-old doctoral candidate at Harvard when my second child, whom I had already named Adam, was prenatally diagnosed with Down syndrome. My doctors and advisors strongly urged a very late-term therapeutic abortion. I had a few hours to make a decision that shook me to my bones: Would I bear and raise a mentally retarded child, or abort the baby I'd already come to love?

As I considered my options, something curious happened to my view of life itself. Adam was considered better off unborn because he would lack characteristics that society values: good looks, high earning potential, *savoir faire*, and so on. But come to think of it, I knew plenty of "normal" people who also lacked these things—like, for example, me. Furthermore, even the most gifted individuals might lose their advantage through accident, illness, or age. The lucky few who avoided all catastrophe would still find death waving coyly from the finish line of their enchanted lives.

In the intensity of a life-or-death decision, all the "real world" values I cherished seemed to dissolve, like sugar in water. What I lost that day was not just the hope of having a perfect child. It was the illusion that anybody ever "has" anyone or anything. I'd been shoved face to face with the naked realization that there is nothing anyone can hang on to forever, nothing we can be, do, or possess that we will not lose.

I decided against the abortion, not out of moral judgment but because of my emotional connection to Adam—and my newfound willingness to accept the fact that the course of any life, not just the life of a handicapped person, is utterly unpredictable. This triggered a period of intense mourning. For months, my inner narrative consisted entirely of a rambling, anguished Elegy for Everything, for the transience and impermanence of all I had once depended on. But then something unexpected began to emerge from the rubble of my preconceptions: a strange, new kind of peace. I felt as though I'd jumped off a cliff, and found that though the fall was frightening, the landing never came. I had nowhere to stand, but the sensation I would later come to call "groundlessness" was not as bad as I had expected. Loosening my grip on achievement, prestige, power, money, or whatever, I found that letting go had a healing resonance I'd never felt while holding on.

In the fifteen years since Adam's birth, it has become increasingly obvious that he is some sort of Zen master wearing a blond-mentally-retarded-boy costume. His approach to life is free from conceptual rigidity or expectation; he simply takes experience as it comes, moment by moment. Sometimes there is pain, sometimes pleasure, but there is no need to judge these things, or to pretend they are not what they are. In one of my favorite Taoist stories, an old man astounds onlookers by swimming happily under a raging waterfall. How does he do it? "It's simple," the man explains. "I go up when the water goes up, and I go down when the water goes down." This is Adam's approach to life, and though I have learning disabilities in this area, I've learned much from his example.

Pema Chödrön once commented that what will happen to us

during the rest of this day is as unknown to us as what will happen at the moment of our death. I loved this thought so much that I repeated it to a couple of friends, who became very upset and told me to shut up. That moment reminded me how much I gained when I lost everything. Managing my life by fearing loss had always felt like a prison, especially since it was so obvious that loss is inevitable. I found inexpressible liberation in accepting the world as it is: transient, fluid, uncontrollable, filled not only with danger but also with breathtaking beauty, adventure, and delight.

One of the few certainties we can rely on is that sooner or later, all of us will have an Adam—an event that rips the rug from under our feet and leaves us nothing to stand on. It's an experience I wouldn't wish on my worst enemies, but I have often wished it for my best friends. If it hasn't happened to you yet, lie back and relax. I promise that it will be here soon enough.

The Human Factor

His Holiness the Dalai Lama and Howard C. Cutler, M.D.

Here's the Dalai Lama at his most down-to-earth. In conversations with Dr. Howard Cutler, he ponders what it's like to have a job. This is a striking example of how great spiritual teachers understand deeply the everyday situations of our lives. We know the Dalai Lama is right when he argues that what makes a job satisfying is the human factor—how much we care for others and they care for us. This should be required reading in all business schools.

As we began a series of dialogues about well being in the workplace, I told the Dalai Lama about my friend who had raised the question of how to practice the art of happiness at work. At the time she raised this question I had asked her specifically what kinds of difficulties she was encountering.

"I don't know," she said, "there's just a lot of aggravation at work right now. And I'm getting it from two fronts, from my boss and also some of my coworkers. My boss is way too demanding. He expects us to stay after hours and work even though we're not getting paid overtime, and he doesn't even appreciate it. He's rude and disrespectful. And I can't stand some of the other people at work too. It's getting to the point where I almost dread going to work each day."

I asked my friend to tell me about what kinds of difficulties she was having with her coworkers, and she launched into a long, convoluted tale of interoffice politics. Having no experience in her field, I couldn't make out much of what she said, but as far as I could understand it had to do with a troublesome, back-stabbing colleague who took over someone else's account and caused a rift among the employees as various factions formed in the department and aligned themselves into several camps. It sounded to me like an episode of the TV show *Survivor*.

In virtually every study of workplace conditions and the factors that contribute to employee satisfaction or dissatisfaction, the social climate of the organization plays a prominent role. Leading scholars in the emerging field of positive psychology, such as James Harter, Frank Schmidt, and Corey Keyes, in reviewing the existing literature on well-being at work, have found social interaction to be an important element in job satisfaction. Numerous researchers, including sociologist Karen Loscocco, while working at SUNY Albany, or Sheila Henderson conducting research at Stanford University, confirmed the key role of social atmosphere in employee satisfaction. In addition to providing greater satisfaction at the workplace, "work-related social support" was also found to be a factor in a person's general state of well-being.

It is of little surprise, therefore, that in my discussions with the Dalai Lama about happiness at work, sooner or later we were bound to touch upon the subject of relationships at work—the human factor.

"There may be many factors or variables that affect the degree to which work contributes to happiness," the Dalai Lama began, "and it depends on each individual's circumstances, make-up, and so on. Still, I think that in talking about work and happiness, there are some general things to keep in mind. I think it is important to remember that in all human activities, whether it is work or some other activity, the main purpose should be to benefit human beings. Now, what is it that we are seeking in our work, what is the purpose of work? Like any other human activity, we are seeking a sense of fulfillment and satisfaction and happiness. Isn't it? And if we are talking about human happiness, then of course human emotions come into play. So we should take special care to pay attention to the human relationships at work, how we interact with one another, and try to maintain basic human values even at work."

"By 'basic human values,' you mean . . ."

"Just basic human goodness. Be a good person, a kind person. Relate to others with warmth, human affection, with honesty and sincerity. Compassion."

The Dalai Lama was still for several moments, as if deeply reflecting on these principles. It was remarkable. He had spent a lifetime speaking about these human values, repeating the same ideas over and over, yet each time he spoke of them it was with a certain freshness, as if he were discovering these concepts for the first time. He seemed to take great delight in speaking about human values no matter how many times he had spoken of them before. So with a tone of genuine interest and enthusiasm he resumed.

"You know one thing that I think is crucial to keep in mind when talking about human values, compassion, and so on, is that these are not simply religious subjects. Compassion isn't something sacred, nor are anger and hatred considered to be profane just from a religious perspective. These things are important not because some religious text says so, but because our very happiness is dependent on them. These states of mind—compassion, human affection—have clear benefits to our physical health, our mental and emotional health, all of our relationships at work or at home, and even are critical for the ultimate benefit of society. They are for our own benefit. When we cultivate compassion the primary beneficiary is really ourselves. After all, humans are social animals; we are built to work cooperatively with others for our survival. No matter how powerful a single person may be, without other human companions, that individual person cannot survive. And certainly, without friends he or she cannot lead a happy and fulfilling life. So, at work if you have a warm heart, human affection, your mind will be calmer and more peaceful, which will give you a certain strength, and also will allow your mental faculties to function better, your judgment and decision-making abilities and so on."

A maroon-robed attendant silently glided into the room and poured some tea. He smiled. As I had observed in the past, there was no mistaking the atmosphere of mutual respect and affection between the Dalai Lama and his staff.

"I think on a basic level we are all human beings," he continued. "We all have the capacity to relate to one another with warmth, with affection, with friendship. So, if we are discussing happiness and satisfaction at work, like in all human activities, the human factor—how we relate to those around us, our coworkers, our customers, our boss—is of prime importance. And I think if one makes a special effort to cultivate good relationships with people at work, get to know the other people, and bring our basic good human qualities to the workplace, that can make a tremendous difference. Then, whatever kind of work we do, it can be a source of satisfaction. Then you look forward to going to work, and you are happier there. You say, *'Oh, I'm going to work to see my friends today!'* " The Dalai Lama exclaimed with such an exuberant tone that I could almost picture him showing up at the factory, lunch pail in hand, greeting his coworkers this way. I couldn't help but smile.

"And this is something you can do yourself to improve your experience at work," the Dalai Lama went on. "Often people wait for the other person to make the first move, but I think that is wrong. That is like when people remain neighbors for a long time, but never get to know one another. So, you must take some initiative, even from your first day on the job, and try to show some friendship to others, introduce yourself, say hello, ask how long have you worked here, and so on. Of course, people will not always be receptive to that. In my own case sometimes I'll smile at someone, and that just makes them look upon me with greater suspicion," he laughed. "So people may have their own problems and frustrations, but then don't give up if they don't immediately respond. Try for one week, or one month. Eventually you may find others responding. Sometimes it's easy to give up, like sometimes I'm in a hotel or somewhere and I'll smile but the person ignores me. And if that remains their attitude, I'll assume the same attitude and ignore them," he chuckled. "I guess that's just human nature. But it shows how one person can influence another's attitude, which implies that even one person can make a big difference. One person can change the atmosphere of the workplace environment. You can see examples, for instance, of a very tense group of coworkers who don't get along, and then a new employee shows up, one who is warm and friendly, and after a while the mood and attitude of the whole group changes for the better. In the same way, sometimes you will see the opposite occur, where people at work are getting along, and are friends, but then someone new will start work there, someone who is a troublemaker, and then that one can affect the whole group and cause conflicts and problems. So, each of us can have an effect on others, and even change the atmosphere at work. And in that respect, a low-level worker might have more impact on one's immediate surroundings at work, at least in one's department, than the boss.

"For example, I know some Tibetans who moved to Switzerland, and went to work in factories there. And even without knowing the language they managed to make friendships, just by smiling and doing their work sincerely, and in mainly nonverbal ways showing that they were just trying to be helpful. There was this one Tibetan who would eat in the cafeteria, where normally people would keep to themselves, or sit in small groups. And one day he decided to buy lunch for a group of his coworkers. Before that people would not ordinarily buy someone lunch unless they knew that person very well, but even though he did not know them well he bought them lunch. Then the next day, another person bought lunch for the group to reciprocate. Then, others started doing that, and soon each day a different person would buy lunch, and through that they became closer friends."

I once heard the Dalai Lama remark that we can use our own lives as a kind of laboratory, where we can experiment with the implementation of the principles he speaks about, and investigate for ourselves the truth of his assertions. In thinking over his ideas about work and happiness during a recent trip to my local supermarket, I amused myself by viewing the shopping trip as if it were a controlled experiment designed by some clever researcher. The controlled experimental conditions: Take a half-dozen identical check-out stations, identical aisles with identical copies of the *National Enquirer*, identical cash registers, and identical racks of chewing gum and razor blades. The experimental variable: add the human factor—insert a different human being behind each cash register.

At this supermarket there are two check-out clerks who have been working here for some years. I've ended up in each of their lines countless times. Jane is a woman in her mid-thirties. She goes about her job efficiently and quickly, yet she rarely says a word, other than calling out for a price check. No matter when I've shopped there, she always seems to have a slightly sullen expression, almost on the verge of a scowl. Dorothy, on the other hand, a jolly lady in her late fifties, couldn't be more different. She always engages in friendly banter with the customers, always smiling and helpful. She asks them about their lives, and remembers what they say—she even remembers what they bought last time. It is a delight to listen to her. You can wait in her aisle, standing in line while the person in front of you unloads 137 items, pulls out a two-inch stack of coupons, and wants to pay with a third-party check, yet one doesn't seem to mind. Well, at least one minds less. Dorothy has a sincere interest in food as well as the customers, and often engages in a running commentary about the person's food choices, swapping recipes as she rings up your purchases, "Oh, I haven't tried that brand of frozen pizza. Is it good?" "I see you bought Twinkies again—let me give you a tip—buy some of the Betty Crocker yellow cake mix, the kind with pudding in the mix, and slice up the pieces thin, then layer it with fresh whipped cream—it's like a homemade Twinkie, at least if your home happens to be in heaven!" (She was right!) She has always struck me as one who genuinely enjoys her work.

The difference between Dorothy and Jane not only illustrates the impact of attitude on job satisfaction, but also how one person can make a difference on those around her. Recently I was restocking a lot of food items at home, so my purchases filled two shopping carts. The bagboy offered to help push one of the carts out to my car, and we spoke as I was loading the groceries into my car. I've always noticed how Dorothy treats her baggers with respect, and some of the younger high-school students relate to her as a mother. As we were loading the groceries, the bagboy was telling me about how much more he enjoys his work on the days that Dorothy works, adding, ". . . and it's not just me. When Dorothy is working, everybody seems to be in a better mood, even the manager. I'm not sure why, but things just seem to go better on the days that she's working."

The prime importance of the human factor at work applies equally to any setting, a supermarket or the stock market, in a boardroom or in a boiler room. As the character played by Nicolas Cage in *The Family Man* exclaimed, "Whether it's on Main Street or on Wall Street, it's all just people!" So, no matter where we work, we've got to find a way to get along well with the people around us.

"Some people work in a really tense environment, and may not be getting along with their coworkers. In those situations, do you have any thoughts on how to improve things?" I asked the Dalai Lama.

"This depends on the person, and their capacity and willingness to try to control their own emotions like anger, jealousy, and so on. We should try our best to accept responsibility for our own emotions, practice tolerance, and try to reduce jealousy, although of course it isn't always easy, and people will have varying degrees of success.

"But generally speaking, one could start by recognizing that we are all interdependent, we all depend on one another for our livelihood. That is the place we could start. The deeper our appreciation of that fact, that reality, the greater our willingness to work cooperatively with others will be. Sometimes we have a sort of feeling that we are separate from others, independent, that kind of feeling that *I earn my own money, I support myself, so who needs others?* Especially when we are young and healthy, there's that tendency to think *I can manage alone; I do not need to care about others.* But no matter what kind of job we have, there are many other coworkers who contribute in their own way to the running of the company that we depend on for our livelihood. Without them, the company simply would not exist, and we would not be able to earn our living, not to mention our customers, our suppliers, or many others who make it possible for us to earn our money."

"That's of course, unless we work alone in our basement, having a job as a counterfeiter, printing up our own money," I joked.

The Dalai Lama chuckled politely at my meager sense of humor, then continued, "In fact, in the context of the workplace, which is what we are talking about here, in order to get along better with others I think the most important thing is to recognize our interconnection, our interdependence. That's the key factor. Have a clear understanding of that reality. At least on that basis one will be more willing to work cooperatively with others, whether one has any particular, special feeling of affection or compassion towards them or not. On that level, on the level of building teamwork, compassion or empathy is not even required. However, if you want to enhance and strengthen the relationship, move it to a deeper and much more satisfying level, then empathy and compassion would be required. You understand?"

"Yes," I nodded.

"So in thinking of other things that can help one deal with

difficult people at work, I think that if one is in a situation where there may be hostile coworkers or demanding supervisors, a wider perspective can sometimes help—realizing that this person's behavior may have nothing to do with me, there may be other causes for their behavior, and not take it too personally. Their hostile outbursts may actually have more to do with unrelated issues, maybe even problems at home. We sometimes tend to forget these simple truths.

"And also I should mention that if we are talking about trying to cultivate a deeper compassion for others, that compassion should be unbiased; ideally it should be directed towards everyone equally. That's genuine compassion, universal compassion. For example, often we think of compassion as something that is directed towards those who are worse off than we are, less fortunate people who are poor or in some difficult circumstances. There, of course, compassion is a completely appropriate response. But often if people are more wealthy than we are, or famous, or enjoying some fortunate circumstances, we feel that they are not appropriate objects for our compassion. Our compassion dries up, and we may feel jealousy instead. But if we look deeper, no matter how rich or famous someone is, he or she is still a human being just like us, subject to the changes of life, of old age, illness, loss, and so on. Even if it is not apparent on the surface, sooner or later they are subject to suffering. They are worthy of compassion on that basis, on the basis of being fellow human beings. So, this relates specifically to the workplace, where we are often in conflict with our supervisors, bosses, but we are more likely to feel envy, fear, or hostility rather than to think of them merely as another human being, as worthy of our compassion as anyone else.

"So, this brings me to the final approach to dealing with difficult people at work, these trying situations. And this depends entirely on the basic outlook and orientation, and personal interest of the individual. In this regard, there are some people who have an interest in spirituality, who are trying to train their mind, to cultivate spiritual values, like compassion, patience, tolerance, and forgiveness. Now for those people, they may use these challenging situations as part of their spiritual practice, and view situations where there are conflicts with difficult coworkers as opportunities to practice these wonderful human qualities, to strengthen these spiritual values. I think it is a wonderful thing if one can use one's place of work as a place of spiritual practice as well. As I usually mention, practicing patience and tolerance does not mean that one should passively allow oneself or others to be harmed in any way—in those cases one needs to take appropriate countermeasures. But this has to do with one's internal response and reaction to conflicts at work, or to situations that may cause emotions like anger, hatred, or jealousy to arise. And this approach is definitely possible. In my experience, for instance, I have met many Tibetans who have been imprisoned, political prisoners, by the Chinese for many years, being beaten, starved, tortured. And yet they were able to use their spiritual practices even in these extreme conditions, and in some cases even strengthening their spiritual practice, while maintaining compassion even towards their captors.

"For example, there was one senior monk who was imprisoned by the Chinese for many years. A group of his students were also in the same prison. I once met one monk, who was one of the students of this senior monk. He told me that all of them were mistreated and abused in this prison, but it was especially hard on the students when they saw their teacher being beaten and humiliated. They became very angry. But the teacher advised them not to be overcome by hatred, that this was in fact an opportunity for inner development. He spoke to them about the importance of maintaining their compassion, even toward their guards, who were sewing the seeds for their own future suffering by their misdeeds."

The Dalai Lama looked at his watch, and realized it was time to close. As our meeting concluded, he suddenly started to laugh heartily. "Anyway," he remarked, "today I've been giving you suggestions about dealing with difficult people at work. Even though I'm talking about these things, if I went to work for a company and was in those kinds of adverse situations with employers or coworkers, I do not know how far I would be able to follow my own advice. I don't know—I might start stomping around, yelling and breaking things, throwing things through windows and breaking glass. I might get fired! And later on if we make a book about these discussions, there's a danger that one of the readers might come to me and say something like, *I've been in this very difficult work situation, so since you have made such a wonderful presentation, be in my place for at least one week! Then you will be in trouble.* Anyway, thank you, Howard. Good night."

"Good night. Sleep well, and I'll see you tomorrow."

The Heart's Intention

Phillip Moffitt

Buddhism is about leading the examined life. When we don't examine our lives closely, we are prey to superficial values, social conditioning, and self-defeating patterns. In this essay, Phillip Moffitt asks us to examine the goals we set for ourselves and see whether they align with our real values.

Once a month, an hour before the Sunday-evening meditation class I teach, I offer a group interview for students who attend regularly. These interviews give them the opportunity to ask questions about their meditation practice or about applying the dharma to daily life. In a recent session, a yogi who dutifully meditates every morning admitted, "I must be confused about the Buddha's teaching on right intention. I'm very good about setting intentions and then reminding myself of them. But things don't ever seem to turn out according to those intentions, and I fall into disappointment. What's wrong with my practice?"

At first, I could only smile in response. What a good question! When I asked her to explain these intentions, she proceeded to describe a number of *goals* for her future—to become less tense at work, to spend more time with her family, to stabilize her finances, and more. She was suffering from a kind of confusion that seems to afflict many bright, hardworking people: mixing up two different life functions that are easily mistaken for each other. All of her goals were laudable, but none would fit within the Buddha's teachings on right intention.

Goals vs. Intentions

Goal making is a valuable skill; it involves envisioning a future outcome in the world or in your behavior, then planning, applying discipline, and working hard to achieve it. You organize your time and energy based on your goals; they help provide direction for your life. Committing to and visualizing those goals may assist you in your efforts, but neither of these activities is what I call setting intention. They both involve living in an imagined future and are not concerned with what is happening to you in the present moment. With goals, the future is always the focus: Are you going to reach the goal? Will you be happy when you do? What's next?

Setting intention, at least according to Buddhist teachings, is quite different from goal making. It is not oriented toward a future outcome. Instead, it is a path or practice that is focused on how you are "being" in the present moment. Your attention is on the everpresent "now" in the constantly changing flow of life. You set your intentions based on understanding what matters most to you and make a commitment to align your worldly actions with your inner values.

As you gain insight through meditation, wise reflection, and moral living, your ability to act from your intentions blossoms. It is called a practice because it is an ever-renewing process. You don't just set your intentions and then forget about them; you live them every day.

Although the student thought she was focusing on her inner experience of the present moment, she was actually focusing on a future outcome; even though she had healthy goals that pointed in a wholesome direction, she was not *being* her values. Thus, when her efforts did not go well, she got lost in disappointment and confusion. When this happened, she had no "ground of intention" to help her regain her mental footing—no way to establish herself in a context that was larger and more meaningful than her goal-oriented activity.

Goals help you make your place in the world and be an effective person. But being grounded in intention is what provides integrity and unity in your life. Through the skillful cultivation of intention, you learn to make wise goals and then to work hard toward achieving them without getting caught in attachment to outcome. As I suggested to the yogi, only by remembering your intentions can you reconnect with yourself during those emotional storms that cause you to lose touch with yourself. This remembering is a blessing, because it provides a sense of meaning in your life that is independent of whether you achieve certain goals or not.

Ironically, by being in touch with and acting from your true intentions, you become more effective in reaching your goals than when you act from wants and insecurities. Once the yogi understood this, she started to work with goals and intentions as separate functions. She later reported that continually coming back to her intentions in the course of her day was actually helping her with her goals.

Doing the Groundwork

What would it be like if you didn't measure the success of your life just by what you get and don't get, but gave equal or greater priority to how aligned you are with your deepest values? Goals are rooted in *maya* (illusion)—the illusionary world where what you want seems fixed and unchanging but in truth is forever changing. It is in this world that *mara*, the inner voice of temptation and discouragement, flourishes. Goals never fulfill you in an ongoing way; they either beget another goal or else collapse. They provide excitement—the ups and downs of life—but intention is what provides you with self-respect and peace of mind.

Cultivating right intention does not mean you abandon goals.

You continue to use them, but they exist within a larger context of meaning that offers the possibility of peace beyond the fluctuations caused by pain and pleasure, gain and loss.

The Buddha's Fourth Noble Truth teaches right intention as the second step in the eightfold path: Cause no harm, and treat yourself and others with lovingkindness and compassion while seeking true happiness, that which comes from being free from grasping and clinging. Such a statement may sound naïve or idealistic—a way for nuns and monks to live but not suitable for those of us who must make our way in this tough, competitive world. But to think this is to make the same error as the woman in my group interview.

In choosing to live with right intention, you are not giving up your desire for achievement or a better life, or binding yourself to being morally perfect. But you are committing to living each moment with the intention of not causing harm with your actions and words, and not violating others through your livelihood or sexuality. You are connecting to your own sense of kindness and innate dignity. Standing on this ground of intention, you are then able to participate as you choose in life's contests, until you outgrow them.

Naturally, sometimes things go well for you and other times not, but you do not live and die by these endless fluctuations. Your happiness comes from the strength of your internal experience of intention. You become one of those fortunate human beings who know who they are and are independent of our culture's obsession with winning. You still feel sadness, loss, lust, and fear, but you have a means for directly relating to all of these difficult emotions. Therefore, you are not a victim, nor are your happiness and peace of mind dependent on how things are right now.

Misusing Good Intentions

When I offer teachings on right intention, students often ask two things: "Isn't this like signing up for the Ten Commandments in another form?" and "What about the old saying 'The road to hell is paved with good intentions'?" First, the Ten Commandments are excellent moral guidelines for us all, but right intention is not moral law; it is an attitude or state of mind, which you develop gradually. As such, the longer you work with right intention, the subtler and more interesting it becomes as a practice.

In Buddhist psychology, intention manifests itself as "volition," which is the mental factor that most determines your consciousness in each moment. Literally, it is your intention that affects how you interpret what comes into your mind.

Take, for example, someone who is being rude and domineering during a meeting at work. He is unpleasant, or at least your experience of him is unpleasant. What do you notice? Do you see his insecurity and how desperately hungry he is for control and attention? Or do you notice only your own needs and dislike, and take his behavior personally, even though it really has little to do with you? If you are grounded in your intention, then your response will be to notice his discomfort and your own suffering and feel compassion toward both of you. This doesn't mean that you don't feel irritation or that you allow him to push you around, but you avoid getting lost in judgment or personal reaction. Can you feel the extra emotional space such an orientation to life provides? Do you see the greater range of options for interpreting the difficulties in your life?

As for those good intentions that lead to hell in the old adage, they almost always involve having an agenda for someone else. They are goals disguised as intentions, and you abandon your inner intentions in pursuit of them. Moreover, those goals are often only your view of how things are supposed to be, and you become caught in your own reactive mind.

Mixing Motives

One issue around cultivating intention that trips up many yogis is mixed motives. During individual interviews with me, people will sometimes confess their anguish at discovering during meditating how mixed their motives were in past situations involving a friend or a family member. They feel as though they're not a good person and they aren't trustworthy. Sometimes my response is to paraphrase the old blues refrain "If it wasn't for bad luck, I wouldn't have no luck at all." It is the same with motives; in most situations, if you didn't go with your mixed motives, you wouldn't have any motivation at all. You would just be stuck.

The Buddha knew all about mixed motives. In the Majjhima Nikaya *sutta* (a discourse of the Buddha) "The Dog-Duty Ascetic," he describes how "dark intentions lead to dark results" and "bright intentions lead to bright results." Then he says, "Bright and dark intentions lead to bright and dark results." Life is like this, which is why we practice. You are not a fully enlightened being; therefore, expecting yourself to be perfect is a form of delusion.

Forget judging yourself, and just work with the arising moment. Right intention is a continual aspiration. Seeing your mixed motives is one step toward liberation from ignorance and from being blinded by either desire or aversion. So welcome such a realization, even though it is painful. The less judgment you have toward yourself about your own mixed motives, the more clearly you can see how they cause suffering. This insight is what releases the dark motives and allows room for bright ones.

Sowing Karmic Seeds

For some people, the most difficult aspect of right intention has to do with the role it plays in the formation of karma. The Buddha classified karma as one of the "imponderables," meaning we can never fully understand it; attempting to do so is not fruitful. Yet we are challenged to work with the truth that every action has both a cause and a consequence.

The primary factor that determines karma is intention; therefore, practicing right intention is crucial to gaining peace and happiness. In Buddhist teachings, karma refers to "the seed from action." This means that any word or action is either wholesome or unwholesome and automatically plants a seed of future occurrence that will blossom on its own accord when the conditions are correct, just as a plant grows when there is the right balance of sunshine, water, and nutrients.

Whether an action is wholesome or unwholesome is determined by the intention that originated it. On reflection, this is common sense. The example often given is that of a knife in the hands of a surgeon versus those of an assailant. Each might use a knife to cut you, but one has the intention to help you heal, while the other has the intention to harm you. Yet you could die from the actions of either. Intention is the decisive factor that differentiates the two. In this view, you are well served by cultivating right intention.

When I'm teaching right intention, I like to refer to it as the *heart's intention.* Life is so confusing and emotionally confounding that the rational mind is unable to provide an absolutely clear intention. What we have to rely on is our intuitive knowing, or "felt wisdom." In the Buddha's time, this was referred to as *bodhichitta,* "the awakened mind-heart."

It is said that a karmic seed may bloom at one of three times: immediately, later in this lifetime, or in a *future* life. Conversely, what is happening to you at each moment is the result of seeds planted in a past life, earlier in this life, or in the previous moment. Whatever your feelings about past lives, the latter two are cause-and-effect phenomena that you recognize as true. But here is a thought to reflect on that is seldom mentioned: Whatever is manifesting itself in your life right now is affected by how you receive it, and how you receive it is largely determined by your intention in this moment.

Imagine that you will have a difficult interaction later today. If you are not mindful of your intention, you might respond to the situation with a harmful physical action—maybe because you got caught in your fear, panic, greed, or ill will. But with awareness of your intention, you would refrain from responding physically. Instead, you might only say something unskillful, causing much less harm. Or, if you have a habit of speaking harshly, with right intention you might only have a negative thought but find the ability to refrain from uttering words you would later regret. When you're grounded in your intention, you are never helpless in how you react to any event in your life. While it is true that you often cannot control what happens to you, with mindfulness of intention you can mitigate the effects of what occurs in terms of both the moment itself and what kind of karmic seed you plant for the future.

Developing Resolve

Buddhist teachings suggest that there are certain characteristics called *paramis*, or perfections, you must develop before you can ever achieve liberation. One of these qualities, right resolve, has to do with developing the will to live by your intentions. Through practicing right resolve, you learn to set your mind to maintaining your values and priorities, and to resist the temptation to sacrifice your values for material or ego gain. You gain the ability to consistently hold your intentions, no matter what arises.

Right intention is like muscle—you develop it over time by exercising it. When you lose it, you just start over again. There's no need to judge yourself or quit when you fail to live by your intentions. You are developing the habit of right intention so that it becomes an unconscious way of living—an automatic response to all situations. Right intention is organic; it thrives when cultivated and wilts when neglected.

Not long ago, the yogi gave me an update on her efforts to practice right intention. She said that for several years, she had pushed and pulled in her relationship, getting irritated with her partner for not spending more time with the family and demanding that he change. One day in meditation, she realized that this was just another example of her getting caught in wanting more.

In truth, there was nothing intrinsically wrong with his behavior. It was just that she wanted to spend more time together than he did. She immediately stopped making demands and was much happier.

Soon after this first realization, she found herself in a situation at work where all of her insecurities were ignited. She was in a meeting during which an action was being proposed that she felt was unfair, and she sensed anger rising in her. But before speaking, she left the room to reflect.

When she returned, she was grounded in her intentions to be nonreactive, to seek out clear understanding, and to not be attached to the outcome. This allowed her to participate in the meeting in a calm, effective manner, saying her truth. Surprisingly, the group came to a conclusion that, although it was not what she thought should happen, was at least something she could live with. "Sometimes I remember to work with my intentions," she told me, "but then at other times, I just seem to develop amnesia and completely forget the whole idea for weeks at a time. It's like I had never been exposed to the teaching. I mean, there is nothing in my mind but my goals. I don't even consider my intention." I assured her that it is like this for almost everyone. It takes a long time to make right intention a regular part of your life.

At times, the benefits of acting from your intentions can seem so clear and obvious that you vow, "I'm going to live this way from now on." Then you get lost or overwhelmed and conclude that it is more than you can do. Such emotional reactions, while understandable, miss the point. If you make right intention a goal, you are grasping at spiritual materialism. Right intention is simply about coming home to yourself. It is a practice of aligning with the deepest part of yourself while surrendering to the reality that you often get lost in your wanting mind.

There are only two things you are responsible for in this practice: Throughout each day, ask yourself if you are being true to your deepest intentions. If you're not, start doing so immediately, as best as you're able. The outcome of your inquiry and effort may seem modest at first. But be assured, each time you start over by reconnecting to your intention, you are taking one more step toward finding your own authenticity and freedom. In that moment, you are remembering yourself and grounding your life in your heart's intention. You are living the noble life of the Buddha's teachings.

In Buddha's Kitchen

Kimberley Snow

You might think that Buddhist centers are oases of calm and clarity, free of neurosis and conflict. Yeah, right. But the point isn't a pretend sanctity. It's to be fully who we are and to find the brilliance and wisdom in that. In this funny, down-to-earth story, professional chef Kimberley Snow adapts to the chaos, eccentricity, and yet underlying sanity of life at a Tibetan Buddhist center.

Three volunteer workers and I were fixing lunch, standing on either side of the long prep table that dominated the room. Huge pots and frying pans hung from the wrought iron rack over the table.

"Whoever put tile floors in this kitchen should be shot," a woman named Celie complained.

"Or be made to stand on them for hours and hours." I sighed and looked around for the thick rubber "fatigue mat." Someone had taken it out back to use as a doormat. Someone was always doing something like that.

Chop, chop, chop.

We worked in silence for a few minutes, then talked about the girl from L.A. who had come in that morning to say she only ate range-free chicken and fresh melon. She hoped that wasn't going to be a problem for the kitchen.

Learning at last to watch my mouth, I hadn't said out loud that it might be a problem for her, but it wouldn't be for the kitchen. Just pretended I hadn't heard. But the more I subvocalized my negative thoughts, the darker my mood became. I remembered yesterday's teaching by Lama Longtalk—not his real name, but it came close—about the man who placed a black stone on a pile for every negative thought he had, a white one for every positive thought. At first, he produced a mountain of black stones, a tiny heap of white ones. At the end of ten years, he had only white stones in front of him. A happy man.

How can anyone watch their thoughts for a single day, much less years and years, I wondered glumly. Am I supposed to be doing that?

The talk in the kitchen turned to the dressing for the beet and apple salad we were having for lunch. Belinda, from New Mexico, slipped the cooked beets out of their skins, then wiped her hands on a new white apron. I knew the red stains would never come out, but I didn't say a word. With another sigh, a deeper one this time, I remembered the good old days when I'd been able to fire someone on the spot, scream at them to get out of my kitchen and never, ever come back. Back in the days when I'd been able to control every aspect of kitchen life like a monarch. Back when they'd called me God.

I'd had a large staff then, especially when we hosted the horse sales and I fed around eight hundred people in one afternoon. I had to run a tight ship. I'd hire every reliable person I had ever worked with for the event. Semireliables (a much larger group) were also on call. I remembered a staff meeting we'd had the week before D day where I explained everything in detail. The bulk food would be brought in the day of the sales: the bread stored in the closet behind the bar, the rest to be taken upstairs, assembled and garnished, then carried downstairs as needed. One person would act as a gofer, nothing else, just a gofer, always available at the wink of an eye to leave and get whatever we needed. Susie in charge of tea and coffee, nothing else. Keep the coffeemaker going;

use the gallon jugs of iced tea to fill the pitchers. Make sure the glasses are full of ice; get it from behind the bar. Pete to see that the buffet table stays fully stocked. When something looks like it's getting low, not when it's already gone, but before that, when it begins to wane, come upstairs and get another platter full of whatever. We'll have the backup platters all ready in the kitchen.

"Any questions?" I asked the assembled group.

A bored silence, then one hand went up. "Anybody got any speed?"

Can't say that I missed the old days, although it was nice to be able to fire people. Somehow it is easier to be God than Buddha, easier to control rather than cooperate. At least at first it seems that way.

The Tibetan Buddhist retreat center I'll call Dorje Ling occupies over two hundred acres of hills and forest dotted with buildings, statues, reflecting pools, a woodworking shop, a small canteen, and numerous cabins snuggled into the bushes. Lines and lines of colorful prayer flags hang from poles or trees behind a row of seven *stupas.*

When I went down to the garden to pick parsley for the soup, I saw, along with regular American people in sweats or tattered jeans, red-robed Asian monks, women with embroidered Tibetan aprons over long wraparound dresses called *chubas.* Several children ran through the grass chasing a ball. A stocky little blond boy, with a plastic machine gun in one hand and a Tibetan prayer wheel in the other, seemed to be the leader. Peacocks, in their own large cage, let out raucous screams at odd intervals. Large dogs drowsed in the sun. Hammering could be heard in the background.

A golf cart flying a red prayer flag was always parked near the side entrance of the main building, that three-story cream-colored stucco structure I'd gazed at so often in the photo on my bulletin board back in Kentucky. Dark red trim on the tall windows flared wide at the bottom, then narrowed toward the top, emphasizing the soaring aspect. The Tibetan-style roof with upturned gables was decorated with hand-painted designs of dragons and clouds.

The building—just like the Bluegrass Horse Center where I'd once been executive chef—grew more private the further up one went. The main shrine room, dining rooms, meeting room, and kitchen took up the first floor, while the monks, lamas, and important visitors lived on the second. The acting head of the retreat center, a Tibetan named Lama Tashi, lived on the third floor with all the painted dragons and clouds.

"Tibetans like noise," an older student from Denmark had told me as we washed up after lunch the first day of the retreat, "and company. If you have a dozen Danes and a dozen tables, you'll get one at each table, eating alone. If you have a dozen Tibetans, they'll all crowd together at one table."

"I somehow thought that retreats were silent." Unlike a Vipassana retreat I'd attended, this one was constant noise. In the shrine room, bells, cymbals, drums, long horns were all part of the ritual. Rather than traveling inward toward a personal still point, here the focus seemed to be on group activity.

"You won't get silence here. Hold on to your ear plugs."

I had heard all about Zen kitchens. The sense of order, focus. Everyone silent, bowing respectfully to each other, to the food, mindful of every minute detail. Zen master Dogen's idea that only senior students should be allowed to cook.

But Japanese Zen Buddhism was very different from Tibetan Vajrayana, and the kitchens of the two differed in the extreme. Forget the bowing, the silence, the respect. Add color, noise, and chaos. Add a kitchen full of people—construction workers looking for a snack, children playing hide and seek in the pantry, visitors using the only phone on the first floor, monks making statues out of butter and oatmeal, senior students melting coconut oil for butter lamps—fit these in the spaces around the kitchen workers and the food, and you've got the sort of kitchen I now worked in.

A high level of energy seemed to sweep through everything at Dorje Ling. Everyone was charged, pumped up with life force, buzzing with activity. And I was right out there in front like a racehorse stamping, pawing the ground, ready to break out of the chute and go.

Coordinate, I decided—after I'd ruined my chances for enlightenment by volunteering to take over the kitchen when the cook's back went out—*coordinate* was the operative word. I didn't have to actually cook for everyone myself—or so they said—just oversee the food. When I started asking around for an assistant, someone pointed me toward a senior student named Lonny who had once been in charge of the kitchen. But when asked if she could help out, Lonny said, "Sorry. I burn everything."

"Oh, I heard that you'd been the main chef a few years ago."

"That's true. Then I was the only cook for twelve people doing a three-year retreat. Seven men over in the right wing of the building and five women in the left. The kitchen in the middle. Literally and figuratively."

"What happened?"

"For the first few months, everyone was really into the practice, glad to be on retreat, grateful that I was supporting them by cooking. By the third year, everything had changed. People had nowhere else to go, so they'd come into the kitchen to freak out, go crazy. By then I was the main moving target of everyone's projections, hopes, and fears.

"The men would ask me to pass on messages to the women. And, of course, vice versa. Early the second year, the women took in a pregnant stray cat, and things just got worse and worse as time went on. The building was crawling with all of these felines, and some of the men found that the pussy cats were upsetting their minds."

"Nothing subtle about *that.*"

"Right. So we had the whole male/female thing, and the cat thing, and then some of the retreatants would become obsessed with the person next to them or across the way, so they'd come into the kitchen where I'd be chopping and talk to me endlessly about this person. Then the other person would come in and do the same. Such venom. At first I'd tried to keep the peace, to mediate, but finally I learned to be very quiet and just try to generate compassion and love for them."

"Did it work?"

"Well, it sure helped me."

"Who did the grocery shopping?"

"Some of the bulk stuff would be delivered, but mainly I went into town every few days. I finally stopped personal shopping for the group except once every two weeks. Made them write out a list and I'd only get a few items for each person. Frightening how fascistic I became, but being the only one shopping for twelve people can get pretty hairy.

"Then, with the food, they'd become obsessed by tiny little things. Oatmeal, for instance. People could fixate on oatmeal for hours, days, weeks. It didn't matter if they liked it or didn't like it, if they wanted me to serve it with raisins and sunflower seeds or with salt and butter. They'd develop this sort of oatmeal tunnel vision. William James said, 'Whatever you attend to becomes your reality.' "

"So these people on the three-year retreat . . . ?" I didn't quite know how to formulate the question. Lonny didn't help. "So the three-year retreat isn't always, um, successful?"

"With some it is, yes, incredibly so. Look at Lama P. He was on that retreat. With others, no. It was a disaster. Partly it depended on their motivation for going into retreat in the first place."

"Motivation?" I had noticed how often this word came up at Dorje Ling.

"If they were hiding from their sexuality or their psychological quirks, then there would be problems. Or if they were motivated by their image of themselves as a spiritual person, they didn't get very far."

"But aren't the ones who choose to go into a long retreat the pick of the crop, so to speak?"

"Not necessarily. Some pretty serious students don't do group retreats. They tend to be quiet about their practice."

Later I found out that Lonny had done years of retreat herself, but never mentioned the fact. Sitting next to her was like nestling down beside a boulder. Solid, stable, nonjudgmental. Yet there was something soft about her, too, something almost flowerlike in her face. An open sweetness, even tenderness, but without sentimentality. Just clarity.

"Do you really burn everything?"

Lonny didn't answer, just looked through my eyes into something deep within me even while drawing me into her heart. This exchange was so sudden that I couldn't have resisted even if I'd wanted to. When Lonny left, I found that I had tears in my eyes.

Over and over I discovered that the senior students—and I could identify them by the fact that they seldom talked about themselves, but always listened attentively—had a certain quality, a certain presence that I had never encountered anywhere else.

From now on, I decided, much too late, I'm going to burn everything and earn the right to sit and meditate. Even as I said this to myself, I knew that my thinking was missing something essential, though I couldn't quite put my finger on it.

The idea of a food fair comes to me during the middle of the morning meditation. I hardly notice the pain in my knees that day as I contemplate a variety of booths: a salad bar, a soup station, potatoes with toppings, rice with. . . . But maybe we shouldn't have rice and potatoes the same day, better on alternate days. When the lunch bell sounds, I'm surprised at how short the session has been.

As always, we end by dedicating the merit generated by our practice to the welfare of all sentient beings, and I realize that I've hardly done any real practice. But doesn't helping to feed real people count? And who's doing the counting?

In Tibetan Buddhism, different types of energy are represented by what are called the five buddha families, and each of the five is associated with a color, among many other qualities. Gold or yellow, for instance, symbolizes the Ratna family's involvement with wealth, enrichment, and generosity. In one of the many ceremonies at Dorje Ling, a specially marked tray is passed around and each person throws a flower onto it. Where the flower lands on the tray indicates the particular buddha family with which the individual has the strongest connection. My flower always fell to the north, on the green area of the Karma family, the one involved in activity. In fact, the person representing this family is usually shown in profile since she doesn't have the time to turn around fully to face you. No matter how hard I try to make my flower hit somewhere else on the tray, it always, always lands on the Karma buddha family.

During the afternoon session, I develop the idea of food booths in more detail. Soups, salads, breads blossom into Soups & Stews, Salads & Fruit, Breads & Sweets. During lunch, I'd found some large plastic bins that fit into even larger tubs that I could pack with ice and use for the salad bar. A trip to the shop reveals cans of spray paint to use on some rusty metal shelves that I'd unearthed. My hope of relaxing into emptiness recedes with each detail, each list.

Fortunately, I've brought my laptop, so at the break, I go back to my cabin and start converting recipes to feed a large group. I've just worked out a few step-by-step work lists when I hear the dinner gong. I'd forgotten to go back after the break! Maybe tomorrow, I tell myself (my face in profile, working away), I can return to sitting.

That night, I don't go into the shrine room at all but into the kitchen, empty and quiet at last. I settle in the storeroom, checking supplies and making lists. More than anything, I want to serve simple, wholesome food that doesn't distract from everyone's retreat, and to create a workable system that gives me time away from the kitchen. I'd forgotten just how much I enjoyed the administrative part of being a chef. The more planning I could do, the better.

"What doing?" Lama Tashi catches me by surprise as I'm sitting on the floor of the pantry surrounded by my laptop and portable printer, by written-over lists and schedules, books, banners of material that say POTATOES and SALADS and such. Born and raised in Tibet, Lama Tashi has a funny way of speaking English that the students both imitate and use as pith instructions. "What doing, do!" is a favorite kitchen slogan to shout at distracted helpers. "Why so much attachment having?" is taped up near the prep table.

"Meditating not?" he asks. I shake my head and try to get up, but he motions for me not to. The laptop is indeed on top of my lap. He just stands there, interested, present. I tell him that I am planning the food for the retreat.

"In Tibet. One pot. Big spoon." He picks up a plastic pail from the corner and mimes dishing out spoonfuls of food to waiting bowls. Does he really expect me to use a pail and a big spoon?

"Lama Tashi, I used to be a professional chef," it comes in a rush, "and I thought that if I just planned enough we could have sort of like a food fair with different booths. One for salads, one for soups, another station for sandwiches, and so on." I'd actually planned to have the shop make small booths and the sewing group run up signs in the colors of the buddha families and string prayer flags between, but I suddenly see all this as the sheerest folly, excessively elaborate in a way that only southern women can manage. Lama Tashi doesn't say a word, just stands there in silence as the contents of my mind open to me in a new and not very flattering light. My plans are not exactly pointless or silly, but I'm so invested in my concept of a dazzling, original food fair that I can barely think of anything else. Not for the last time in the presence of a Tibetan lama, I feel as if I am operating on several planes at once, one of which allows me to see the full extent of my grasping and ignorance. My attachment is truly staggering. But I take it in without guilt or recrimination, simply with unprecedented clarity. Simultaneously, I can also see that my motivation is good, that I do want to help.

"You good worker," Lama Tashi says, nodding approvingly. "But you *so* busy being you!" He flashes a big smile and is gone.

Only Love Dispels Hate

Geri Larkin

The Dhammapada *is one of Buddhism's most beloved texts, a simple statement of eternal truths in spare, beautiful poetry. It is recited every day in Buddhist homes and temples around the world. Geri Larkin is the guiding teacher at a Zen center in Detroit, where she adapted the* Dhammapada *for an inner city audience. Here's a selection from her rendering, followed by a story of Zen life in Detroit.*

The Twin Verses

Our minds create everything.
If we speak or act with an impure mind
suffering is as certain
as the wheel of a bike that moves
when we start to pedal.

In the same way
if we speak or act with a pure mind
happiness will be ours—
a shadow that never leaves.

"He abused me; he beat me; he defeated me;
he robbed me."

If we cling to such thoughts
we live in hate.

"She abused me; she beat me; she defeated me;
she robbed me."
If we release such thoughts
our hate dissolves.

Hatred has never stopped hatred.
Only love stops hate.
This is the eternal law.

So many people fail to realize that
in quarreling
we ourselves are destroyed.

Those who recognize
this truth
restrain their quarrels.

If we live our lives obsessing
about pleasant things,
our senses unrestrained—
eating too much, being lazy—
temptations will destroy us
even as the wind
uproots a weak tree.

On the other hand,
if we are heedful,
restrain our senses,
keep our consumption moderate,
have faith in the Dharma—
and in ourselves—
if we are humble

and abide in our spiritual path,
temptation cannot destroy us
any more than the wind can overturn
a mountain.

A person without integrity,
who has no self-control,
who cannot be truthful,
is not worthy of wearing the yellow robe
of a monk.
Yet one who
keeps his word,
who practices self-control
and lives truthfully,
is worthy of wearing
the monk's robe.

If we mistake the unessential
for the essential
and the essential for the unessential
we can never realize enlightenment.

Only when we see the essential as essential
and the unessential as unessential
can we fall into awakeness.

Even as rain penetrates a poorly roofed house
so does lust
for things, people, and experiences
penetrate an untrained mind.
But rain cannot penetrate
a well-roofed house,
and desire cannot penetrate a well-trained mind.

The person who gives in to impure thoughts
suffers in this life and beyond.

She suffers
greatly
when she sees
the mistakes she has made.

But if she does good deeds
she is joyful
in this life and beyond.
Seeing the purity of her deeds
she rejoices greatly.

Evildoers suffer now and later.
Realizing that they have been evil,
they suffer.
Even later evildoers suffer
from remorse
and wave upon wave of woe.

Those who perform good deeds
do not experience remorse and woe.
Instead
they are happy now
and they are happy later—
in this world
and the next
they know bliss.

You can recite all the sacred texts you want
but if you do not act accordingly
how will you benefit?
Without actions we are like
accountants
who count the wealth of others
but have little of their own.

We will not share the fruits of a holy life—
not ever.

Those who act
from compassion and wisdom—
however many holy texts they read—
those who let go of
greed, hatred, and delusion,
those who let go of all clinging,
who are able to follow the path to freedom
and know peace;
these are the ones
who will share the fruit
of the holy life.

Are You Nuts?

Melanie and I are sitting at the kitchen table, overwhelmed. "This is too much," we both think. The trash strewn all over this block alone is more than we can keep up with, even if we do a garbage pickup every morning instead of once a week.

On the nights when I'm awake at three a.m., I can stand at my bedroom window and watch drug transactions across the side street. I'm pretty sure it's cocaine changing hands, but it could be heroin. The water main on the front sidewalk sprang a leak recently, and it took ten days for city workers to show up to repair it, leaving us with a growing floodwater to jump across each morning to get to our respective cars. The security guys didn't show up for weeks to set up the system in Melanie's first-floor bedroom windows. Ango, our abbot, had to call them a lot. Only when he phoned to tell them how sad their response was making him did anyone appear at our door. And then they charged us an hourly rate that would have made a corporate attorney proud.

The view beyond our front porch is of an abandoned apartment house. It's four-storied, with boarded up windows, mostly.

Graffiti galore. Weeds and trash surrounding it. Behind it, smelling like a dead animal, an overgrown vacant lot the size of four football fields. Behind the field, a huge eight-lane highway. We can hear the traffic through the night.

And yet.

Shunryu Suzuki once advised his students to "shine one corner." We can't solve the problems of Detroit from our little corner. But we can pick up the trash—for a quarter of the block anyway. And we can say good morning to everyone we see, and mean it. We can take a freshly baked pie to our neighbor, a nurse who works the midnight shift, and we can chant for peace and pure awakeness for all beings during evening practice.

When we first started Still Point Zen Buddhist Temple, in the fall of 2000, well-intentioned friends outside of Detroit warned us about moving into such a dangerous neighborhood. Inner-city Detroit. The Cass Corridor. Were we nuts?

Hate never dispels hate.

Move in we did. Replaced a bullet-shattered billboard in the front of the temple with new glass. It's still there, hole-free. Started picking up the garbage on the church lawn and haven't stopped. Hung chimes—beautiful, expensive chimes—on a tree branch at the temple's front door. Anyone could steal them. No one has.

Started building *stupas*, small piles of rocks, to remind ourselves that enlightenment can happen at any time, anywhere, and that every place is a sacred space. The stupas are still standing.

Then, in July 2001, we bought a building for an abbey, a big old brick house, a house with ten bedrooms and at least fourteen years of neglect. It's a ten-minute walk from the temple, past the abandoned apartment house, the field, and the highway. Two Dumpsters worth of garbage went out the abbey's front door in the first two weeks. A "freebie" garage sale was available to anyone who would haul stuff away. We started scraping and painting. For days at a time one person or another, all but one of them volunteers, stood on too-high ladders trying to get the house's wood trim painted before the first frost.

A printing company made a huge peace pole for the front lawn. It stands about eight feet tall and has spiritual instructions carved into it in big red letters. "Pay attention!" "Do no harm!" "Just this moment!" "Only do good!" Every day someone from the neighborhood stops to read the words, looks up at the house, smiles—usually a curious smile—and walks on.

For our first two months in the abbey a man stood in front of the house for about an hour every afternoon. He was waiting for a bus. He never smiled. His face was so disfigured—by a bullet wound, it looked like—that he wouldn't even turn to fully face the house when he watched us painting, cleaning, and sorting. Almost every day, for one reason or another, I walked past him. Sometimes it was to throw something into the Dumpster. Sometimes it was to carry a ladder to the back of the house, or to paint. Sometimes I was racing to the hardware store before it closed because someone needed a particular tool to keep going.

He always felt pretty angry when I passed. I'd say hi anyway. We all did. But he never smiled. Never responded. Sometimes someone'd add, "How are you today?" knowing there wasn't going to be an answer.

Then one day the man didn't show up. He was gone for a month, and we missed him. Even though he'd never spoken, he'd still been company.

Just as suddenly as he'd disappeared, he came back on Wednesday afternoon. Because the day was noticeably colder and shorter than the last time I'd seen him, I was concentrating on finishing the painting of the porch ceiling. Moving too fast for myself I was making a mess, wasting paint and time as I stopped to clean up after myself by the half-hour. Curses started showing up, first in my mind and then out of my mouth. I kept going anyway, knowing it would be spring before we could paint again. Five months away.

Just as the sun went down, making it too dark to see, I finished the last corner. A clean gray porch ceiling—slate gray—was ready for winter. Rushing down the walk to put the ladder away I almost slammed into the man.

Skidding to a stop I smiled, glad to see him.

"Hi."

He looked at me for what felt like forever. I suddenly realized that he had heard me swearing, especially the "Sweet Mary Joseph Jesus" that I'd learned from my Irish grandmother at the ripe old age of five.

"I've been watching you. You're doing good work."

And he smiled back at me for the first time.

Only love dispels hate. This is the eternal law.

Now when we see him, which isn't very often, this man tells us about the neighborhood, its history and people. One day he told me all about his hopes for Detroit, for the children; told me it could be the city of the future, with its potential. He's right, of course. And he's a wonderful storyteller, knows the juiciest stories, the ones about the prostitutes who used to live in my house, and the ones about the children who filled it when it when it was an orphanage. He knows the heartbreaks and the miracles and who used to live with whom and who's been fighting since grade school. Next time I see him, maybe he'll come in for tea.

A Deeper Maturity

Norman Fischer

A group of parents at the famed San Francisco Zen Center asked Norman Fischer, a poet and former abbot at the center, to help guide their sons, aged eleven to thirteen, through the difficult passage of adolescence. He worked with the boys for two years, and their discussions led him to reflect on what maturity really means, on what it means at any age to grow up.

I suppose that most of us think of maturity as simply a matter of timing. Seeds grow into seedlings, seedlings into plants, and plants bear fruit. All living things develop naturally, and people do too, coming to a stage of possibility, competence, or ripeness when they are ready to. Of course we grow up. Time passes, the body changes, the mind changes, the emotions change. We become adults.

But this natural maturity, though basic and important, doesn't really make us grown-ups. It is only a beginning, a necessary foundation. Beyond this there must also be emotional maturity, spiritual maturity, and maturity of character. This deeper sort of maturity doesn't come naturally. Many of us never develop it, for it takes a particular kind of thoughtfulness and care beyond what is natural and socially established as a minimal standard for adulthood.

This deeper and more subtle growth requires a fuller vision of maturity, a firm and clear commitment to move toward that vision, and a context and a vehicle for getting there. Here was where the boys and I had work to do, if we could figure out how to do it. We had to find a way to discover and evoke this deeper sense of maturity so that it could become real to us. It couldn't be something that I was presumed to have in me and could therefore pass on to them, like liquid that can be poured from one bottle into another. I could make speeches at them if I wanted to, but what good would that do? They had heard enough speeches in their lives already. And what good would it do me to repeat to them things I thought I knew about life? No, mutual discovery was the only pathway, for them and for me. We would have to enter exploratory ground together, traveling fresh, without assuming anything. The vital question, for me as much as for them, became: What is true maturity anyway?

It's a good question, one that needs to be pondered for a long time. There are answers to life's most important questions, but they are never final; they change as we change. Maybe true maturity is finding a way of keeping such questions alive throughout our lifetime. For when there are no more questions, we stop maturing and begin merely to age.

To explore this question of maturity, the boys and I thought of people we knew who we felt were truly grown up and tried to discover what it was about those people that made them seem grown up to us. Out of these discussions we began to develop a working list of qualities that we felt were present in most people whose emotional and spiritual lives were deeply mature. Most of these people, we found, seem to be responsible without being boring, experienced without being closed-minded, self-accepting without being shut off to change and improvement, loving without being corny, stable without being inert, and strong without being brittle. We discussed all of these qualities at length, being as concrete and personal as possible. Out of our conversations came, eventually, a rough list of qualities that we felt marked a mature person—qualities we felt we wanted to study and point toward in our efforts to truly become grown-ups. The first of these quantities was responsibility.

When the topic of responsibility comes up, I find myself suddenly seized with an attack of scruples and am inspired to speak in a deep, archetypal, stentorian voice (like the voice of God on those childhood records) that trails off into vague distances. I suppose this is how most of us view the notion of responsibility—as the opposite of creativity, spontaneity, and growth. No wonder we resist growing up, and no wonder we become boring when it finally seems we must admit that we are adults and had better start acting like it.

But responsibility doesn't have to be like that. In its truest and most literal sense, responsibility is simply the capacity to respond. Being responsible is an inherently lively quality. It is the capacity to react completely and freely to conditions. Being responsible has nothing to do with control and conformity. Quite the contrary, responsibility is the willingness to confront nakedly and clearly what's in front of you on its own terms and to be called forth fresh by what occurs. The Greek root of the word *response* means to offer, to pledge. To be responsible is to offer yourself to what happens to you, to pledge yourself to your life.

Being responsible in this sense isn't easy. Because it is so active and creative, responsibility is the enemy of all forms of laziness. It requires discovery and self-transcendence. To respond with authenticity, to really be present with what your life is, you have to let go of self-concern and preconception as much as possible and be true to your situation. You must have the courage to let yourself be overcome by what happens to you.

This reminds me of the story of one of our Zen Center priests, who arrived at the center in an odd way. Riding his motorcycle in the mountains one day and coming across a dirt road, he decided to see where it led. The road ended up at our monastery, Tassajara, which was just then opening. The young man came in to look around and was so intrigued by what he saw that he decided to stay for a few days, which became a few months, and then a few years. Eventually he ordained, studied traditional carpentry in Japan, and came back to America to help build the Zen Center's finest temple buildings. He had driven down a mountain road only to see what was there, but because he was willing to respond fully to what he encountered and give himself to it completely, his life turned into a life of benefit.

A mature person is someone who is willing to hear the call, no matter how faint or unexpected it may be, and respond. It is not necessary, however, to look around for things to be responsible for if nothing appears. But when something does appear, you are ready to respond with all of your attention and loving care, and with no excuses, no avoidance, no fanfare. You just roll up your sleeves and do it.

In his well-known text *Instructions to the Head Cook,* the Japanese Zen master Dogen recounts the story of a seminal encounter he had with an old Chinese monk who was serving his monastery as head cook. Although Dogen wanted the old monk to stay with him and engage in conversation about religious matters, the old man said he could not. Since he was head cook, it was his duty to go out in the hot sun to dry mushrooms, a job that had to be done immediately so that the mushrooms would be ready for the evening meal. When Dogen implored him to stay and to get an underling to take care of the mushrooms instead, the old man said, "You do not understand. I am head cook. If I do not do this job, who will do it? And if I do not do it now, when will I do it?"

There is a deep simplicity in taking responsibility in this way. The head cook wasn't trying to prove anything, to get credit for anything, or even to accomplish anything. He was simply occupying his place, fulfilling his role. Although we might now be alert enough to notice it, being responsible in this way has reverberations beyond what we can predict or control. For life's endless possibilities arise in response to our passion to give ourselves fully to what we are doing wherever we are. Our tomorrows can be neither saved up nor created out of our heads; they flow out of our present engagement. Responsibility, far from limiting or shutting down our lives, provides the potential for opening. Even if responsibility seems to keep us in one place for a very long time (as with the young priest who rode his motorcycle) or to press our nose to the grindstone (as with the head cook), we don't feel this as restriction. When we give ourselves to our situation we're letting go of preferences and habits and trusting what's in front of us, with faith that it will provide the wisdom we need. To truly be responsible is to recognize that reality is smarter than we are.

Another clear characteristic of maturity—one that any of us would mention—is experience. A grown-up is someone who is experienced and, through having lived long enough to have seen many things, has a point of view and a measure of savvy about how life works. There is certainly no substitute for the experience that accumulates as the years go by, but it is also possible to be alive for a long time and not really experience our living, not really see our life. The human capacity for self-deception and blindness runs deep. We may be alive, but we have not necessarily lived. If we accumulate experiences without really engaging with them, then our experience tends to make us stodgy and boring. As we catalog and define our experiences, possessing them without ever really being possessed by them, we begin to expect that new situations will just be repetitions of old ones. Soon we feel as if we've seen it all before. We know what to expect. Our point of view gradually becomes a set of blinders rather than a searching flashlight.

But if we pay close and open attention to our experiences, life's larger patterns begin to come into view. We see that all things are transitory and unique. Nothing repeats. We understand that, though always instructive, the past can never us tell what the future will be. Within the larger pattern that experience reveals, there are endless variations. Insofar as we see this, our life experience increases our wonder at and appreciation of all that happens. With little life experience, we might be naïvely excited by the novelty of a person we meet or an event that occurs. But when we truly appreciate our experience, we respond to that newness with a deeper understanding of its meaning and wonder as we relate it to what we have seen before. Far from dampening our sense of wonder, real experience refreshes and mellows it.

Some years ago I attended a peace conference in Belfast, Northern Ireland, with His Holiness the Dalai Lama. We were sitting in a large auditorium listening to the stories of people who had been victims of what is called in Ireland "the troubles," the long, violent conflict between Protestants and Catholics. One person was blind. One was wheelchair-bound. Another was emotionally scarred from having seen his father shot down before his own eyes when he was a child. When I glanced over at His Holiness, I saw that he was weeping like a baby, leaning his head on his assistant's shoulder. A few moments later he was being photographed with two Irish religious leaders, one a Catholic priest, the other a Protestant minister. It happened that both men had bushy white beards. For some reason His Holiness thought this was very funny, so he reached up and gave their beards a tug. I remember that he almost fell off the podium with laughter. The next day *The Irish Times* carried a front-page color picture of the Dalai Lama laughing hysterically while "bearding" the two shocked clergymen. It seemed amazing to me that His Holiness could be so shattered with sadness one moment, and then so freely—almost inappropriately—merry the next. A man who has seen and felt so much, and carries a great burden of responsibility, the Dalai Lama nevertheless seems to hold his experience lightly.

We often think of growing up as a slow and inevitable process of dying to life, something to be avoided for as long as we can. We contrast maturity with childhood or youth, which we see as full of excitement and promise. Certainly we encounter a lot of sadness as life goes on. The older we get, the more trouble we've seen, and there's no doubt that life will show us the face of loss. Time passes, youth fades, and people disappear from our lives. And time will also introduce us to bitterness, disappointment, and defeat.

But it is exactly in digesting and accepting the profundity of our difficulties that life opens up to us. The truly experienced person knows and feels the preciousness, fragility, and impermanence of life. Certainly the Dalai Lama has known his share of suffering and has taken it in with all seriousness. But the experience of suffering hasn't dampened his enjoyment of life.

In Japanese culture an appreciation of life—of the beauty of a flower, the peacefulness of a shrine, the purity of a mountaintop scene—seems to be tied to a recognition of impermanence. Often life's most moving moments are found right in the middle of sadness and loss. The twelfth-century Japanese Buddhist poet Saigyo penned this verse:

> Winter has withered
> Everything in this mountain place:
> Dignity is in
> Its desolation now, and beauty
> In the cold clarity of its moon

Self acceptance is another key quality of the mature person. Someone who lives long enough, and with enough heart, to truly understand his or her experience, will gradually come to self-acceptance. Observing accurately and without shame our thoughts, deeds, and feelings over time, we begin to see a clear picture of our character. We let go of our expectations and illusions about ourselves and settle with confidence into who we really are. As we become familiar with our weaknesses and all the trouble they have caused us, we are less dismayed at them and do not run away from them as often; this new response, in turn, brings us a calmness that helps us stop indulging our weaknesses.

We also come to appreciate our strengths enough to see that we don't have to make a big deal out of them. We don't need to keep reminding ourselves and everyone else about our strengths. Instead we can simply enjoy and make use of them. As time goes on and our self-acceptance deepens, the very idea of strengths and weaknesses seems off the mark because the closer we look, the harder it is to distinguish between the two. All human qualities have a flip side: we're loving, but we meddle; we're fearful, but we're helpfully prudent; we're critical, but we are very perceptive. It's all a dance. As we realize this, it seems increasingly silly to judge ourselves one way or the other.

Still, no matter how well we know ourselves and how much we achieve a steadiness of character, we are never immune to mistakes. With self-acceptance we know this, and we try to make use of our mistakes, learning from them as best we can. Over time we see how often our worst mistakes and most ignominious failures have turned out to be our greatest teachers. Some of our greatest disasters turn out to have powerfully positive consequences for our lives, even though it can take a long time for us to recognize it. Given all of this, we become less worried about making mistakes, although we are regretful when we make them, especially when others are hurt in the process. Zen master Dogen famously referred to his long life of spiritual endeavor as "one continuous mistake."

Sometimes our mistakes can be helpful to others: if we show that there can be dignity in making mistakes, others can learn from us that they don't have to live in constant fear of error. Many times in my life I have witnessed mistakes that my teachers made—being headstrong or stubborn, being angry when it was inappropriate, being nervous when I wanted them to be clear-headed and cool. Sometimes they said or did things impulsively, or even deliberately, that they shouldn't have said or done. Most of the time I appreciated these mistakes, for they made me see my teacher's humanness and vulnerability. Far from seeing the mistake-making as a flaw that lowered the estimation of my teacher in my eyes, I saw it as a wonderful badge of his or her humanity, which helped me to accept my own imperfection more easily.

I remember the one-hundredth birthday party of my friend and teacher Charlotte Selver, who has been teaching and practicing sensory awareness, a powerful mindfulness training, for more than seventy-five years. After birthday cake and a champagne toast, people gathered around to recount stories from Charlotte's life, incidents that revealed her wisdom. After many tales were told of the wonderful and perceptive things that Charlotte had said or done in the presence of her students, one man said that what he cherished the most were the stupid arguments that Charlotte and Charles, her husband of many years, used to have, often right in the middle of a workshop session. "It was the way you did it," the man said. "So wholeheartedly, without embarrassment or justification. Somehow it gave me permission to be myself without feeling there was some ideal I was supposed to be living up to."

Self-acceptance is paradoxical: we see and accept our essential character, the personality that seems to define us, but at the same time we know that character is actually in constant flux. When we feel this dynamic interplay between change and constancy and accept the paradox of human character, we see how we can avoid being trapped by ourselves, as so many people are. Since we accept who we are, and are no longer driven to improve; we're not constantly self-critical and off-balance. On the other hand, since we know that who we are isn't fixed but rather is always subtly being reinvented by conditions, we know that we can and will grow and improve if only we pay attention and stay present for what happens to us. With self-acceptance we are confident that we can trust what happens. We begin to realize how much power and subtlety there is in simply seeing ourselves without distortion, without shame, without guilt or desire.

A short and instructive Zen dialogue I am very fond of evokes this profound sense of self-acceptance. A monk named Hui Chao asks his teacher, "What is Buddha?" The teacher replies, "You are Hui Chao." A mature person appreciates the simple fact of being himself or herself, knowing that in the entire cosmos there is now and will only ever be one temporary occurrence of this person. He or she also knows that something deeply unique and necessary is being expressed through his or her life.

Such profound self-acceptance tenderizes the heart and opens our empathy for others, for we recognize that the precious and unique person we are has been formed and is being formed through our relations with others. We are always creating each other—our moods, our personalities, and our attitudes are always connected to the moods, personalities, and attitudes of others. Experiencing our own suffering without excuse or attempt to escape, we know that others have suffered as we have. Deeply reflecting on all this, we become open to and capable of love. We come to understand the profound truth that there is nothing but love and therefore nothing is more worthwhile, more pervasive, or more necessary.

We think of love as a big enthusiastic feeling. Certainly emotion is part of what love is, but it's not limited to that. Our society's focus on romantic relationships seems natural and delightful, at least if you are in a relationship yourself that is reasonably happy. But love is a much larger container than romance. A person can be loving whether or not he or she is in love with someone. I have many friends who are monks and nuns, among whom are the most loving and mature individuals I know. They are living proof that the power of love, and of loving connection that is deep and satisfying, is a mark of maturity for all of us, regardless of the nature of our relationships.

Love is practical and down-to-earth. It exists in the rough and tumble of real human relationship, with all its problems and misunderstandings. Love requires human warmth and contact. It also requires all the other qualities of maturity I have already discussed—responsibility, experience, and self-acceptance—insofar as we have developed them. Love evokes the healing power of simple human kindness. Mature people are not aloof, coolly distant, or stuck within themselves. They might not all be jolly extroverts, but they all have the capacity for meeting others with some degree of warmth and interest.

In my own work with Zen students over the years, I have felt the awesome power of love. Although it may seem extravagant to say so, the truth is that I love the people with whom I practice Zen. I get to know many of them over time and to see their lives unfold, with all the inevitable triumph and tragedy. Sharing all this with them, admiring their courage and sincerity in facing what they face and their determination to keep on devotedly with the practice, how can I not love them? If there is any benefit in our practicing together, all of it comes from this loving relationship, which has a healing power one cannot measure or truly understand.

In Zen literature the word *intimacy* is often used as a synonym for enlightenment. In the classical Zen enlightenment stories, a monk or a nun is reduced simultaneously to tears and laughter as he or she suddenly recognizes that nothing in this world is separate, that each and every thing, including one's own self, is nothing but the whole, and that the whole is nothing but the self. What are such stories telling us if not that love is much wider and deeper than an emotion? Love is fruition of, the true shape of, one's self and all that is.

Attending to the Deathless

Ajahn Amaro

"When the heart is released from clinging," said the Buddha, "then consciousness does not land anywhere. That state, I tell you, is without sorrow, affliction, or despair." Here is a teaching by Ajahn Amaro on the consciousness that is beyond all conditions—even life and death itself—and how at this very moment we can rest in the space of the deathless.

A great passage in the *suttas* [Buddhist scriptures] presents an exchange between two of the Buddha's elder monks. Venerable Sariputta is the Buddha's chief disciple, the one most eminent in wisdom and also in meditative accomplishments. Although he had no psychic powers whatsoever, he was the grand master of meditators. The other elder disciple of the Buddha, Venerable Anuruddha, had spectacular psychic powers. He was the one most blessed with "the divine eye"; he could see into all the different realms.

The two disciples were an interesting mix. Sariputta's weakness was Anuruddha's great gift. Anyway, shortly before his enlightenment, Anuruddha came to Sariputta and said, "With the divine eye purified and perfected I can see the entire ten-thousand-fold universal system. My meditation is firmly established; my mindfulness is steady as a rock. I have unremitting energy, and the body is totally relaxed and calm. And yet still my heart is not free from the outflows and confusions. What am I getting wrong?"

Sariputta replied, "Friend, your ability to see into the ten-thousand-fold universal system is connected to your conceit. Your persistent energy, your sharp mindfulness, your physical calm, and your one-pointedness of mind have to do with your restlessness. And the fact that you still have not released the heart from the outflows and defilements is tied up with your anxiety. It would be good, friend, if rather than occupying yourself with these concerns, you turned your attention to the deathless element." (By the way, the Pali Canon has a lot of humor in it like this, although it's rather similar to British humor and is sometimes easy to miss.) So of course Anuruddha said, "Thank you very much," and off he went. Shortly thereafter, he realized complete enlightenment. This was very understated humor.

The point of their discussion, however, is really quite serious. As long as we are saying, "Look at how complicated my problems are," or "Look at my powers of concentration," we will stay stuck in samsara. In essence, Sariputta told his colleague, "You're so busy with all of the doingness and the effects that come from that, so busy with all of these proliferations, you'll never be free. You're looking in the wrong direction. You're looking *out*, looking at the meditation object *out there*, the ten-thousand-fold universal system *out there*. Just shift your view to the context of experience and attend to the deathless element instead."

All it took was a slight shift of focus for Anuruddha to realize: "It's not just a matter of all the fascinating objects or all the noble stuff I have been doing—that's all conditioned, born, compounded, and deathbound. The timeless dharma is being missed. Look within, look more broadly. Attend to the deathless."

There are also a few places in the suttas where the Buddha talked about the same process with respect to development of concentration and meditative absorption. He even made the point that when the mind is in first *jhana*, second *jhana*, third *jhana*, and all the way out to the higher formless *jhanas*, we can look at those states and recognize all of them as being conditioned and dependent. This, he said, is the true development of wisdom: the mindfulness to recognize the conditioned nature of a state, to turn away from it and to attend to the deathless, even while the state is still around. When the mind is concentrated and very pure and bright, we can recognize that state as conditioned, dependent, alien, and something that is void or empty. There is the presence of mind to reflect on the truth that all of this is conditioned and thus gross, but there is the deathless element. And in inclining toward the deathless element, the heart is released.

In a way it is like looking at a picture. Normally the attention goes to the figure in a picture and not the background. Or imagine being in a room with someone who is sitting in a chair. When you look across the room you would probably not attend to the space in front of or beside that person. Your attention would go to the figure in the chair, right? Similarly, if you've ever painted a picture or a wall, there's usually one spot where there's a glitch or a smudge. So where does the eye go when you look at the wall? It beams straight in on the flaw. In exactly the same way, our perceptual systems are geared to aim for the figure, not the ground. Even if an object looks like the ground—such as limitless light, for example—we still need to know how to turn back from that object.

Incidentally, this is why in Buddhist meditation circles there's often a warning about deep states of absorption. When one is in one, it can be very difficult to develop insight—much more so than when the mind is less intensely concentrated. The absorption state is such a good facsimile of liberation that it feels like the real gold. So we think, "It's here, why bother going any further? This is really good." We get tricked and, as a result, we miss the opportunity to turn away and attend to the deathless.

In cosmological terms, the best place for liberation is in the human realm. There's a good mixture of suffering and bliss, happiness and unhappiness here. If we are off in the *deva* (god) realms, it's difficult to become liberated because it's like being at an ongoing party. And we don't even have to clean up afterwards.

We just hang out in the Nandana Grove. Devas drop grapes in our mouths as we waft around with flocks of adoring beings of our favorite gender floating in close proximity. And, of course, there's not much competition; you're always the star of the show in those places. Up in the *brahma* realms it's even worse. Who is going to come back down to grubby old earth and deal with tax returns and building permits?

This cosmology is a reflection of our internal world. Thus the brahma realms are the equivalent of formless states of absorption. One of the great meditation masters of Thailand, Venerable Ajahn Tate, was such an adept at concentration that as soon as he sat down to meditate he would go straight into *arupa-jhana,* formless states of absorption. It took him twelve years after he met his teacher, Venerable Ajahn Mun, to train himself *not* to do that and to keep his concentration at a level where he could develop insight. In those formless states, it is just so nice that it's easy to ask, "What's the point of cultivating wise reflection or investigating the nature of experience? The experience itself is so seamlessly delicious, why bother?" The reason we bother is that those are not dependable states. They are unreliable and they are not ours. Probably not many people have the problem of getting stuck in *arupa-jhana.* Nonetheless, it is helpful to understand why these principles are discussed and emphasized.

This gesture of attending to the deathless is thus a core spiritual practice but not a complicated one. We simply withdraw our attention from the objects of the mind and incline the attention towards the deathless, the unborn. This is not a massive reconstruction program. It's not like we have to *do* a whole lot. It's very simple and natural. We relax and notice that which has been here all along, like noticing the space in a room. We don't notice space, because it doesn't grab our attention; it isn't exciting. Similarly, *nibbana* (Sanskrit: nirvana) has no feature, no color, no taste, and no form, so we don't realize it's right here. The perceptual systems and the naming activity of the mind work on forms; that's what they go to first. Therefore we tend to miss what's always here.

Actually, because it has no living quality to it, space is the worst as well as the best example, but sometimes it is reasonable to use it.

Unsupported Consciousness

In the Theravada teachings, the Buddha also talked about this quality in terms of "unsupported consciousness." This means that there is cognition, there is knowing, but it's not landing anyplace; it's not abiding anywhere. "Attending to the deathless" and "unsupported consciousness" are somewhat synonymous. They are like descriptions of the same tree, from different angles.

In describing unsupported consciousness, the Buddha taught:

> Wherever there is something that is intended, something that is acted upon or something that lies dormant, then that becomes the basis for consciousness to land. And where consciousness lands, that then is the cause for confusion, attachment, becoming and rebirth, and so on.
>
> But if there is nothing intended, acted upon or lying latent, then consciousness has no basis to land upon. And having no basis to land, consciousness is released. One recognizes, "Consciousness, thus unestablished, is released." Owing to its staying firm, the heart is contented. Owing to its contentment, it is not agitated. Not agitated, such a one realizes complete, perfect nibbana within themselves.

The Buddha used a whole galaxy of images, similes, and forms like this because they spoke to different people in different ways. In another passage the Buddha asked his disciples, "If there was a house with a wall that faced out towards the east and in that wall there was a window, when the sun came up in the morning, where would the shaft of sunlight fall?"

One of his monks replied, "On the western wall."

The Buddha then asked, "And if there's no western wall, where would the sunlight land?"

The monk answered, "On the ground."

Then the Buddha responded, "And if there's no ground, where will it land?"

The monk replied, "On the water."

The Buddha pushed it a bit further and asked, "And if there's no water, where will it land?"

The monk answered correctly when he said, "If there is no water, then it will not land."

The Buddha ended the exchange by saying, "Exactly so. When the heart is released from clinging to what are called the four nutriments—physical food, sense contact (sight, sound, smell, taste, touch), intention, and consciousness—then consciousness does not land anywhere. That state, I tell you, is without sorrow, affliction, or despair."

Consciousness: Invisible, Radiant, Limitless

In several instances, the language of the Tibetan Dzogchen tradition seems strikingly similar to that of the Theravada. In Dzogchen, the common description of the qualities of *rigpa,* nondual awareness, is "empty in essence, cognizant in nature, and unconfined in capacity." A different translation of these three qualities is "emptiness, knowing and lucidity, or clarity." In the Pali scriptures, the Buddha talks about the mind of the *arahant* [one who has attained liberation] as "consciousness which is unmanifest, signless, infinite. and radiant in all directions." The Pali words are *viññanam* (consciousness), *aniddassanam* (empty, invisible or signless, nonmanifestative), *anantam* (limitless, unconfined, infinite), and *sabbato pabham* (radiant in all directions, accessible from all sides).

One of the places the Buddha uses this description is at the end of a long illustrative tale. A monk has asked, "Where is it that earth, water, fire, and wind fade out and cease without remainder?" To which the Buddha replies that the monk has asked the wrong question. What he *should* have asked is, "Where is it that earth, water, fire, and wind can find no footing?" The Buddha then answers this question himself, saying it is in "the consciousness which is invisible, limitless, and radiant in all directions" that the four great elements "and long and short, and coarse and fine, and pure and impure can find no footing. There it is that *nama-rupa* (body-and-mind, name-and-form, subject-and-object) both come to an end. With this stopping, this cessation of consciousness, all things here are brought to an end."

Such unsupported and unsupportive consciousness is not an abstract principle. In fact, it was the basis of the Buddha's enlightenment. As the Buddha was sitting under the bodhi tree, the hordes of Mara attacked him. Armies were hurling themselves at the Buddha and yet nothing could get into the space under the tree. All the weapons and spears they threw turned into rays of light; the arrows that they fired turned into flowers that came sprinkling down around the Buddha. Nothing harmful to the Buddha could get into that space. There was nowhere for it to land. Sight, sound, smell, taste, and touch, long and short, coarse and fine, pure and impure are all aspects of body and mind. They represent attributes of all phenomena. Yet none of them could find a footing. The Buddha was in a nonstick realm. Everything that came toward him kept falling away. Nothing stuck; nothing could get in and harm the Buddha in any way. To get a better sense of this quality of unsupported consciousness, it's helpful to reflect on this image. Also very useful are the phrases at the end of the passage just quoted, particularly where the Buddha says, "When consciousness ceases, all things here are brought to an end."

The Anatomy of Cessation

The concept of cessation is very familiar in the Theravada tradition. Even though it's supposed to be synonymous with nibbana, it's sometimes put forth as some event that we're all seeking, where all experience will vanish and then we'll be fine: "A great god will come from the sky, take away everything, and make everybody feel high." I don't want to get obsessed about words, but we suffer a lot or get confused because of misunderstandings like this. When we talk about stopping consciousness, do you think that means "Let's all get unconscious?" It can't be that, can it? The Buddha was not extolling the virtues of unconsciousness. Otherwise thorazine or barbiturates would be the way: "Give me the anesthetic and we're on our way to nibbana." But obviously that's not it. Understanding what is meant by stopping or cessation is thus pretty crucial here.

I've known people, particularly those who have practiced in the Theravada tradition, who have been taught that the idea of meditation is to get to a place of cessation. We might get to a place where we don't feel or see anything; there is awareness but everything is gone. An absence of sight, sound, smell, taste, touch, the body—it all vanishes. And then these students are told, "This is the greatest thing. That's what there is to look forward to." The teacher encourages them to put tremendous hours and diligence into their meditation. When one of these students told her teacher that she had arrived at that kind of state, he got really excited. He then asked her, "So what did it feel like?" and she said, "It was like drinking a glass of cold water but without the water and without the glass." On another occasion she said, "It was like being shut inside a refrigerator."

This is not the only way of understanding cessation. The root of the word *nirodha* is *rudh,* which means "to not arise, to end, check or hold"—like holding a horse in check with the reins. So *nirodha* also has a meaning of holding everything, embracing its scope. "Stopping of consciousness" can thus imply that somehow everything is held in check rather than that it simply vanishes. It's a redrawing of the internal map.

A story from the time of the Buddha might help to expand our understanding of what this means. One night while the Buddha was meditating, a brilliant and beautiful *devata* [deity] named

Rohitassa appeared in front of him. He told the Buddha, "When I was a human being, I was a spiritual seeker of great psychic power, a sky walker. Even though I journeyed with great determination and resolution for one hundred years to reach the end of the world, I could not come to the end of the world. I died on the journey before I had found it. So can you tell me, is it possible to journey to the end of the world?"

And the Buddha replied, "It is not possible to reach the end of the world by walking, but I also tell you that unless you reach the end of the world, you will not reach the end of suffering."

Rohitassa was a bit puzzled and said, "Please explain this to me, Venerable Sir." The Buddha replied, "In this very fathom-long body is the world, the origin of the world, the cessation of the world, and the way leading to the cessation of the world."

In that instance the Buddha used the same exact formulation as in the Four Noble Truths. The world, or *loka,* means the world of our experience. That's how the Buddha almost always uses the term "the world." He's referring to the world *as we experience it.* This includes only sight, sound, smell, taste, touch, thought, emotion, and feeling. That's it. That's what "the world" is—my world, your world. It's not the abstracted, geographical planet, universe-type world. It's the direct experience of the planet, the people, and the cosmos. Here is the origin of the world, the cessation of the world, and the way leading to the cessation of the world.

He said that as long as we create "me and my experience"—"me in here" and "the world out there"—we're stuck in the world of subject and object. Then there is *dukkha.* And the way leading to the cessation of that duality is the way leading to the cessation of suffering. Geographically, it is impossible to journey to the end of the world. Only when we come to the cessation of the world, which literally means the cessation of its otherness or thingness, will we reach the end of dukkha, unsatisfactoriness. When we stop creating sense objects as absolute realities and stop seeing thoughts and feelings as solid things, there is cessation.

To see that the world is within our minds is one way of working with these principles. The whole universe is embraced when we realize that it's happening within our minds. And in that moment when we recognize that it all happens *here,* it ceases. Its thingness ceases. Its otherness ceases. Its substantiality ceases.

This is just one way of talking and thinking about it. But I find this brings us much closer to the truth, because in that respect, it's held in check. It's known. But there's also the quality of its emptiness. Its insubstantiality is known. We're not imputing solidity to it, a reality that it doesn't possess. We're just looking directly at the world, knowing it fully and completely.

So, what happens when the world ceases? I remember one time Ajahn Sumedho was giving a talk about this same subject. He said, "Now I'm going to make the world completely disappear. I'm going to make the world come to an end." He just sat there and said, "Okay, are you ready? . . . The world just ended. . . . Do you want me to bring it back into being again? Okay, . . . welcome back."

Nothing was apparent from the outside. It all happens internally. When we stop creating the world, we stop creating each other. We stop imputing the sense of solidity that creates a sense of separation. Yet we do not shut off the senses in any way. Actually, we shed the veneer, the films of confusion, of opinion, of judgment, of our conditioning, so that we can see the way things really are. At that moment, dukkha ceases. There is knowing. There is liberation and freedom. There is no dukkha.

Is the Sound Annoying You?

If people were trying to meditate and wanted to shut the world out, Ajahn Chah used to give them a very hard time. If he came across a nun or a monk who had barricaded the windows of their heart and was trying to block everything out, he would really put them through it. He drew in one monk of this type as his attendant for a while and he would never let him sit still. As soon as he saw the monk close his eyes to "go into meditation" he would immediately send him off on some errand. Ajahn Chah knew that cutting yourself off was not the place of true inner peace. This was because of his own years of trying to make the world shut up and leave him alone. He had failed miserably. Eventually he was able to see this is not how to find completion and resolution.

Years ago, when he was a wandering monk, living on his own on a mountainside above a village, he kept a strict meditation schedule. In Thailand they love outdoor, nightlong film shows because the nights are cool compared to the very hot days. Whenever there was a party, it tended to go on all night. About fifty years ago, public address systems were just starting to be used in Thailand and every decent event had to have a PA going. It was blasted as loud as possible all through the night. One time, Ajahn Chah was quietly meditating up on the mountain while there was a festival going on down in the village. All the local folk songs and pop music were amplified throughout the area. Ajahn Chah was sitting there, seething and thinking, "Don't they realize all the bad karma involved in disturbing my meditation? They know I'm up here. After all, I'm their teacher. Haven't they learned anything? And what about the five precepts? I bet they're boozing and out of control," and so on and so forth.

But Ajahn Chah was a pretty smart fellow. As he listened to himself complaining, he quickly realized, "Well, they're just having a good time down there. I'm making myself miserable up here. No matter how upset I get, my anger is just making more noise internally." And then he had this insight: "Oh, the sound is just the sound. It's me who is going out to annoy it. If I leave the sound alone, it won't annoy me. It's just doing what it has to do. That's what sound does. It makes sound. This is its job. So if I don't go out and bother the sound, it's not going to bother me. Aha!"

As it turned out, this insight had such a profound effect that it became a principle that he espoused from that time on. If any of the monks displayed an urge to try and get away from people or stimulation—the world of things and responsibilities—he would tend to shove them straight into it. He would put that monk in charge of the cement-mixing crew or take him to do every house blessing that came up on the calendar. He would make sure that the monk had to get involved in things because he was trying to teach him to let go of seeing meditation as needing sterile conditions—to see, in fact, that most wisdom arises from the skillful handling of the world's abrasions.

Ajahn Chah was passing along an important insight. It's pointless to try to find peace through nullifying or erasing the sense world. Peace only comes through not giving that world more substantiality or more reality than it actually possesses.

Touching the Earth

Sometimes when I use the example of the Buddha sitting under the bodhi tree, people still feel that this is a negation of the sense world. There is an intimation of condescension, a looking down on that. We become afraid when we hear people talking about dispassion towards the sense world as it can offend our habits of life affirmation.

The balance—and this is something we can experience for ourselves—is not in negation. It comes when we stop creating each other and allow ourselves to relax into a pure quality of knowing. In not fabricating the world, ourselves, or our stories, there is a gentle relaxation and, ironically, we find ourselves far more attuned to life than ever. This cannot happen while we are busy carrying around "me and you" and "it's my life" and "my past" and "my future" and the rest of the world with all its problems. Actually, the result of this relinquishment is not a kind of numbness or a distancing but an astonishing attunement.

Buddhist cosmology and the stories of the suttas always have a historical, a mythical, and a psychological element to them. When we talk about the Buddha under the bodhi tree, we sometimes wonder, "Was it actually *that* tree? Are we sure that he *really* sat beside the river Nerañjara near Bodhgaya? How can anyone know it was actually there?" The story goes that perhaps the Buddha did sit under a tree, or a Nepalese prince sat under a tree, and something happened (or stopped happening) somewhere in India a couple of thousand years or so ago. In other words, there are both historical and mythological aspects to the story. But the most crucial element is how this maps onto our own psychology. How does this symbolize our experience?

The pattern of the story is that even though the Buddha has totally penetrated the cycles of dependent origination and his heart is utterly free, Mara's army doesn't retreat. Mara has sent in the horrors, he has sent in his beautiful daughters, he's even sent in the parental pressure factor: "Well, son, you could have done a great job. You're such a natural leader, you would have made a great king. Now there's only your half-brother, Nanda, and he's a bit of a wimp, no good on the battlefield. Well, I guess if you're going to do this monk thing, the kingdom is going to go to rack and ruin. But that's all right, it's fine. You just do whatever you want to do. Just be aware that you're ruining my life; but don't worry, it's fine, it's okay."

The forces of allure, fear, and responsibility are all there. Yet the Buddha doesn't just close his eyes and escape into blissful absorption. As the armies of Mara come at him, he looks straight at them and says, "I know you, Mara. I know what this is." The Buddha doesn't argue with Mara or give rise to aversion towards Mara. He remains undeluded; he doesn't react against what's happening in that moment. No matter what Mara's armies do, none can get into that space under the bodhi tree. All their weapons turn to flowers and incense and beams of light illuminating the *vajra* [immutable] seat.

But even when the Buddha's heart is totally liberated, Mara still won't retreat. He says to the Buddha, "What right do you have to claim the royal seat at the immovable spot? I'm the king of this world. I'm the one who should be sitting there. I'm in charge here. I'm the one who deserves to be there, aren't I?" And he turns around to his horde, his army 700,000 strong, and they all say, "Yes, indeed, Sire!" "See," says Mara, "everyone agrees. I belong there, not you. I'm supposed to be the great one."

What happens then is that, just as Mara has called his witnesses to back him up, the Buddha calls on the mother goddess, Maer Toranee, as his witness. The Buddha reaches down to the ground, touches the earth, and calls forth the earth mother. She appears and says, "This is my true son. He has every right to claim the vajra seat at the immovable spot. He has developed all the virtues necessary to claim the sovereignty of perfect and complete enlightenment. You do not belong there, Mara." The mother goddess then produces a flood from her hair and the armies of Mara are all washed away. Later they come back full of apologies, offering gifts and flowers and asking for forgiveness: "Terribly sorry about that, Mother. I didn't really mean it."

It's very interesting that Buddha thus did not become a fully enlightened, teaching Buddha without the help of the mother goddess and then, later, of the father god. It was Brahma Sahampati, the creator god, the C.E.O of the universe, who came and asked the Buddha to teach. Without those two figures, he would not have left the immovable spot and he wouldn't have started teaching. So, mythologically, there are some interesting little quirks to the tale.

The Buddha's gentle gesture of touching the earth is a magnificent metaphor. It is saying that even though we might have this enlightened, free space internally, it needs to be interfaced with the phenomenal world. Otherwise, there is no completion. This is why meditating with the eyes open is, in a way, such a useful bridge. We cultivate a vast internal space, but it is necessarily connected to the phenomenal world. If there is only an internal, subjective experience of enlightenment, we're still caught. Mara's army won't retreat. The hassles are everywhere—the tax returns, the permits, the jealousies. We can see that they are empty, but they are still coming at us from all directions.

But in reaching out to touch the earth, the Buddha recognized, yes, there is that which is transcendent and unconditioned. But humility demands not simply holding to the unconditioned and the transcendent. The Buddha recognized and acknowledged that "There is the conditioned. There is the sense world. There is the earth that makes up my body and my breath and the food that I eat."

That gesture of reaching out from the transcendent is saying, How could fully engaging with the sense world possibly corrupt the innate freedom of the heart? This freedom cannot be interrupted, corrupted, or confused by any sense experience. Therefore why not allow it all in? By openly, freely acknowledging the limited—needing to call the great mother to bear witness, for example—the unlimited manifests its full potential. If there is hesitancy and the caution to keep the conditioned at bay, that betrays a basic lack of faith in the natural inviolability of the unconditioned.

Another phrase that expresses this same principle is *cittam pabhassaram, akandukehi kilesehi,* meaning "The heart's nature is intrinsically radiant; defilements are only visitors" (Anguttara Nikaya 1.61). It's pointing out the fact that the heart's nature is intrinsically pure and perfect. The things that appear to defile this purity are only visitors passing through, just wandering or drifting by. The heart's nature cannot truly be corrupted by any of that.

Like a Mirror, Like a Rainbow, Like the Heart of the Sun

Dilgo Khyentse

The Dzogchen teachings of Tibet are renowned for their direct description of the nature of mind. Here is an outstanding example from the great Dilgo Khyentse Rinpoche (1910–1991). He was one of the most important Buddhist teachers of the twentieth century, a man of unfathomable depth who was a teacher and guide to many other great lamas. This teaching was given in traditional fashion as a commentary on an earlier text, in this case verses 51 to 69 of The Hundred Verses of Advice, *which were given by the Indian teacher Kamalashila to the people of the Tibetan village of Tingri. If you've ever longed for a clear and precise description of how things really are—the way they're seen by a Buddha—this may be the closest you'll ever get.*

In a state of emptiness, whirl the spear of pure
awareness;
People of Tingri, the view is free of being caught by
anything at all.

Your view should be as high and vast as the sky. Pure awareness, once it manifests within the mind's empty nature, can no longer be obscured by the negative emotions, which become its ornaments instead. The changeless state which is the realization of the view is not something which comes into existence, remains, or ceases; within it, awareness observes the movement of thoughts like a serene old man watching children at play. Confused thoughts cannot affect pure awareness any more than a sword can pierce the sky.

Lady Peldarbum said to Jetsun Milarepa:

> When I meditated on the ocean,
> My mind was very comfortable.
> When I meditated on the waves,
> My mind was troubled.
> Teach me to meditate on the waves!

The great yogi responded:

> The waves are the movement of the ocean.
> Leave them to subside by themselves in its vastness.

Thoughts are the play of pure awareness. They arise within it, and dissolve back into it. To recognize pure awareness as where your thoughts come from is to recognize that your thoughts have never come into existence, remained, or ceased. At that point, thoughts can no longer trouble your mind.

When you run after your thoughts you are like a dog chasing a stick; every time a stick is thrown, you run after it. But if, instead, you look at where your thoughts are coming from, you will see that each thought arises and dissolves within the space of that awareness, without engendering other thoughts. Be like a lion, who, rather than chasing after the stick, turns to face the thrower. You only throw a stick at a lion once.

To take the uncreated stronghold of the nature of mind, you

have to go to the source and recognize the very origin of your thoughts. Otherwise, one thought will give rise to a second, then a third, and so on. In no time, you will be assailed by memories of the past and anticipation of the future, and the pure awareness of the present moment will be completely obscured.

There is a story about a practitioner who was feeding the pigeons outside with the rice he had offered on his altar, when he suddenly remembered the numerous enemies he had had before devoting himself to the dharma. The thought came to him, "There are so many pigeons at my door now; if I had had that many soldiers then, I could easily have wiped out my enemies."

This idea obsessed him until he could no longer control his hostility, and he left his hermitage, assembled a band of mercenaries, and went to fight his former enemies. The negative actions he then committed all began with that one simple, deluded thought.

If you recognize the emptiness of your thoughts instead of solidifying them, the arising and subsiding of each thought will clarify and strengthen your realization of emptiness.

> In a state without thoughts, without distraction
> abandon the watcher;
> People of Tingri, the meditation is free of any torpor
> or excitement.

When your mind remains in pure awareness, with no thought of past or future, without being attracted by external objects or occupied by mental constructions, it will be in a state of primordial simplicity. In that state, there is no need for the iron hand of forced vigilance to immobilize your thoughts. As it is said, "Buddhahood is the natural simplicity of the mind."

Once you have recognized that simplicity, you need to maintain that recognition with effortless presence of mind. Then you will experience an inner freedom in which there is no need to block the arising of thoughts, or fear that they will spoil your meditation.

In a state of natural spontaneity, train in being free of
any holding back;
People of Tingri, in the action there is nothing to
abandon or adopt.

Preserve that state of simplicity. Should you encounter happiness, success, and other favorable conditions, take them as like a dream or an illusion. Do not get attached to them. And should you be struck by illness, calumny, or other trials, physical or mental, do not let yourself be discouraged. Rekindle your compassion by wishing that through your own suffering the sufferings of all beings might be exhausted. Whatever the circumstances, do not get either elated or depressed, but remain free and at ease in imperturbable serenity.

The four bodies, indivisible, are complete in your
mind;
People of Tingri, the fruit is beyond all hope and doubt.

Buddhahood may seem far away, a distant goal almost beyond reach, but in truth the emptiness that is the essential nature of your mind is nothing other than the "absolute body," or *dharmakaya.* The clarity that is its natural expression is the "body of perfect endowment," or *sambhogakaya.* The all-pervading compassion that emanates from it is the "body of manifestation," or *nirmanakaya.* The intrinsic oneness of these three bodies is the "body of the nature as it is," or *svabhavikakaya.* These four bodies, or dimensions, of a Buddha have always been present within you. It is only because you do not know that they are there that you think of them as being somewhere outside and far away.

"Is my meditation correct?" you wonder, restlessly. "When am I finally going to make some progress? I'll never attain the level of my spiritual master." Torn between hope and fear, your mind is never at peace.

According to your mood, you practice intensely one day, and

the next day not at all. You cling to the agreeable experiences that arise when you attain sustained mental calm, but feel like abandoning the meditation when you cannot slow down the flood of thoughts. That is not the way to practice meditation.

Whatever state of mind you find yourself in, keep up a regular practice, day after day, observing the movement of your thoughts and following them back to their source. You cannot expect to be able to maintain the flow of your concentration day and night from the very start.

When you start meditating on the nature of the mind, it is preferable to practice in short, frequent sessions. With perseverance, you will progressively recognize and realize the nature of your mind, and this realization will become more and more stable. By that point, thoughts will have lost their power to disturb and enslave you.

> The root of both samsara and nirvana is to be found
> within your mind;
> People of Tingri, the mind is free of any true reality.

It is our own minds that lead us astray into the cycle of existence. Blind to the mind's true nature, we fixate on our thoughts, which in truth are simply the manifestations of that nature. But through fixation, pure awareness is frozen into solid concepts such as "self" and "other," "desirable" and "repulsive," and many more. That is how we create samsara.

If we can melt the ice of these fixations by following a teacher's instructions, pure awareness recovers its natural fluidity. To put it another way, if you cut through a tree at the base of the trunk, the trunk, branches and leaves all fall together. Similarly, if you cut through thoughts at their source, the whole delusion of samsara will collapse.

Everything we experience—all the phenomena of samsara and nirvana—appears with the vivid clarity of a rainbow, and yet, like a rainbow, is devoid of any tangible reality. Once you recognize the nature of phenomena—manifest and at the same time empty—your mind will be freed from the tyranny of delusion.

To recognize the ultimate nature of the mind is to realize the state of Buddhahood, and to fail to recognize it is to sink into ignorance. In either case, it is your mind, and your mind alone, which liberates or binds you.

That does not mean, however, that the mind is an entity to be worked on, like a piece of clay which a potter can change into any shape. When the teacher introduces the disciple to the nature of the mind, he is not pointing to some concrete object. When the disciple seeks and finds that nature, he does not take hold of some entity that can be grasped. To recognize the nature of the mind is to recognize its emptiness. That is all. It is a realization that takes place in the realm of direct experience, and cannot be expressed in words.

To expect such a realization to be accompanied by clairvoyance, miraculous powers, and other extraordinary experiences would be to delude yourself. Just devote yourself to recognizing the empty nature of the mind!

> Desire and hate appear, but like birds in flight should leave no trace behind;
> People of Tingri, in meditation be free of clinging to experiences.

Generally speaking, we feel attachment to our family, to our belongings, and to our position, and aversion to anyone who hurts or threatens us. Try turning your attention away from such external objects and examine the mind that identifies them as desirable or hateful. Do your desire and anger have any form, color, substance, or location? If not, why is it that you fall so easily under the power of such feelings?

It is because you do not know how to set them free. If you allow your thoughts and feelings to arise and dissolve by themselves, they will pass through your mind in the same way as a bird flies through the sky, without leaving any trace. This applies not only to attachment and anger, but also to the experiences of meditation—bliss, clarity, and the absence of thought. These experiences result from perseverance in practice and are the expression of the inherent creativity of the mind. They appear like a rainbow, formed as the rays of the sun strike a curtain of rain, and to become attached to them is as futile as it would be to run after a rainbow in the hopes of wearing it as a coat. Simply allow your thoughts and experiences to come and go, without ever grasping at them.

> The unborn absolute body is like the very heart of the sun—
> People of Tingri, there is no waxing or waning of its radiant clarity.

The dharmakaya, the absolute dimension, the ultimate nature of everything, is emptiness. But it is not mere nothingness. It has a cognitive, radiant clarity aspect that knows all phenomena and manifests spontaneously. The dharmakaya is not something produced by causes and conditions; it is the primordially present nature of the mind.

The recognition of this primordial nature is like the sun of wisdom rising and piercing through the night of ignorance. The darkness is dissipated instantly; the shadows cannot remain. The clarity of the dharmakaya does not wax and wane like the moon, but is like the unchangeable brilliance that reigns at the center of the sun.

> Thoughts come and go like a thief in an empty house—
> People of Tingri, in fact there is nothing to be gained or lost.

Convinced of the reality of an entity called "I" and its thoughts, we follow after those thoughts and feelings and act upon them, creating karmic results, good or bad. In reality, thoughts are like a thief in an empty house, where the thief has nothing to gain and the owner has nothing to lose. To realize that thoughts never really come into existence, and can therefore neither remain nor cease to exist, is enough to render them harmless. Thoughts liberated in this way as they arise have no impact and bring no karmic effect. There will be nothing to fear from negative thoughts, and nothing to hope for from positive ones.

> Sensations leave no imprints, like drawings made
> on water;
> People of Tingri, don't perpetuate deluded
> appearances.

We are naturally attached to comfort and pleasure and bothered by physical and mental suffering. These innate tendencies lead us to seek out, maintain, and try to increase whatever gives us pleasure—comfortable clothing, delicious food, agreeable places, sensual pleasure—and to avoid or destroy whatever we find unpleasant or painful.

Constantly changing and devoid of any true essence, these sensations rest on the ephemeral association of the mind with the body, and it is useless to be attached to them. Rather than being dragged along and trapped by your perceptions, just let them dissolve as soon as they form, like letters traced on the surface of water with your finger disappearing as you draw them.

> Thoughts of attachment and aversion are like rainbows
> in the sky;
> People of Tingri, there is nothing in them to be grasped
> or apprehended.

People can be so dominated by their craving or their hatred that they are even willing to lose their lives to satisfy it, as wars so tragically illustrate. Your own thoughts and feelings of attachment and aversion may seem very solid and compelling, but if you examine them carefully you will see that they have no more substance than a rainbow. To devote your life to trying to satisfy such impulses, to hunger for power, pleasures, and riches, would surely be as puerile as a child wanting to catch a rainbow.

In practice, whenever a strong desire or a burst of anger inflames your mind, look closely at your thoughts and recognize their fundamental emptiness. If you allow them to, those thoughts and feelings will dissolve by themselves. When you can do the same with the next thought and with all that follow, they will lose their hold over you.

> Mind's movements dissolve by themselves, like clouds
> in the sky;
> People of Tingri, in the mind there are no reference
> points.

When banks of clouds gather in the sky, the nature of the sky is not impaired. Nor, when they disperse, is it improved. The sky is made neither more vast or pure, nor less. It is not changed or affected at all. The nature of the mind is just the same. It is not altered by the arising of thoughts, nor by their disappearance.

The essential nature of the mind is emptiness. Its natural expression is clarity. These two aspects of the mind can be distinguished for descriptive purposes, but they are essentially one. Fixating on the notion of emptiness or of clarity alone as if these were independent entities is a mistake. The ultimate nature of the mind is beyond all concepts, definitions and partial views.

A child might think, "I could walk on those clouds!" If he actually found himself in the clouds, however, he would find nowhere to set foot. In the same way, your thoughts appear to be solid until you examine them. Then you find that they are without any substance. This is what we call the simultaneous appearance and emptiness of things.

Without fixation, thoughts are freed by
themselves—like the wind,
People of Tingri, which never clings to any object.

The wind blows through the sky and flies across continents without ever settling anywhere. It sweeps through space leaving no trace whatsoever. Let thoughts pass through your mind in the same way, leaving no karmic residue and never altering your realization of innate simplicity.

Pure awareness is without fixation, like a rainbow in
the sky;
People of Tingri, experiences arise quite unimpededly.

Pure awareness, the enlightened mind, which is simply the mind liberated of all delusion, transcends the very notions of existing or not existing.

"Where there is attachment, there is no view," were the words that the great Sakya master Jetsun Trakpa Gyaltsen heard from Manjushri, the Buddha of wisdom, during a vision. Enlightenment cannot be said to exist, because even the Buddhas have not seen it. Nor can it be said not to exist, because it is the source of samsara and nirvana. As long as concepts such as existing and not existing persist, you have not realized the mind's true nature.

A rainbow gleaming in the sky, although it could be called a manifestation of the sky, is really nothing other than the sky itself. Similarly, the experiences that arise in your mind when you meditate—the good experiences that lead you to believe you have attained realization, and the bad ones that discourage you—in fact have no substantial existence of their own. The saying goes, "Meditators taken in by their experiences are like children lured by a rainbow." Lend no importance to such experiences, and they will never be able to lead you astray.

Realization of the absolute nature is like the dream of
a mute;
People of Tingri, there are no words to express it.

For someone without the faculty of speech, a beautiful dream, clearly remembered though it might be, is impossible to describe in words. In the same way, the nature of the mind is beyond any description; no words can define its ultimate nature, the dharmakaya. You could say it exists, but there is nothing you can show of it but emptiness. Or you could say it is nothing at all, but then how do you explain its myriad manifestations? The ultimate nature of the mind defies all description and cannot be grasped by discursive thought.

> Realization is like a youthful maiden's pleasure;
> People of Tingri, the joy and bliss just cannot be
> described.

With the dawn of realization, the mind becomes perfectly free, at ease, fulfilled, vast, and serene. This realization, however, is inexpressible, like the joy of an adolescent in the flower of youth.

> Clarity and emptiness united are like the moon
> reflected in water;
> People of Tingri, there is nothing to be attached to and
> nothing to impede.

Everything we perceive, all phenomena throughout samsara and nirvana, arises simply as the play of the mind's natural creativity. This "clarity" of the mind—the distinct appearance of phenomena to our perception—is the radiance of the mind's empty nature. Emptiness is the very essence of clarity, and clarity is the expression of emptiness. They are indivisible.

The mind, like a reflection of the moon in the still surface of a lake, is brilliantly apparent, but you cannot take hold of it. It is vividly present and at the same time utterly intangible. By its very nature, which is the indivisible union of emptiness and clarity, nothing can obstruct it and it can obstruct nothing, unlike a solid object, such as a rock, with a physical presence occupying space and excluding other objects. In essence, the mind is insubstantial and omnipresent.

> Appearances and emptiness inseparable are like the
> empty sky;
> People of Tingri, the mind is without either center or
> periphery.

The mind apprehends forms, sounds, and other phenomena, and experiences happiness and suffering. Yet the world of appearances has never existed in itself. When you analyze it, there is only emptiness. Just as physical empty space provides the dimensions in which whole worlds can unfold, so too does the empty nature of the mind provide the space for its own expressions to appear. And just as physical space is limitless, with no center or periphery, so too the mind is without beginning or end, in both space and time.

> The mind with no thought and no distraction is like
> the mirror of a beauty;
> People of Tingri, it is free of any theoretical tenets.

Once you have recognized the nature of the mind, you no longer need to restrict yourself to a conscious recollection of that nature, nor to modify it in any way. At that point, the mind cannot even be said to be in "meditation," because it naturally stays at rest in a state of serene integration. There is no need to concentrate on the details of a particular visualization, such as the form of a deity. The mind will not stray into the distraction and delusion that characterize the ordinary state because it stays continually and effortlessly in its own nature.

Awareness is not affected by agreeable or disagreeable perceptions. It simply stays as it is, in the same way that a mirror when it reflects people's faces is neither enraptured by their beauty nor offended by their ugliness. And just as a mirror reflects all forms faithfully and with absolute impartiality, so too an enlightened being clearly perceives all phenomena without his realization of the ultimate nature being affected in any way.

An image reflected in a mirror is neither part of the mirror nor is it elsewhere than in the mirror. In the same way, the phenomena we perceive are neither in the mind nor outside it. Indeed, a true realization of the ultimate nature of things goes utterly beyond any concepts of being or non-being. Thus Nagarjuna said in the *Root Stanzas of the Middle Way*: "Since I affirm nothing, no one can refute my point of view."

> Awareness and emptiness inseparable are like
> reflections in a mirror;
> People of Tingri, nothing is born there and nothing
> ceases.

The empty nature of the mind is not a state of blank torpor or mere nothingness. Rather, it has the faculty of knowing, a naturally present clarity which we call awareness, or enlightened consciousness. These two aspects of the mind's nature, emptiness and awareness, are essentially one, like a mirror and the reflection in it.

Thoughts take form within emptiness and dissolve there, as the reflection of a face appears and disappears in a mirror. Since the reflection of the face never was actually in the mirror, it does not cease to be when it is no longer reflected there.

Nor does the mirror itself ever change. Before you start out on the spiritual path, you are in the supposedly impure state of samsara that, in relative terms, is governed by ignorance. Once you engage in the path, the different states you go through are a mixture of ignorance and knowledge. At the end of the path, at the moment of awakening, nothing remains but awareness. Throughout all the stages of the path, although it might look as if some transformation is taking place, the nature of the mind itself never changes. It is not corrupted at the beginning of the path; it is not improved at the end.

The Great Spring

Natalie Goldberg

Natalie Goldberg is one of American Buddhism's best writers and a well-known teacher of the creative process. Here she tells the story of her return to Minnesota, where she studied with the Zen teacher Katagiri Roshi, and how she resolved a koan *many Buddhists struggle with—the meaning of their teacher's death.*

I lived for a year and a half recently in St. Paul, Minnesota, practicing Zen with one of Katagiri Roshi's dharma heirs. Roshi had been dead for a long time and still I missed him and did not know how to complete the relationship that had begun over twenty years before. I was frozen in the configuration we had together when he died—he was always the teacher and I forever would be the student. Now over a decade had passed. I wanted to move on, and in order to do that it seemed I had to move back to that northern state of long winter shadows, a place I left fifteen years earlier to plant my roots in Taos, New Mexico. It seemed I had to go back to that cold place in order to unfreeze.

A few months before the move, though, I pulled a muscle in my groin that would not let me cross my legs in the traditional zazen position. This did not please me. I'd been sitting cross-legged for twenty-five years, so my reflex even at a fancy dinner party was to have my legs intertwined on the upholstered oak chair under the pink linen tablecloth.

Structure in the zendo had been everything to me: straight back, butt on black round cushion, eyes unfocused, cast down at a forty-degree angle. Bells rung on time. Clip, clip. Everything had order. In a chaotic world it was comforting. Sitting in a chair in the zendo with feet flat on the floor seemed silly. If I was going to sit in a chair, I might as well have a cup of tea, a croissant—hell, why not be in a café or on a bench under an autumn tree.

So I did go every single day, like a good Zen student, except in the wrong direction—not to the Zen center in downtown St. Paul, but to Bread and Chocolate, a café on Grand Avenue. I walked there slowly, mindfully, and it was grand. I didn't bring a notebook. I just brought myself and I had strict regulations: I could only buy one chocolate chip cookie. And I ate that one attentively, respectfully, bite after bite at a table next to big windows. I felt the butter of it on my fingers, the chips still warm and melted. In the past, seven good bites would have finished it off. But the eating was practice now, the café a living zendo. Small bites. Several chews. Be honest—was this mindfulness or a lingering? This cookie would not last. Oh, crisp and soft, brown and buttery. How I clung. The nearer, the more appreciative was I, as it disappeared.

"Life is a cookie," Alan Arkin pronounced in *America's Sweethearts.* I fell over the popcorn in my lap with laughter. One of the deep, wise lines in American movies. No one else in the theater was as elated. No one else had eaten the same single cookie for months running. I gleefully quoted Arkin, the guru, for weeks after. I could tell by people's faces: this, the result of all her sitting?

But nothing lasts forever. My tongue finally grew tired of the taste day after day. Was this straw in my mouth, this once great cookie? In the last weeks I asked only for a large hot water with lemon and wanted to pay the price for tea, but they wouldn't let me. I had become a familiar figure. So I left tips in a paper cup, and I sat. Not for a half hour or until the cookie was done—I sat for two, often three hours. Just sat there, nothing fancy, alongside an occasional man chopping away at a laptop, a mother, her son and his young friends, heads bent over brownies, eating their after-school snack, an elderly couple sighing long over steaming cups, a tall, retired businessman reading the *Pioneer Press.* I sat through the whole Bush/Gore campaign and then the very long election, through a young teenage boy murdered on his bike by the Mississippi, the eventual capture of the three young men who did it for no reason but to come in from the suburbs for some kicks, and the sad agony of the boy's parents who owned a pizza parlor nearby.

St. Paul is a small city with a big heart. If I was still enough, I could feel it all—the empty lots, the great river driving itself under bridges, the Schmidt brewery emitting a smell that I thought meant the town was toasting a lot of bread, but found out later was the focal point of an irate neighborhood protest. In early fall when the weather was warm I sat on the wood-and-wrought-iron bench that was set out in front of the café under a black locust. I even sat out there in slow drizzles and fog when the streets were slick and deserted. After fifteen years in New Mexico, the gray and mist were a great balm.

Sometimes if I was across the river in Minneapolis I sat at Dunn Brothers Café on Hennepin, and then, too, at the one in Linden Hills. Hadn't this always been my writing life? To fill spiral notebooks, write whole manuscripts in local luncheonettes and restaurants? But now here was my Zen life, too, happening in a café at the same square tables, only without a notebook. Hadn't I already declared that Zen and writing were one? In and out I'd breathe. My belly would fill, my belly would contract. I lifted the hot paper cup to my lips, my eyes now not down on the page but rather unfocused on the top of the chair pushed under the table across from me.

My world of meditation was getting large for me. By leaving the old structure, I was loosening my tight grip on my old Zen teacher. I was finally letting go of him. I was bringing my zazen out into the street. But who wants to let go of something you love? I did all this, but I did not recognize what was happening to me.

There is a recorded interview of me on a panel with an old dharma friend on December 21, 2001. It was a Saturday evening, the second winter of my return to Minneapolis, and the weather had tipped to thirty below. I'd just been driven across town by a kind young Zen student. No, not driven—the car slipped across black ice. I was so stunned by the time I was in front of the audience, most of my responses to the moderator's questions were, "You can find the answer to that in one of my books." I only knew no matter how deluded you may be, the land told you you would not last forever. As a matter of fact, driving home that night might be the end of you.

By the last days of February, even the most fastidious homeowners—and believe me, St. Paul is full of them—had given up shoveling their walks. In early March I looked out my apartment window to the corner of Dale and Lincoln near posh Crocus Hill and watched the man across the street blaze out of his large many-floored, old pale blue clapboard house, jacket flying open, with a long ax in his hand. While bellowing out months of confinement in piercing yelps, he hacked away at the ice built up by the curb. Behind him stood a massive crabapple, its branches frozen and curled in a death cry.

I had scheduled, for mid-April, a day-long public walking and writing retreat. I doubted now that it would take place. Where would we walk? In circles around the hallway of the zendo? My plan had been to meet at the zendo, write for two rounds, then venture out on a slow mindful stroll, feeling the clear placement of heel, the roll of toes, the lifting of foot, the bend of knee, the lowering of hip, as we made our way through the dank, dark streets of industrial St. Paul, across railroad tracks and under a bridge, to be surprised by a long, spiral, stone tunnel, opening into Swede Hollow along a winding creek and yellow grass (after all, when I planned it the year before, wasn't April supposed to be spring?), then climbing up to an old-fashioned, cast-iron, high-ceilinged café with a good soup and delicious desserts where we could write again at small tables. I would not tell the students where we were going. I would just lead them out the zendo door into the warehouse district with cigarette butts in wet clusters, gathered in sidewalk cracks. We would walk past the Black Dog Café and the smokers hunched on the outside stoop and near the square for the Lowertown farmers' market where impossible summer and fresh-grown produce would arrive again.

In this city of large oaks, magnificent elms, and maples, I managed to return to practice Zen at a zendo surrounded by concrete, where one spindly young line of a tree gallantly fought by a metal gate to survive. I'd renamed the practice center "The Lone Tree Zendo." And, yes, in truth, I did actually go there early mornings and Saturdays and Sundays, for weekend and week-long retreats. I was working on koans, ancient teaching stories that tested the depth of your realization. I had to present my understanding and it never came from logic or the thinking brain. I had to step out of my normal existence and come face-to-face with images from eighth- to tenth-century China: a rhinoceros fan, a buffalo passing through a window, an oak tree in the courtyard. The northern cold penetrated me as deeply as these koans. No fly, no bare finger could survive—even sound cracked. I was gouged by impermanence.

The first miserable weekend in April came. I looked at the roster of twenty-four faithful souls who had registered for the writing retreat. Two women from Lincoln, Nebraska, were flying in. A woman from Milwaukee—a six-hour drive away—was leaving at 3:30 a.m. to make the 9:30 beginning. Such determination. Only in the Midwest, I thought. I noted with delight that Tall Suzy and her friend from Fargo were coming. She'd studied with me back in New Mexico. Mike, the Vietnam vet, from Austin, Minnesota, was driving up too. I nervously fingered the page with the list of names.

The workshop date was the Saturday before Easter. The day

came and miraculously it was in the low sixties. I hustled over early to Bread and Chocolate to grab a cookie and touch the recent center of my universe, and then arrived a few minutes late for class. Everyone was silently meditating in a circle. I swirled into my place.

"We are going out for most of the day. You'll have to trust me. Remember: no good or bad. Just one step after another. We'll see different things. This is a walk of faith."

After two initial writing sessions we bounded outside, eager to be in the weak yet warming sun. But the weekend desolation of industrial St. Paul sobered us. One step after another. This was a silent walk so no one could complain—not that a Midwesterner would do such a thing. But I, an old New Yorker, had to shut up too. I couldn't encourage, explain, apologize. We just walked barefaced on this one early April day, slow enough to feel this life. Over the still frozen ground to the tracks, crushing thin pools of ice with our boots. A left foot lifted and placed, then a right. The tunnel was ahead. Half of us were already walking through the yellow limestone spiral, built in 1856, a miracle of construction that seemed to turn your mind. Eventually we all made it through to the other side, to sudden country, the hollow, and the first sweetness of open land. Long, pale grasses, just straightening up after the melting weight of snow, and thin, unleafed trees gathered along the lively winding stream.

We had walked an hour and a half at the pace of a spider. I'd forgotten what this kind of walking does to you. You enter the raw edge of your mind, the naked line between you and your surroundings drops away. Whoever you are or think you are cracks off. We were soul-bare together in the hollow, the place poor Swedish immigrants inhabited a hundred years ago in cardboard shacks. Some people broke off and went down to the stream, put their hands in the cold water. I sat on a stone with my face in the sun. Then we continued on.

We didn't get to the café until almost two o'clock. The place was empty. We filled the tables and burst into writing. I remember looking up a moment into the stunned faces of two people behind the counter. Where did all these people suddenly come from? And none of them are talking?

I'd forgotten how strenuous it was to walk so slow for so long. I was tired.

When it was time to leave, I had planned to follow the same route back. Oh, no, the students shook their heads and took the lead almost at a trot. A short cut across a bypass over noisy 94 to the zendo. We arrived breathless in twenty minutes. Back in the circle, I inquired, "How was it?"—the first spoken words.

I looked around at them. My face fell. I'd been naïve. They ran back here for safety. That walk had rubbed them raw. One woman began: "When we reached the tunnel, I was terrified to go through. It felt like the birth canal."

Another: "I didn't know where it would lead. I looked at all of us walking like zombies and began to cry. I thought of the Jews going to the chambers."

I remembered two kids in the hollow stopping their pedaling and straddling their bikes, mouths agape, staring at us. I had taken comfort in numbers and didn't worry about how we appeared to the outside. Of course, we must have looked strange.

What happened to us? they asked.

I checked in with my own body right then. Oh, yes, I felt the way I did after a five- or seven-day retreat, kind of shattered, new and tremulous. They were feeling the same.

One woman said, "I physically felt spring entering the hollow. It was right there when I slowed up enough to feel it. I opened my hand and spring filled it. I swear I also saw winter leaving. Not a metaphor. The real thing."

They were describing experiences I'd had in the zendo after long hours of sitting. But I'd thought that only within the confines of those walls and with that cross-legged position I loved, could certain kinds of openings occur. I'd wanted so badly to cling to the old structure I learned with my beloved teacher, the time-worn, true way handed down from temples and monasteries in

Japan, that he'd painstakingly brought to us in America. Yes, I loved everything he taught me, but didn't the Buddha walk around a lot? What I saw now, with these students as witnesses, was that it was me who had confined my mind, grasped a practice I learned in my thirties, feeling nothing else was authentic.

Nat, what about writing? You'd said it was a true way, but even you didn't truly believe it. You only wanted to be with your old teacher again when you came back to Minnesota a year ago. You'd returned to St. Paul, it turns out, not to let go, but to find him. Like a child, you'd never really believed he'd died. Certainly you'd discover him again up here, but your body couldn't sit in the old way. You happened upon him, but all new.

What was Zen anyway? There was you and me, living and dying, eating cake. There was the sky, there were mountains, rivers, prairies, horses, mosquitoes, justice, injustice, integrity, cucumbers. The structure was bigger than any structure I could conceive. I had fallen off the zafu, that old round cushion, into the vast unknown.

I looked again at these students in a circle. This day we were here and we experienced we were here. I could feel Roshi's presence. I thought he had died. No one had died. And in a blink of an eye none of us were here, only spring would move to summer, if we were very lucky and no one blew up the world. But maybe there were other summers and winters out there in other universes. Nothing like a Minnesota winter, of course—that single solid thought I probably would die clinging to, like a life preserver, the one true thing I'd met after all my seeking.

After the last student left, I bent to put on my shoes. I was tired of being pigeonholed as a writer. Limited to one thing. Not Zen separate from hamburgers, not writing divided from breath. Only the foot placed down on this one earth.

If we can sit in a café breathing, we can breathe through hearing our father's last breath, the slow crack of pain as we realize he's crossing over forever. Good-bye, we say. Good-bye. Good-bye. Toenails and skin. Memory halted in our lungs: his foot, ankle, wrist. When a bomb is dropped it falls through history. No one act, no single life. No disconnected occurrence. I am sipping a root beer in another café and the world spins and you pick up a pen, speak and save another life: this time your own.

That night at three a.m., one of those mighty Midwestern thunderstorms suddenly broke the dark early sky in an electric yellow. I gazed out the cold glass pane. Either in my head or outside of it—where do thoughts come from?—three words resounded: The Great Spring. The Great Spring. Together my students and I had witnessed the tip of the moment that green longed for itself again. I realized in all these years, Roshi had never been outside of me.

The Threshold

Bonnie Myotai Treace

Live on the threshold, says Zen teacher Bonnie Myotai Treace, not seeking certainty or security. In the openness where past answers have dissolved and future ones have not yet solidified, you will find reality.

What is the gate of Zen? Is there a way to live in the threshold of every moment? Pablo Neruda writes in the opening stanzas of his verse "Poetry":

> And it was at that age . . . Poetry arrived
> in search of me. I don't know, I don't know where
> it came from, from winter or a river.
> I don't know how or when,
> no, they were not voices, they were not
> words, nor silence
> but from a street I was summoned,
> from the branches of night,
> abruptly from the others,
> among violent fires
> or returning alone,
> there I was without a face
> and it touched me.

In practice, we explore this threshold, this place where old and new meet in a body. We explore the "liminal"—the realm in which we're touched beyond personality, beyond the limits of what we understand or have assigned ourselves as our life. A practitioner of Zen is most basically one whose life is awakening each moment to that threshold, the still point where all the possibilities exist. To practice is to release oneself from the momentum of the past, the karma of what seems to be indicated as the only next step. It is to turn one's face towards the unknown as a way of life.

Maezumi Roshi once wrote, "Once through the gate, the discovery is made that the gate is not actually a barrier or an opening through which to pass. It's simply reality presenting itself." Usually we either regard that threshold, that barrier gate, as a place of stopping or as a place of incipient going. Maezumi Roshi points to the place where there is neither coming nor going, neither speech nor silence, no momentum—and yet utter obligation to all things. This is what touched Neruda. But what is it?

Anthropologist Victor Turner also takes up that moment at the threshold in a book called *Ritual Process.* He describes it as "the liminal—the time and space of transition integral to all rites of passage. Entering this condition, a person leaves behind his or her old identity and dwells in a threshold state of ambiguity, openness and indeterminacy." It's easy to see that every *koan,* in a sense, is simply that: "Entering . . . a threshold state of ambiguity, openness and indeterminacy. . . ." In other words, not knowing. Every liturgy is that liminal realm. Everything, every breath, is the threshold.

What tends to happen as we become used to—or familiar with—the language and devices of Zen, its rhetoric of gates and barriers, is that we cease to recognize what its real demand is, what its real offering is. What happens when Neruda enters this state in which he surrenders his path, his direction? When he's summoned from the street, from where he thought he was heading, from what he thought he was doing? Suddenly, his life is up for grabs—his face is missing, his identity can't be found, and that allows a life larger than his own to touch him. A life beyond his agenda, his ideas, begins at that moment. But at root in all the gate-barrier-threshold teachings is the essential question, "What is it that touches the mind at such a moment?"

Surrendering path and face, letting go of our self-ideas about direction: how is that accomplished? Ambiguity may not seem so attractive when we're craving certainty as if it were water. Allowing reality to arrive, or as Maezumi Roshi said, "to present itself," isn't easy. The fact that we can't grasp or guarantee it is reality's challenge. To live in that threshold, to let one's life *be* that threshold itself, is to not be dependent on the temporary comforts of knowing something, of being someone, of going somewhere. This is why practice can be so fundamentally uncomfortable; until we let go, we are holding on, and that simply hurts.

We can see the challenge of the threshold in the life of Patacara, who lived in India at the time of the Buddha. Patacara was a very strong young woman. When her parents picked out a prospective husband for her, she secretly married instead a servant who had long been her lover. In this detail, we get an indication that she was, from the beginning, not much of a rule-follower. The consequence of that allegiance to her own heart was rejection by her family. She and her husband had to leave and make their home in a distant part of India.

It was the custom in that culture for a woman to return to her mother's house when it was time to give birth. When her first child was due, Patacara was delayed by her husband in starting her journey, and gave birth in the woods. When she was pregnant the second time, her husband was again resistant, so she began the trek without him. He soon followed, and found his family deep in the woods as a fierce storm began kicking up. As he gathered wood to build a shelter for his child and pregnant wife, he was bitten by a snake and quickly died. Patacara gave birth alone. She sheltered her newborn and her other child with her body as the storm raged on.

In grief over her husband's unexpected death, she also realized that she and her children would no longer be welcome in his village. Her only option was to proceed to her parents' home and beg to be welcomed. To get there, she had to cross a large river, now a torrent because of the storm.

Unable to make the crossing with both children, she told the toddler to stay put and entered the water carrying the newborn. She crossed the river, settled the newborn into a nest of leaves, and began to make her way back for her other child. But when she reached mid-river, to her horror, she saw a hawk swoop down, pick up the baby, and begin carrying it away as prey. She cried out, trying to get the hawk to release it, but it ignored her. Her older child, hearing her shriek, thought she was calling him to come to her. He ran into the water towards her, and she watched as he was swept up in the waves and drowned.

Like Job, Patacara is brought to a level of sadness so low it is hard to imagine. Somehow, she made her way out of the river and continued walking toward her old home. Along the road, she met someone from the town, and asked them about her family. This person told her that during the storm, her family's house collapsed and they were killed. She went mad with grief, and no longer tried to protect herself. She wandered—naked, disheveled, disoriented.

So far, the story is largely about what is happening to Patacara, but let's look at what she is doing instead. She has lived according to her heart, and has persevered against all odds. And now she has exhausted all reference systems, if you will. Nothing has protected her from suffering, and she knows it. She now sees through all of the things that had been of value to her. No one can get near her. She sees every offer of false hope for what it is. "I'll take care of you" is no longer a promise she can believe. "I'll be there for you"—she knew that no one could guarantee that. All the games were over. In the deepest sense, she *is* naked.

Unwilling to organize herself to fit into her culture, she kept wandering. When she came upon the Jeta grove where the Buddha was teaching, his disciples found her frightening and appalling. But when the Buddha saw her, he rose and followed her. He placed himself in her path and, when they met, said, "Sister, it is time to recover your presence of mind." Patacara came to her senses, realized she was naked, and gratefully covered herself with a cloak. Then she asked the Buddha to help her.

It's important to recognize what's happening in this story. It's easy to say that the Buddha did something, gave her something. But realize that she heard not simply the words of Shakyamuni Buddha, but the timeless Buddha voice which calls us to wake up, to recover our presence of mind. She heard her first Dharma talk, if you will. And she had emptied herself of games and illusions so completely that she *could* hear it.

After listening to Patacara's tragic story, the Buddha told her that throughout her many lives, she "had shed more tears for the loss of loved ones than there was water in the oceans." This, too, is critical. In her hearing of the Buddha voice, we can see what happens when our life is recognized. The Buddha mind meets us in our suffering, when we drop all the devices we use to buffer ourselves against it.

Then the Buddha reminded her that "at your death, even had they all been living, your family could only look on in helpless despair. Only the Dharma can help you." Hearing this, Patacara decided to ordain and was taken into the nun's community, which welcomed her.

What did she realize? The Buddha told Patacara, "Recover your presence of mind." What happens when we ordain into the truth of this boundless mind itself? When we recognize that no one can help us come home because we've never left? Patacara was freed.

She went on to become a great teacher. She had thirty disciples, which for a woman of her time was pretty odd. She is, in a sense, the star of the *Therigata*, the enlightenment poems of the Buddhist nuns and laywomen. Her voice appears in the collection more often than any other. Her enlightenment poem, which gives us an indication of what she realized, says:

> Bathing my feet
> I watched the bath water

Spill down the slope.
I concentrated my mind
The way you train a good horse.

Then I took a lamp
And went into my cell.
Checked the bed and sat down on it.
I took a needle and pushed the wick down.

As the lamp went out
My mind was freed.

It's akin to what we encounter in Neruda's absent face, that sheerness and dailyness, that everything-ness of awakening. "Show me your face before your parents were born," the koan says. "For Neruda," the poet and essayist Jane Hirshfield writes, "that face becomes a poetry of all things: a long praise-song to salt in the mines and in the ocean, to a wristwatch ticking in the night's darkness like a tiny saw cutting time, to the dead body of a fish in the market. In the light of the poet's abundance of heart and imagination, we remember the threshold is a place at once empty and full. It is on the margins, where one thing meets another, and in the times of transition, that ecosystems are most rich and diverse—birds sing, and deer, fish, and mosquitoes emerge to feed at dawn and at dusk."

But at such a threshold, we're not sure of that richness. We're not sure of mosquitoes. We're not sure of deer or stars. We're not sure of anything. We're just, as the anthropologist Turner said, "in a state of ambiguity, openness and indeterminacy." We're in a state of beginner's mind. We're in a state of self-forgetting, that state which the Buddha called "presence of mind." It's almost redundant: recover your presence, and recover your mind. Don't "know" about your situation. *Be profoundly present.*

"Only afterward," the anthropologist writes, "may the initiate enter into new forms of identity and relationship, rejoining the everyday life of the culture—but now as an adult or married person, as healer or holder of clan secrets." This is the ritual process of the threshold, celebrated in a marriage ceremony, celebrated in *Jukai* [a Zen initiation], celebrated in becoming a student. When may we initiate the new forms of relationship? When we've forgotten the self, when we've dropped the face. The ten ox-herding pictures depict this same process: in the final one, entering the marketplace with bliss-bestowing hands, all relationships are transformed, all things are radiant.

But our transitions trigger a great deal of initial fear; we feel like we're going to somehow fall apart if we go forward. That's why steps seem so hard to take before we take them. A wonderful martial arts teacher once counseled several of us who were pulling back in class that we had to practice in class just as we'd practiced learning how to walk. In order to walk, a child needs to first develop a willingness to fall, because basically walking is nothing but falling and recovering. If willingness to fall isn't there, you just never give walking a shot. Life crawls on, but you never really become an upright human being.

The willingness to step into the unknown and possibly take a fall is to surrender to the threshold. When what's falling is everyone you love, or your sense of yourself or your direction—life in the liminal calls us from the street. To let it touch us, we have to practice our fears.

In the Buddhist scripture collection known as the *Abhidharma*, they list five great fears. Since I first read that list, I've often reflected on how whatever fear I had coming up might fit into the ancient file system.

The *Abhidharma*'s five great fears are:

Fear of death,
Fear of the loss of livelihood,
Fear of unusual states of consciousness,
Fear of loss of reputation,
Fear of speaking before a public assembly.

What are we afraid of? The uncountable millions of things—from the mystery of mortality, to the intractable sense of loss when there is no one to love or no one to love us, to the abuses of cruel people, or an indifferent, chaotic world. But right in that moment of fear is the place where either life becomes a threshold, or a curse. Daido Roshi always says, "If you miss the moment, you miss your life." We don't need a grand plan: "I'll live my life as a threshold." It's enough to practice now. It's enough to practice *this.* "You have cried more tears than there is water in the ocean," the Buddha said. He began his teaching there, with the recognition that life is suffering, fearful, plagued by insatiable thirsts. "It is time to recover your presence of mind," the Buddha said. It is time. Not Patacara's time. Your time. My time. Not later, not when we feel differently.

Not long ago I was visiting with my mom, who lives in an apartment complex which increasingly houses solitary elderly women. They blow my heart open, because in one sense you can look at them and just see this fabric of misery. Here's the broken hip and the arthritis, the diabetes and the widowhood and the uncaring children. . . . It's almost overwhelming. But then it dawns on me how every day, every moment—they have not opted for any of the not-so-difficult-to-figure-out exits. You know. Leap off the tenth floor, and stop this story. And yet, they stay in a kind of attention to, "What about today? What's at this threshold?" They don't say it like that. They'd think that was the corniest, stupidest thing they'd ever heard. But they breathe it. They live it. They show it.

"A number of specific characteristics mark this state of being 'betwixt and between'" in the liminal world, writes Jane Hirshfield. Again, the anthropologist: "First, the initiate undergoes the removal of both identity and status—he or she becomes nameless; conventional clothing is foregone; the usual constraints of gender no longer apply." And this is ritualized in the receiving of the robe in Zen training. It's obvious in the story of Patacara shedding her clothes, her currency of communicating appropriateness or protection.

"Ordinarily forbidden behavior is now allowed, or, conversely, the person may enter into an extreme discipline equally foreign to conventional life." Like attending one's mind, not running from every discomfort. "Often there is a period of silence, of non-doing, of fasting or going without sleep. Threshold persons are treated as outsiders and exiles, separated from the group, reviled, ignored." The Zen monk leaves home, becoming *unsui*, Japanese for "clouds and water." This is Patacara with no place to land. In a way, it is the gesture of being in *sesshin* [Zen meditation retreat]—removing yourself from that street, dwelling in mystery, willing to be misunderstood by those who do not understand why you'd do such a thing.

"Possessing nothing, they descend into invisibility and darkness, and—symbolically or literally—abandoning both the physical and the ideological structures of society for a wilderness existence." The desert fathers entered the desert; the forest monks and nuns entered the forest. This is the wilderness in which there is no path. There's no guidance in the true wilderness. We create the superstructure of training to hold and encourage that liminal life—come see the teacher, come hear the talk—but in fact there is nothing that a teacher can give you. Why? Because you are already whole. Patacara was already whole. That's why when encouraged—when sparked—by the Buddha's words, "Recover your presence of mind," she could. It's why when a teacher says, "Trust yourself," you can.

I'd like to end as I began, with a poem. Jane Hirshfield writes, in a piece called "Late Prayer," of a time of difficulty—when she was struggling to invoke, to invite, to pray for the bodhi mind of living in the threshold:

> Tenderness does not choose its own uses.
> It goes out to everything equally,
> circling rabbit and hawk.

Look: in the iron bucket,
a single nail, a single ruby—
all the heavens and hells.
They rattle in the heart and make one sound.

We don't get to choose whether it's ruby or nail, whether it's kindness and grace and flow, or abuse and pain and awkwardness. What we *can* ordain into is that it's one sound in the heart. It's one threshold. It's one moment. May we recover it in presence of mind.

A Deep Inquiry into the Meaning of Freedom

Charles Johnson

More than other Americans, says Charles Johnson, black Americans have contemplated the meaning of identity, liberty, and community. He offers in this essay a brief history of how African American thinkers from DuBois to King have reflected on these issues, and argues that black Americans' quest for freedom realizes its most profound and revolutionary meaning in Buddhist practice.

The black experience in America, like the teachings of Shakyamuni Buddha, begins with suffering.

It begins in the violence of seventeenth-century slave forts sprinkled along the west coast of Africa, where debtors, thieves, war prisoners, and those who would not convert to Islam were separated from their families, branded, and sold to Europeans who packed them into pestilential ships that cargoed twenty million human beings (a conservative estimate) to the New World. Only 20 percent of those slaves survived the harrowing voyage at sea (and only 20 percent of the sailors, too), and if they were among the lucky few to set foot on American soil, new horrors and heartbreak awaited them.

As has been documented time and again, the life of a slave—our not-so-distant ancestors—was one of thinghood. It is, one might say, a frighteningly fertile ground for the growth of a deep appreciation for the First and Second Noble Truths, as well as a living illustration of the meaning of impermanence. Former languages, religions, and cultures were erased, replaced by a Peculiar Institution in which the person of African descent was property, systematically—legally, physically, and culturally—denied all sense of self-worth. A slave owns nothing, least of all himself. He desires and dreams at the risk of his life, which is best described as relative to (white) others, a reaction to their deeds, judgments, and definitions of the world. And these definitions, applied to blacks, were not kind. In the nation's pulpits, Christian clergy in the South justified slavery by picturing blacks as the descendants of Ham or Cain; in his *Notes on the State of Virginia*, Thomas Jefferson dismissed slaves as childlike, stupid, and incapable of self-governance. For 244 years (from 1619 to 1863), America was a slave state with a guilty conscience: two and a half centuries tragically scarred by slave revolts, heroic black (and abolitionist) resistance to oppression, and, more than anything else, physical, spiritual, and psychological *suffering* so staggeringly thorough it silences the mind when we study the classic slave narratives of Olaudah Equiano or Frederick Douglass, or see the brutal legacies of chattel bondage in a PBS series like *Africans in America.* All that was over, of course, by the end of the Civil War, but the Emancipation Proclamation did not bring liberation.

Legal freedom instead brought segregation, America's version of apartheid, for another hundred years. But "separate" was clearly not "equal." The *experienced* law of black life was disenfranchisement, anger, racial dualism, second-class citizenship, and, as the great scholar W. E. B. Du Bois put it in his classic *The Souls of Black Folk* (1903), "double-consciousness." Can anyone doubt that if there is an essence—an *eidos*—to black American life, it has for three centuries been craving, and a quest for identity and liberty, which, pushed to its social extremes, propelled this pursuit beyond the relative, conceptual realities of race and culture to a deeper investigation of the meaning of freedom?

If the teachings of Shakyamuni Buddha are about *any*thing, they are about a profound understanding of identity and the broadest possible meaning of liberty—teachings that sooner or later had to appeal to a people for whom suffering and loss were their daily bread. In the century after the Emancipation Proclamation each generation of black Americans saw their lives disrupted by race riots, lynchings, and the destruction of towns and communities, such as the Greenwood district of black homes, businesses, and churches in Tulsa, Oklahoma on May 31, 1921. These Jim Crow years witnessed the birth of blues and a white backlash that fed poisonous caricatures of black people into popular culture and the national consciousness—films like *Birth of a Nation*, the writings of the Plantation School, and endless stereotypes that distorted black identity in newspapers and magazines—images that made the central questions of the black self "Who *am* I? American? African? Or something other? Can reality be found in any of these words?"

During these centuries of institutionalized denial, black Americans found in Christianity a spiritual rock and refuge. Although first imposed on some slaves by their owners as a way of making them obedient, Christianity in black hands became a means for revolt against bondage. Then, in the twentieth century, the black church provided consolation in a country divided by the color line. It became a common spiritual, social, economic, and political experience and was the place where black people could reinterpret Christianity and transform it into an instrument for worldly change. It became a racially tempered institution, one that raised funds to help the poor and to send black children off to college.

Historically, no other institution's influence compares with that of the black church, and I believe it will continue to be the dominant spiritual orientation of black Americans. It provides a compelling and time-tested moral vision, a metaphysically dualistic one that partitions the world into good and evil, heaven and hell; posits an immortal soul that no worldly suffering can harm; and through the agapic love of a merciful Father promises in the afterlife rewards denied in this one. Christianity, in part, made black Americans a genuinely Western people, on the whole identical in their strivings and sense of how the world works with Northern Europeans in the Judeo-Christian tradition.

But as early as 1923, Du Bois reflected deeply on the nature of black desires and a Western weltanschauung in a speech entitled "Criteria of Negro Art." It was published in *The Crisis*, the official publication of the National Association for the Advancement of Colored People, which Du Bois himself edited, and in this document he raises fundamental spiritual questions—what Buddhists might call Dharma doors—for a people whose dreams were long deferred.

> What do we want? What is the thing we are after? As it was phrased last night it had a certain truth: We want to be Americans, full-fledged Americans, with all the rights of American citizens. But is that all? Do we want simply to be Americans? Once in a while through all of us there flashes some clairvoyance, some clear idea, of what America really is. We who are dark can see America in a way that white Americans can not. And seeing our country thus, are we satisfied with its present goals and ideals?
>
> If you tonight suddenly should become full-fledged Americans; if your color faded, or the color line here in Chicago was miraculously forgotten; suppose, too, you became at the same time rich and powerful;—what is it that you would want? What would you immediately seek? Would you buy the most powerful of motor-cars and outrace Cook County? Would you buy the most

> elaborate estate on the North Shore? Would you be a Rotarian or a Lion or a What-not of the very last degree? Would you wear the most striking clothes, give the richest dinners and buy the longest press notices?
>
> Even as you visualize such ideals you know in your heart that these are not the things you really want. You realize this sooner than the average white American because, pushed aside as we have been in America, there has come to us not only a certain distaste for the tawdry and flamboyant but a vision of what the world could be if it were really a beautiful world; if we had the true spirit; if we had the Seeing Eye, the Cunning Hand, the Feeling Heart; if we had, to be sure, not perfect happiness, but plenty of good hard work, the inevitable suffering that always comes with life; sacrifice and waiting, all that—but, nevertheless, lived in a world where men know, where men create, where they realize themselves and where they enjoy life. It is that sort of a world we want to create for ourselves and for all America.

Others echoed Dr. Du Bois's question "What do we want?" As early as the 1920s, some black Americans were quietly investigating Far Eastern philosophies such as Hinduism and the Theravada and Mahayana traditions of Buddhism after experiencing Du Bois's "flashes of clairvoyance." Preeminent among these spiritual seekers was Jean Toomer, who regarded himself as "a psychological adventurer: one who, having had the stock experiences of mankind, sets out at right angles to all previous experience to discover new states of being." His classic work, *Cane* (1923), kicked off the Harlem Renaissance, the first outpouring of black American creativity after World War I. It is fitting, in a way, that *Cane*, a provocatively mystical work of fiction and poetry inaugurated the Renaissance, which scholar Alain Locke described as the dawn of "The New Negro." Furthermore, the year after its publication, Toomer began the first of many summers in Europe studying, then teaching, the philosophy of Georges I. Gurdjieff, which remains an original restatement of esoteric wisdom influenced by Tibetan and Sufi teachings.

In 1931, Toomer self-published a remarkable collection of aphorisms entitled *Essentials.* Therein, he observed that "*I* is a word, but the worm is real," letting us know that the self was in part a product of language, which can conceal as much as it reveals about the world. He understood, as the earliest Buddhists did, that "the assumption of existence rests upon an uninterrupted series of pictures" and, more important, that "whatever is, is sacred." And he knew that all things were interdependent and transitory. He was no stranger to the renunciation of an illusory, empirical ego. Although his work after *Cane* was rejected by publishers and he slipped into literary obscurity until the 1960s, Toomer was a spiritual trailblazer whose creative "journey to the east" inspired post-1960s authors, myself among them, to probe the "multiple simultaneous world" he first charted and to take to heart such aphorisms as "the realization of nothingness is the first act of being" and "we do not possess imagination enough to sense what we are missing."

If Toomer felt alone in his time ("It is as if I have seen," he said, "the end of things others pursue blindly"), he might have been comforted by the fact that some black American soldiers returning from service overseas came home with exposure to Dharma—exposure that only increased as black soldiers brought back Korean and Japanese Buddhist wives. In his superb novel *Kingsblood Royal* (1947), Sinclair Lewis writes the story of a white man who discovers he has a black ancestor; he seeks to better understand people of color and realizes the great diversity of black Americans in his town—among them, writes Lewis, are Buddhists.

By the mid-1950s, as the Beats looked toward Zen, so did a few black musicians and poets; and of course by then the Civil Rights Movement was under way, led magnificently by Dr. Martin Luther King, Jr., who took Mahatma Gandhi as his inspiration.

After a pilgrimage to India in 1959, where he visited ashrams and sought to learn more about nonviolence not simply as a political strategy but as a way of life, King came back to America determined to set aside one day a week for meditation and fasting. In the 1960s, he nominated for the Nobel Peace Prize the outstanding Vietnamese Buddhist teacher Thich Nhat Hanh. King was, at bottom, a Baptist minister, yes, but one whose vision of the social gospel at its best complements the expansive, Mahayana bodhisattva ideal of laboring for the liberation of all sentient beings ("Strangely enough," he said, "I can never be what I ought to be until you are what you ought to be. You can never be what you ought to be until I am what I ought to be"). His dream of the "beloved community" is a *sangha* by another name, for King believed, "It really boils down to this: that all of life is interrelated. We are caught in an inescapable network of mutuality, tied in a single garment of destiny."

The fourteen-year public ministry of Dr. King is emblematic of the philosophical changes that affected black Americans in the 1960s. Another milestone is the remarkable success of Soka Gakkai in attracting black Americans for three decades. Its members include entertainers with the high visibility of Herbie Hancock and Tina Turner. Although I do not belong to this Nichiren Buddhist group, which, according to writer Jane Hurst, represents 50,000 to 150,000 Americans (with 25–30 percent of these being black and Hispanic), my sister-in-law in Chicago and her friends are practitioners who have chanted *Namu-myōhō-renge-kyō* since the early 1970s.

In a recent conversation with my sister-in-law and one of her associates, I was informed that Soka Gakkai's initial attraction for them came about because they discovered that through chanting they could transform their lives and, in fact, that they alone were the architects of their own suffering and happiness. For my sister-in-law, raised Baptist and impoverished in a housing project on Chicago's South Side, the black church with its white Jesus had always been an unsatisfying experience, one from which she felt emotionally distant since childhood; for her friend, a woman raised as a Catholic, Soka Gakkai provided—through its explanation of karma and reincarnation and its foundation in the *Lotus Sutra*—a reason for the individual suffering she saw in the world, convincing her this was not due to the will of God but instead was based causally on each person's actions in this life and previous ones. Global peace is their goal. Chanting is their tool for self-transformation, empowerment, and experiencing the at-oneness with being they both had sought all their lives. *Namu-nzyōhō-renge-kyō*, they said, invested them with boundless energy, individual peace, and, as my sister-in-law's friend put it, "a natural high like I never had before."

Many white Buddhists new to the Zen and Tibetan traditions dismiss Soka Gakkai for what they consider its skewed, Christian-oriented, materialistic version of Buddhism. For me, Soka Gakkai is but one branch on the Bodhi tree. Yet its success in recruiting black Americans indicates that people of color find in Buddhism the depths of their long-denied humanity; centuries-old methods of meditation—very empirical—for clearing the mind of socially manufactured illusions (as well as personally created ones); an ancient phenomenology of suffering, desire, and the self; and a path (the Eightfold Path) for a moral, civilized way of life.

The emphasis in Buddhist teachings on letting go of the fabricated, false sense of self positions issues of race as foremost among *samsaric* illusions, along with all the essentialist conceptions of difference that have caused so much human suffering and mischief since the eighteenth century. It frees one from dualistic models of epistemology that partition experience into separate, boxlike compartments of Mind and Body, Self and Other, Matter and Spirit—these divisions, one sees, are ontologically the correlates of racial divisions found in South African apartheid and American segregation and are just as pernicious.

More than anything else, the Dharma teaches mindfulness, the practice of being here and now in each present moment, without bringing yesterday's racial agonies into today or projecting oneself—one's hopes and longings—into a tomorrow that never comes. You watch the prismatic play of desires and emotions (for example: joy, fear, pride, and so-called black rage) as they arise in awareness, but without attachment or clinging to name and form, and then you let them go. One is especially free, on this path, from the belief in an enduring "personal identity," an "I" endlessly called upon to prove its worth and deny its inferiority in a world that so often mirrors back only negative images of the black self. Yet one need not cling to "positive" images either, for these, too, are essentially empty of meaning. Indeed you recognize emptiness (*sunyata*) as the ultimate nature of reality. In my own fiction, I have worked to dramatize that insight in novels such as *Oxherding Tale* (1982), a slave narrative that serves as the vehicle for exploring Eastern philosophy; *Middle Passage* (1990), a sea adventure tale about the slave trade (and a rather Buddhist African tribe called the Allmuseri); and *Dreamer* (1998), a fictional account of the last two years of Martin Luther King's life that highlights his globally ecumenical spirituality.

Buddhist insights continue to multiply among contemporary black authors. In *Right Here, Right Now*, a recent novel by Trey Ellis, which won a 1999 American Book Award, we are offered the story of a black man who creates a new world religion that borrows heavily from Buddhism and underscores the central theme of impermanence and change. And Octavia Butler, a MacArthur fellow and much celebrated science-fiction writer, features in *Parable of the Sower* (1993) a narrator in 2024 who broods on the fact that "everyone knows that change is inevitable. From the second law of thermodynamics to Darwinian evolution, from Buddhism's insistence that nothing is permanent and all suffering results from our delusions of permanence to the third chapter of Ecclesiastes ('To every thing there is a season . . .'), change is part of life, of existence, of the common wisdom. But I don't believe we're dealing with all that that means. We haven't even begun to deal with it."

Canonical Zen documents like the "Ten Oxherding Pictures" of twelfth-century artist Kakuan Shien also appear in recent black poetry. In the preeminent journal of black letters, *Callaloo* (vol. 22, no. 1), the distinguished poet Lucille Clifton re-visioned the Ch'an teachings of the "Ten Oxherding Pictures" in which the stages of Zen understanding are depicted by a man who follows the footsteps of an ox, which, untamed, represents ego. He finally glimpses the ox, slowly tames it, then trains it to do what he wants, not what ego wants. Only after he has completely transformed himself does he happily ride his ox into the marketplace. Clifton writes these lines for the eighth picture, in which both the ox and oxherder disappear; here, the emptiness suggests the dissolution and arising of forms, and the essence of interdependence is represented by a circle:

> *The Ox and the Man Both Gone Out of Sight*
> man is not ox
> I am not ox
> no thing is ox
> all things are ox.

Through meditation, Du Bois's flashes of clairvoyance are sharpened and the internalized racial conflict of "double-consciousness" is transcended, enabling those of us who live in a violent, competitive society steeped in materialism to grasp the truth of impermanence (*anitya*) that first turned twenty-nine-year-old prince Siddhartha Gautama from the ephemeral sense pleasures of his palace to the pursuit of liberation and enlightenment. After he had abandoned experiencing the world through concepts and representations, after he realized the cessation of mental constructions, he perceived the interdependence of all things, how—as Thich Nhat Hanh says—"Everything is made of everything else, nothing can be by itself alone" (*anatman*) in a universe of ceaseless change and transformation. Then and only then is it possible to realize Dr. King's injunction that we "love our enemies" in the struggle for justice because once one approaches the "enemy" with love and compassion, the "enemy," the Other, is seen to be oneself.

All things, we learn, are ourselves. Thus, practice necessarily leads to empathy, the "Feeling Heart" Du Bois spoke of, Toomer's sense that all is sacred, and the experience of connectedness to all sentient beings. No matter how humble the activity—whether it be walking, sitting, eating, or washing the dishes—one approaches it with mindfulness, acting and listening egolessly as if this activity might be the most important thing in the world, for indeed all that is, has been, and will be is contained in the present moment. In this nondiscursive, expansive spirit, discrimination is inconceivable. After the practitioner has charged his battery, so to speak, in meditation, he eagerly works and creates to serve others—all others—with humility, a boundless joy in giving, fearlessness, and disinterest in all personal "rewards." And though the number of black Buddhists is small, they are growing in an increasingly multicultural America with the promise of more black people turning the Wheel of Dharma as a new millennium dawns. For through the Dharma, the black American quest for "freedom" realizes its profoundest, truest, and most revolutionary meaning.

Depression's Truth

Traleg Kyabgon

Whatever ego wants, Buddhism recommends the opposite. Chögyam Trungpa Rinpoche said that disappointment was the most valuable emotion, from a spiritual point of view. He also recommended boredom. In a similar vein, here is an essay by Traleg Rinpoche on why depression can be helpful. In depression you find intelligence and accuracy, because, let's face it, the reality of the world offers us some pretty good reasons to be depressed.

Depression is something we all experience. For some people depression is mild, while for others it is very intense and debilitating. For some people it lasts for a short time and then disappears, while for others it may persist over many years, or even an entire lifetime. We generally think of depression as a terrible state to be in: it is something we think we have to overcome, and we go to great lengths to hide it from others. This is probably because when we suffer from depression, our energy levels and motivation go down and we become withdrawn, uncommunicative, irritable, resentful, and basically very difficult to be with. There is also often a lot of anger, jealousy, or envy mixed with depression, because seeing someone who is happy only makes our depression worse. The point is that depression, in terms of its symptoms, can be debilitating and paralyzing because of what the Buddhists call the "conflicting emotions" associated with it. When we are depressed, our self-esteem and self-confidence plummet. We begin to doubt ourselves. We begin to think that we have become a failure at everything.

Western psychotherapists say that you can learn a person's reasons for experiencing depression if you look into their biographical or biological history. From the Buddhist point of view, though, the fundamental understanding is that depression is based on our interpretations of our life situations, our circumstances, our self-conceptions. We get depressed for not being the person we want to be. We get depressed when we think we have not been able to achieve the things that we want to achieve in life.

But depression is not necessarily a bad state to be in. When we are depressed, we may actually be able to see through the falsity and deceptive nature of the samsaric world. In other words, we should not think, "When I am depressed my mind is distorted and messed up, while when I am not depressed I am seeing everything clearly."

According to Buddhism, the world that we perceive—the world we interact with and live in—is insubstantial. Through the experience of depression and despair we can begin to see things more clearly rather than less clearly. It is said that we are normally charmed or bedazzled by the world, like a spell has been put on us by the allure of samsaric excitements and entertainment. When we get depressed, though, we begin to see through that—we are able to cut through the illusions of samsara. Depression, when we work with it, can be like a signal, something that puts a brake on our excesses and reminds us of the banality of the samsaric condition, so that we will not be duped into sliding back into the old habits again. It reminds us of the futility, insignificance, and nonsubstantiality of the samsaric condition.

That is extremely important, according to Buddhism, because if we are not convinced of the illusory nature of the samsaric condition, we will always be two-minded. We will have one foot in the spiritual realm and the other in the samsaric realm, never being fully able to make that extra effort.

We are not talking, though, about chronic or clinical depression here, depression that has gotten way out of hand. We are talking about the kind of depression that makes us stop and think and reevaluate our lives. This kind of depression can aid us in terms of our spiritual growth, because it makes us begin to question ourselves. For all these years we may have been thinking, "I'm this kind of person," "I'm that kind of person," "I'm a mother," "I'm an engineer," or whatever. Then suddenly that familiar world crumbles. The rug is pulled out from under our feet. We have to have experiences like that for our spiritual journey to be meaningful; otherwise we will not be convinced of the nonsubstantial nature of the samsaric world. Instead, we will take the world of everyday life to be real.

With a genuinely constructive form of depression, we become nakedly in touch with our emotions and feelings. We feel a need to make sense of everything, but in new ways. Making sense of everything from the samsaric point of view does not work. All the old beliefs, attitudes, and ways of dealing with things have not worked. One has to evaluate, say and do things differently, experience things differently. That comes from using depression in a constructive fashion.

Depression can be used to curb our natural urges to lose control, to become distracted and outwardly directed, dispersing our energy in all directions. The feeling of depression always reminds us of ourselves; it stops us from becoming lost in our activities, in our experiences of this and that. A genuinely constructive form of depression keeps us vividly in touch with our feelings. In that sense, a modest form of depression is like a state of mental equilibrium.

Everything we experience is normally experienced from an egoistic or narcissistic point of view. But a constructive form of depression takes away the brashness, the security, and the illusory forms of self-confidence that we have. When we are depressed, instead of thinking with such confidence, "I know what is going on, I know where things are at," we are forced to be more observant and to question our assumptions, attitudes, and behavior. That is what we have to do if we are to make progress on the spiritual path.

The individual is then open to new ways of doing things, new and creative ways of thinking. As the Buddhist teachings say, we have to ride with life, we have to evolve. Life itself is a learning process and we can only evolve and learn when we are open. We are open when we question things, and we only question things when we are aware of our inadequacies as much as our abilities. Being aware of what we do not know is more important than being aware of what we do know: if we concentrate on what we do not know, we will always be inquisitive and want to learn. And we want to learn if there is that slight experience of depression, which in Tibetan is called *yid tang skyo pa,* which has the connotation of being tired of all that is unreal, of all that is sham and illusory. The mood of depression can, in fact, propel us forward.

Even though many people who experience depression say that they feel stuck, the feeling of depression can be a motivating force. The Christian mystics used the expression, "dark night of the soul," which means that you have to experience the darkness in order to go forward. You cannot just embark on the mystical journey and expect everything to be hunky-dory. You have to have the experience of the carpet being pulled out from under your feet and you have to experience yourself dangling and questioning, filled with doubts and uncertainties, not knowing what the hell is going on. As Lao Tzu says, "Those who say they know, don't know, and those who say they don't know, know." I suppose he is making a similar kind of point, in that the true intuitive knowledge necessary on the spiritual path comes from doubt, uncertainty, and not knowing. The arrogance of knowing is expiated.

In other words, the spiritual path does not just consist of things that massage the ego or make the ego feel good and comfortable. The ego has to be continuously and repeatedly challenged in order for us to grow spiritually. One of the first things that the ego has to learn is that nothing in this world is stable or absolutely true.

In order to deal with depression effectively, we must cultivate five qualities in our meditation: courage, awareness, joy, love, and compassion. Cultivating courage means that we have to have the willingness to allow ourselves to be in a depressed state. If depression is the state that we find ourselves in, we should not become alarmed and regard it as a sign of something terrible. We have to have the courage not to recoil from our experience but simply allow it to arise. It is not helpful to indulge in negative internal dialogues like, "How long is this depression going to last? Is it going to get worse? How am I going to be able to cope with myself? What will people think of me?" Approaching everything that we experience courageously will result in those experiences having no effect on us: on the contrary, we will become empowered by them.

This sort of courage is based on a fundamental conviction that we are capable of dealing with whatever it is that arises, rather than thinking that somehow or other what arises is going to have an adverse effect on us. When we start to think that our experience is going to affect us adversely, then fear, anxiety, and all of those things come up. But when we are able to say, "Whatever arises is O.K.," we do not have to be so self-protective. By allowing the depressive mood to be there—if that is what comes up—we are showing courage. If we have that kind of courage we are not harmed. More damage is done by hiding behind our illusions and delusions; when we do that, the conflicting emotions become insidious.

Most damage takes place due to lack of courage. This lack of courage is almost like a pathological need to protect ourselves. We think, "I won't be able to handle this, it will be too much. I will be destroyed. I will go crazy." We indulge in all kinds of negative monologues. This is the reason our minds get disturbed, not because we have had such-and-such experience. It is not our experiences but our reactions to them that cause damage. We have to forget about our fear that we will somehow be harmed by our negative experiences. If we concentrate more on the courageous mental act of being able to accommodate and accept, we will provide room for the depressive state of mind to be there and we will no longer react to it with alarm.

Having courage in meditation practice means that there automatically will be awareness there. Awareness means being able to see what is going on. If we do not show courage in our meditation there will be no awareness either, because we will instinctively recoil from our meditative experiences. As soon as something disturbing or unpleasant arises, such as a depressive mood, we will recoil. We have to practice awareness in relation to things that we think of as harmful, as well as the things we regard as innocuous. Through showing courage, we can be aware of what we have allowed ourselves to experience.

Awareness is not a state, but a process: an "aware-ing." All the mental states that arise in the mind are also processes. This is an important thing to notice. Even if you are in a depressed mood, you see that the mood changes—if you are aware. If you are not aware, there is no change, no transmutation, no movement. But if you are aware, you will notice that subtle permutations of change are continuously taking place: you will see that the experience of the depressed mood itself fluctuates. Normally we assume that it is the same depression, but it is never the same. It is always presenting itself differently.

This kind of attention is one of the things that Buddhism encourages us to exercise through the practice of meditation, because not noticing things is what leads us to solidify our experiences. When that solidification takes place, our minds become fixated on things and awareness is instantly dissipated. We are no longer in touch with our own mental state. When we are directly in touch with our mental state, we can see the changing hues of our depressive mood.

One sign of depression is a person's posture. In meditation, we pay attention to our posture. We do not sit with our shoulders slouched, looking defeated and forlorn. It is said that the shoulders should be extended and the chest out, showing some kind of majesty and royal bearing. That has to be included in the practice of awareness.

The way to stay in touch with our mental state is simply by paying attention to what we are experiencing in the moment. But when Buddhists talk about "being in the now," they often think that the "now" has no relevance to the past or the future. That is not true. The way to experience the present moment is not by ignoring the relationship between our present experience and where that experience has come from or where it might be going. The past and the present are embodied in the experiences that we have as human beings. Whatever experiences we have, we have them because of the past; we cannot have an experience that is totally disconnected from our past.

The reason why a particular experience arose in the first place is because of our past. That is the reality of karma. Our present mental state is the product of previous mental states and previous life experiences. In other words, what we are experiencing now is the fruit of what we have experienced in the past. When we pay attention to what we are experiencing now, through awareness, we are able to determine our future karma by making it take a different course. If we do not pay attention, our future karma will not be altered.

Besides courage and awareness, we need to cultivate joy in order to work with depression. Joy here does not mean elation, which is always a bad sign. When we are feeling really high, we crash really hard. In this context, joy means a sense of physical and mental well-being. That is, if we have good experiences in meditation, we do not feel too excited, and if we have bad experiences, we do not feel too down and hopeless. Joy in Tibetan is called *dga' ba*; it means not being like a yo-yo, basically. In either elation or depression, according to the Buddhist teachings, there is no real joy—we are just being swept along by our emotional currents. When we are happy we are so happy—and we become completely overwhelmed by that—and when we are unhappy the emotion is so strong we cannot bear it.

Joy is more about being on an even keel. This does not mean that we cannot sometimes feel really uplifted and joyous. But if we have a joyful disposition—an underlying mental attitude of joy—then we do not completely break down when things do not go our way, or lose it to the other extreme when things go well. Instead there is a sense of equilibrium. The fact is, we do not know what to expect: sometimes things will be wonderful, and other times things will be terrible. But having practiced meditation—having dealt with our depression and other states of mind—there can be that underlying sense of joy.

So dealing with our present situation is the most important thing, according to Buddhism. We should not always be thinking that things should be different, that something else should be happening based on our own wishes. If we stop doing that, we will experience joy.

Along with courage, awareness, and joy, we need love and compassion in order to work with our depression. In Buddhism, love and compassion are related to how we view ourselves and others. When we are depressed, we do not feel worthy of receiving love, let alone giving love. We do not feel worthy of receiving the gift of compassion from others, let alone capable of giving the gift of compassion. But through the practice of meditation on love and compassion—called "mind training" in Buddhism—we begin to realize that we have something to give and that we can give it. When that feeling returns, we feel more connected to other beings.

The gift of love or compassion is in the act of giving itself. We do not have to receive something in return to make these gifts worthwhile. The simple existence of others is what makes them worthwhile, because without others we would be solitary, lonely, cut-off, and miserable people. Life would be far less rich if other people were not part of our world. It is said in the teachings that even people who cause us difficulties help us to grow if we are able to deal with them properly.

Practicing love and compassion—along with courage, awareness, and joy—will keep what Winston Churchill referred to as his "black dog" at bay. That does not mean we will get rid of our depression overnight, but we do not have to. The negative effects of depression will gradually decrease and our ability to make use of depression in a constructive fashion will increase.

If we are able to meditate and learn to develop courage, awareness, joy, love, and compassion, we will grow and depression will dissipate. We do not have to get rid of it—depression will get worn out by itself. That is important. Thinking of depression as an enemy and trying to conquer or overcome it, at least from the Buddhist point of view, is a self-defeating task. Our task in meditation is not to do that, but rather to learn the skills necessary to deal with whatever it is that we are experiencing.

I Don't Want to Kill Bambi

Noah Levine

Noah Levine, wild son of a famous Buddhist writer, is finally disillusioned by his life of booze, violence, and punk rock. Camping alone in the woods, he turns to the gentleness inside he has so long denied.

In 1991 I attended my first meditation retreat with Jack Kornfield and Mary Orr at Mount Madonna Center in Watsonville, California. I chose that retreat because my father, the author Stephen Levine, had told me a lot about Jack and I had read his books. Jack had been a monk in Thailand for several years in his twenties but had been teaching meditation in the West since the early seventies. My father had attended courses with him in the early days and now it was my turn to dive a little deeper into this meditation stuff.

Arriving at the retreat, I was filled with both excitement and fear. I was looking forward to giving my spiritual practice a jump-start but afraid of being bored stiff. It didn't help that I was the only twenty-year-old there and certainly the only punk rocker. Looking around, I didn't see anyone even close to my age. This was my father's scene, not mine. But when the retreat started and we began the sessions of sitting and walking meditation I knew I was in the right place. With my eyes closed and my mind focused on the sensations of breathing, I began to forget about all the differences between me and everyone else.

The retreat was not without its challenges; several times a day I considered leaving, making up all sorts of reasons why I shouldn't be there. It was helpful that Jack had known me since I was a kid. When I introduced myself to him he was very kind and seemed genuinely happy that I was there. Mary was also very supportive. In the interview about my meditation practice I told her I was thinking about leaving early. She said that she understood, that it was natural to want to leave. That she too wanted to leave retreats sometimes but was always happy that she had stayed when they were over. She reminded me that there was only one day left and said that she had faith in me and that she knew I could make it. I believed her. I wasn't so sure about myself, but if she had faith in me that was enough. It turned out that Mary was from Santa Cruz and had a couple of weekly meditation groups. It was good to meet her and nice to know that there were groups I could attend.

After my talk with her I went for a walk and thought about what she had said. I sat down under a huge redwood tree and began to meditate. Her confidence in me gave me confidence in myself. As each breath came and went I let go a little bit more each time, surrendering to the present moment. My mind began to wander to the days of my childhood playing innocently among the redwoods. I was transported to a time in my youth when I had sat down alone in the wood near my house and felt peaceful. I relished the memory or fantasy or whatever it was for a while before bringing my attention back to the present time. I must have sat there for some time because when I opened my eyes it was getting dark. It was time for dinner and then the nightly Dharma talk. In the morning, after breakfast, I could pack up my stuff and get out of there, but for now I was contented to stay till the end.

That night, it was during Jack's Dharma talk about meditation and spiritual life that I got my first sense of inspired purpose. As I sat there listening I began to fantasize about becoming a meditation teacher. It was almost as if I just knew that eventually it would happen. One day I would teach. A quiet sense of direction took me to a place I had never been before.

I knew that even though the retreat had been difficult, I had found a meditation practice that I deeply resonated with. The simplicity of the technique and the profundity of the results had already given me a glimpse of the freedom and happiness I had always been seeking.

After living alone for a while and slowly transitioning out of the whole tough guy/biker/hard-line/Straight Edge identity, I began really getting more involved in a program of addiction recovery. I now focused my time and energy on meditation and service. I ended up moving in with some friends I knew from the program. I was going to lots of meetings and trying to help other alcoholics and drug addicts. I was going to junior college and trying to turn my life toward some kind of career that would be in the helping professions. I decided that working in the medical field would be a good way to give back to society. Through helping people who were sick or injured maybe I could begin to repay my debt to society for all of the damage I had caused in my insanity and addiction.

It was around that time that my friend Darren accidentally killed himself while building a house for himself and his fiancée. The skill saw had slipped off the wood he was cutting and severed the femoral artery in his thigh. He was alone and bled to death fairly quickly. Darren had been sober for a long time and I had known him from the streets from when I was still drinking. When I got sober he was one of the only friendly faces in the program. At his funeral I ran into some of the street punks I hadn't seen in years. Everyone was dealing with the grief in his or her own way. Toby was way high on smack. Johnny, Mark, and Stinky were all drinking beers in the parking lot. Talia and Louie looked like they were doing pretty well, dressed nicely and sitting up front with the family, but I didn't get a chance to talk to them. I was feeling pretty torn up and confused. Although we hadn't been the closest friends, Darren was one of the only kids I knew from the streets who had been in my life consistently since I got clean. When he died I had to question my beliefs and practices. Why would the so-called loving Higher Power take the life of someone like him? Unable to feel my sadness, I got so angry I couldn't even stay at the funeral, so I left early.

I was kind of crazy for a few days after the funeral, annoyed by all of the dramatic attitudes of the people in the meetings who hardly even knew him. I walked out of meetings as I had walked out of his funeral. It took about a week before I could feel the sadness of his loss. It was when I was alone, in my car listening to Suicidal Tendencies, his favorite band, that I began to realize how much I was going to miss him and how much it had meant to me to have him around.

As each of my friends has died, so has a part of me, my past. This time too I was left here to deal with the world and all of life's difficulties. I felt totally alone and friendless, with Toby still getting high and all the others spread out across their lives.

I had grown up in some of the most beautiful and wild areas of this country, the redwood forests of northern California and the high deserts of New Mexico, but I had always preferred to spend my time in town, on the sidewalk. I was never much into camping or hiking; that shit was for tree huggers and cowboys.

When I first got sober and started in on recovery and would hear about serenity, I always equated it with some place outside myself. I had a picture in my mind of a peaceful meadow filled with wildflowers, butterflies, and grazing animals. I felt that peace was for hippies and that as a punk rocker it had been my duty to fight against those passive, useless people, to foster some real changes, or at least to leave a path of destruction so that someone would know I had existed. My vision in those days was to enter a serene meadow with a flame-thrower, smoking a cigarette, and burn down the whole fucking place, destroying everything and killing Bambi.

I was really afraid of what I would find in the quiet moments. I was afraid of being bored and boring. Filled with grief and rage that had fueled years of drug abuse and violence (even in sobriety it was still there), I was afraid of what I might find if I slowed down enough to see what was really behind my negative attitudes and actions.

Yet after having practiced meditation for a while I began to truly experience moments of serenity, and my fear of peace began to lessen. Once I saw that serenity had nothing to do with nature and was simply another state of mind that could be experienced in any surrounding, I became more and more attracted to spending time in the mountains and on the coast. The more my mind began to quiet, the more I found myself wanting to be surrounded by natural beauty. I began taking hikes and spending afternoons on the coastline of northern California, between Santa Cruz and San Francisco, just wandering about offering prayers and practicing meditation.

Just after a retreat with Ajahn Amaro and Sister Sundara, I decided I was ready to do some solitary practice, alone in the wilderness, sitting under a tree like Buddha had.

I packed up my car with a tent, a sleeping bag, some food, and a copy of my father's book, *A Gradual Awakening*, which was my meditation bible at the moment. I was working full-time at the hospital and taking classes at the junior college, so I had only a couple of days to camp. My friends thought I was crazy. "Why would you want to go camping alone?" I was asked. I just said I was going to do some soul-searching or something, and they were like, "Whatever, dude, you're turning into a real fucking hippy." They were right, I was. But I was a lot fucking happier than they were, so fuck it.

I chose big Basin State Park as my destination for that first solo outdoor practice period and adventure, partially because it was close to where I was living in Santa Cruz at the time and partly because it is home to some of the largest and oldest redwood trees in the world. I felt drawn to being in the presence of these ancient trees and figured it would be a safe and inviting place to come to some sort of peace with my fear of being alone in nature.

On the drive up to the mountains I stopped at a small Burmese monastery that was on the way and sat in the shrine room for a few minutes. Before departing I offered some incense to the Buddha image and asked for protection on my journey. My mind was filled with the comment a friend had made about how I was turning into a real fucking hippy. But I knew I was following a path that led to somewhere I had always wanted to be.

As I pulled into the parking lot of the campgrounds, Ice Cube was busting on my stereo, "I ain't the one to get played like poo butt, see I'm from the streets so I know what's up." I turned off the car and jumped out. Before walking over to the ranger's station to reserve a campsite I took a few deep breaths of the fresh mountain air and bent my head back to see the sky through the tops of the redwood trees. NWA was still reverberating in my mind but that was fine; I didn't feel like there was anything incompatible with my love of gangster rap and my spiritual aspirations.

The very cute girl in the ranger station was sweet and helpful. I asked if there were any campsites that were more secluded and she showed me maps of the different available sites. One was located at the very end of the campground, blocked off by a large fallen tree—she said that she had been there and that it was one of the best sites they had.

"I'll take it," I said. For a moment I was tempted to invite her to come with me but I resisted the urge, partially out of fear of rejection but mostly just because I knew I needed to be alone for a couple of days.

Driving from the ranger's station up to the area where my campsite was, I turned off the music, feeling that I had already arrived at my destination and that it was time to begin my practice and start relaxing. Pulling into my parking space, I tensed up, seeing all of the other campers and how close together everyone was packed in. I had come for solitude, not to hear the hillbillies next door getting drunk all night. With more than just a little annoyance, I packed up my gear and made the hike through the very full campsite, past the little kids with peanut butter and jelly smeared across their faces, past the guy with the three cases of beer and the portable radio, past the group of hippies with all the newest North Face camping gear—until, finally, I reached the end of the campground.

For a moment I couldn't even find my spot; every other site I had passed seemed occupied. At the end of the trail where the path began to turn back down toward the parking lot there was a huge fallen redwood on my right and beyond that a hill. After a moment I remembered the map the ranger had shown me and I realized that my site was on the other side of the great big tree. I noticed a small trail that led around the tree. I took it and as I turned the corner I saw my campsite. There was a picnic table, a fire pit, and a large, smooth surface for my tent. I instantly breathed a sigh of relief. Even though there were other campers just a few yards away, at least they were out of sight. I felt like I was really alone but also found some comfort in the fact that I was not too alone.

I began setting up camp. Starting to feel pretty hungry, I pulled out some of the trail mix I'd brought and had a snack. It tasted better than I remembered and I took my time chewing it, recalling the instructions for the eating meditation that I had learned on retreat: chew slowly, taste every mouthful, don't add anything to it. Setting up the tent was the next order of business. I had borrowed the tent from a friend so it was somewhat of a puzzle as to how to put the thing together. I struggled for several minutes, attempting to set the damn thing up. I didn't have a clue about what I was doing. I gave up and searched the carrying bag for the instructions. They were clear and easy to follow; once I knew what to do the tent was set up in a matter of minutes. I faced it toward the mountain to further give myself the sense of being alone with the wilderness.

I unloaded the rest of my pack and stored my clothes neatly in the tent. I put my books on the picnic table and got my food organized for the weekend and then I began to gather some wood for the fire. Once that was done and I was all set up, I sat on the picnic table for a while, surveying the scene, taking in all the sights and sounds. The smell of someone else's campfire was in the air. I realized that this was the first time I had ever set up a tent alone. I had been camping before with friends but this was the only time I had set everything up myself. I felt a moment of pride and had the sense that my life was finally going in the right direction—hoping that all the trouble was behind me. I just wanted to spend the rest of my life trying to help others. All I wanted was to find more of the happiness and satisfaction I had been discovering through spiritual practice.

I picked up *A Gradual Awakening*. It opened at the chapter on daily meditation practice. I realized that in all the busyness of packing and preparing to come camping I had not yet done any meditation that day, not counting my mindful munching on the trail mix. I read a few pages and felt inspired to do some meditation but I also felt pretty hungry—and it was going to get dark soon. So rather than meditate I decided to get the fire going and cook some food.

It was Ramen noodle soup and some fresh vegetables for dinner. I had been attempting to go vegetarian. I was still eating fish sometimes but I had renounced all other flesh foods. I also had some fresh sourdough bread for sandwiches the next day but thought it would go well with my vegetable noodle soup instead. The fire was blazing and I got the water boiling quickly, so I added my carrots, onions, and broccoli. The noodles and soup base went in last and about five minutes later I had a fragrant pot of campfire soup. I let it cool down and then dipped in a piece of bread to get started.

My meal tasted incredibly good. I intentionally ate very slowly, trying to taste every bite and remembering to put the spoon down between each mouthful. Sometime ago my dad had been speaking with me about mindful eating—hadn't he said that he thought it could be as powerful a practice as sitting meditation? The taste of the noodle soup under the evening sky certainly brought me into the present moment as much as paying attention to my breath ever had.

I was just about finished eating and the twilight was well set in. Something was moving nearby, rustling in the bushes on the hillside above me. I looked up and saw a deer, carefully picking its way down the slope. I became very still, sitting, watching the deer as she continued her walk down the hillside. She stopped a couple of times to nibble at some leaves or to straighten up, lifting her head to listen for the sound of a possible predator.

My mind was strangely calm—I was amazed at the sight of the lone deer moving toward my camp. I had never been so close to a wild animal before. A couple of experiences I had as a kid flashed into consciousness: smelling the stench of deer jerky hanging to dry in the garage of our neighbor's house in Santa Fe when I was seven and, when I was eleven, being sickened by the sight of a deer killed and gutted by my friend Ricky's father in Colorado. Now, looking at that exquisite, delicate, living being that was almost at my tent, those disturbing memories evaporated.

It seemed like she was playing some sort of game, to see how close she could get without freaking out and running off. I sat as still as I possibly could, watching and waiting to see when she would realize that I was sitting there, then turn and take off, back up the hill to find the rest of her family. She continued past my tent, sniffing around while carefully avoiding the fire pit, then walked right up to the table where I was sitting. She was only a couple of feet away. She stopped and looked directly at me. For a moment I had no idea what to do; I was mesmerized by the dreamlike experience of being face-to-face with this being. Then, very slowly, I picked up a piece of bread and held it out—my palm was flat and the bread just sat there as an offering on my outstretched hand.

She tensed for a moment, but instead of making a break for it, she took a step forward and her wide eyes relaxed. She sniffed at the piece right before me, within arm's reach. She began to nibble on the bread in the palm of my hand. I could feel her little lips scraping my hand as she ate. I was perfectly still but my heart was racing with excitement by then. I was amazed at the unfolding of the scenario—I couldn't believe that it was happening to me, of all people.

I decided to try to take a step further. Slowly, I reached up with my other hand and lightly touched her head and nose. She continued to eat, not seeming to mind or even really notice that I was stroking her gently between the eyes. They sparkled in the dim light and her fur felt silky. I tried to pet her ears as well but she shook her head.

She finished eating her piece of bread and, without even looking at me again, walked off, just as slowly as she had approached. I watched her until she disappeared over the crest of the hill.

For a long time I sat contemplating what had just happened, wondering what to do next. I found myself making up all kinds of elaborate fantasies: that she must have been sent by God to tell me that everything was going to be all right; that I had been forgiven for all of my early life's violence against nature.

Later that night when I was tucked snugly into my sleeping bag I reflected on the stories my father had told me of Ram and Sita when I was a child, and I remembered that tale of the evil Demon King Ravana, who had one of his sidekicks turn himself into a golden deer to lure Ram and Laxman away from Sita so that she could be kidnapped.

I recalled the childhood stories of Bambi and Thumper—and how I had taken to saying I wanted to burn the fields of serenity and kill Bambi. No! I didn't what to kill Bambi anymore, I didn't want to kill anything anymore, I just wanted to live my life and let go of the past.

How We Get Hooked

Pema Chödrön

The American nun Pema Chödrön is famed for her teachings on how to find the wisdom in difficult states of mind. When we experience fear, discomfort, or uncertainty, she tells us to find the courage to stay with it, because in the long run the real suffering comes from attempting to escape. In this teaching, she offers a clear diagnosis of how we trap ourselves into further suffering and how we can break the pattern.

You're trying to make a point with a coworker or your partner. At one moment her face is open and she's listening, and at the next, her eyes cloud over or her jaw tenses.

What is it that you're seeing?

Someone criticizes you. They criticize your work or your appearance or your child. At moments like that, what is it you feel? It has a familiar taste in your mouth, it has a familiar smell. Once you begin to notice it, you feel like this experience has been happening forever.

The Tibetan word for this is *shenpa.* It is usually translated as *attachment,* but a more descriptive translation might be *hooked.* When shenpa hooks us, we're likely to get stuck. We could call shenpa "that sticky feeling." It's an everyday experience. Even a spot on your new sweater can take you there. At the subtlest level, we feel a tightening, a tensing, a sense of closing down. Then we feel a sense of withdrawing, not wanting to be where we are. That's the hooked quality. That tight feeling has the power to hook us into self-denigration, blame, anger, jealousy, and other emotions that lead to words and actions that end up poisoning us.

Remember the fairy tale in which toads hop out of the princess's mouth whenever she starts to say mean words? That's how being hooked can feel. Yet we don't stop—we can't stop—because we're in the habit of associating whatever we're doing with relief from our own discomfort. This is the shenpa syndrome. The word *attachment* doesn't quite translate what's happening. It's a quality of experience that's not easy to describe but which everyone knows well. Shenpa is usually involuntary and it gets right to the root of why we suffer.

Someone looks at us in a certain way, or we hear a certain song, we smell a certain smell, we walk into a certain room and boom. The feeling has nothing to do with the present, and nevertheless, there it is. When we were practicing recognizing shenpa at Gampo Abbey, we discovered that some of us could feel it even when a particular person simply sat down next to us at the dining table.

Shenpa thrives on the underlying insecurity of living in a world that is always changing. We experience this insecurity as a background of slight unease or restlessness. We all want some kind of relief from that unease, so we turn to what we enjoy—food, alcohol, drugs, sex, work, or shopping. In moderation what we enjoy might be very delightful. We can appreciate its taste and its presence in our life. But when we empower it with the idea that it will bring us comfort, that it will remove our unease, we get hooked.

So we could also call shenpa *the urge*—the urge to smoke that cigarette, to overeat, to have another drink, to indulge our addiction, whatever it is. Sometimes shenpa is so strong that we're willing to die getting this short-term symptomatic relief. The momentum behind the urge is so strong that we never pull out of the habitual pattern of turning to poison for comfort. It doesn't necessarily have to involve a substance; it can be saying mean things, or approaching everything with a critical mind. That's a major hook. Something triggers an old pattern we'd rather not feel, and we tighten up and hook into criticizing or complaining. It gives us a puffed-up satisfaction and a feeling of control that provides short-term relief from uneasiness.

Those of us with strong addictions know that working with habitual patterns begins with the willingness to fully acknowledge our urge, and then the willingness not to act on it. This business of not acting out is called refraining. Traditionally it's called renunciation. What we renounce or refrain from isn't food, sex, work, or relationships per se. We renounce and refrain from the shenpa. When we talk about refraining from the shenpa, we're not talking about trying to cast it out; we're talking about trying to see the shenpa clearly and experiencing it. If we can see shenpa just as we're starting to close down, when we feel the tightening, there's the possibility of catching the urge to do the habitual thing, and not doing it.

Without meditation practice, this is almost impossible to do. Generally speaking, we don't catch the tightening until we've indulged the urge to scratch our itch in some habitual way. And unless we equate refraining with loving-kindness and friendliness towards ourselves, refraining feels like putting on a straitjacket. We struggle against it. The Tibetan word for renunciation is *shenlok*, which means turning shenpa upside-down, shaking it up. When we feel the tightening, somehow we have to know how to open up the space without getting hooked into our habitual pattern.

In practicing with shenpa, first we try to recognize it. The best place to do this is on the meditation cushion. Sitting practice teaches us how to open and relax to whatever arises, without picking and choosing. It teaches us to experience the uneasiness and the urge fully, and to interrupt the momentum that usually follows. We do this by not following after the thoughts and learning to come back to the present moment. We learn to stay with the uneasiness, the tightening, the itch of shenpa. We train in sitting still with our desire to scratch. This is how we learn to stop the chain reaction of habitual patterns that otherwise will rule our lives. This is how we weaken the patterns that keep us hooked into discomfort that we mistake as comfort. We label the spinoff "thinking" and return to the present moment. Yet even in meditation, we experience shenpa.

Let's say, for example, that in meditation you felt settled and open. Thoughts came and went, but they didn't hook you. They were like clouds in the sky that dissolved when you acknowledged them. You were able to return to the moment without a sense of struggle. Afterwards, you're hooked on that very pleasant experience: "I did it right, I got it right. That's how it should always be, that's the model." Getting caught like that builds arrogance, and conversely it builds poverty, because your next session is nothing like that. In fact, your "bad" session is even worse now because you're hooked on the "good" one. You sat there and you were discursive: you were obsessing about something at home, at work. You worried and you fretted; you got caught up in fear or anger. At the end of the session, you feel discouraged—it was "bad," and there's only you to blame.

Is there something inherently wrong or right with either meditation experience? Only the shenpa. The shenpa we feel toward "good" meditation hooks us into how it's "supposed" to be, and that sets us up for shenpa towards how it's not "supposed" to be. Yet the meditation is just what it is. We get caught in our idea of it: that's the shenpa. That stickiness is the root shenpa. We call it ego-clinging or self-absorption. When we're hooked on the idea of good experience, self-absorption gets stronger; when we're hooked on the idea of bad experience, self-absorption gets stronger. This is why we, as practitioners, are taught not to judge ourselves, not to get caught in good or bad.

What we really need to do is address things just as they are. Learning to recognize shenpa teaches us the meaning of not being attached to this world. Not being attached has nothing to do with this world. It has to do with shenpa—being hooked by what we associate with comfort. All we're trying to do is not to feel our uneasiness. But when we do this we never get to the root of practice. The root is experiencing the itch as well as the urge to scratch, and then not acting it out.

If we're willing to practice this way over time, *prajna* begins to kick in. Prajna is clear seeing. It's our innate intelligence, our wisdom. With prajna, we begin to see the whole chain reaction clearly. As we practice, this wisdom becomes a stronger force than shenpa. That in itself has the power to stop the chain reaction.

Prajna isn't ego-involved. It's wisdom found in basic goodness, openness, equanimity—which cuts through self-absorption. With prajna we can see what will open up space. Habituation, which is ego-based, is just the opposite—a compulsion to fill up space in our own particular style. Some of us close space by hammering our point through; others do it by trying to smooth the waters.

We're taught that whatever arises is fresh, the essence of realization. That's the basic view. But how do we see whatever arises as the essence of realization when the fact of the matter is, we have work to do? The key is to look into shenpa. The work we have to do is about coming to know that we're tensing or hooked or "all worked up." That's the essence of realization. The earlier we catch it, the easier shenpa is to work with, but even catching it when we're already all worked up is good. Sometimes we have to go through the whole cycle even though we see what we're doing. The urge is so strong, the hook so sharp, the habitual pattern so sticky, that there are times when we can't do anything about it.

There is something we can do after the fact, however. We can go sit on the meditation cushion and re-run the story. Maybe we start with remembering the all-worked-up feeling and get in touch with that. We look clearly at the shenpa in retrospect; this is very helpful. It's also helpful to see shenpa arising in little ways, where the hook is not so sharp.

Buddhists are talking about shenpa when they say, "Don't get caught in the content: observe the underlying quality—the clinging, the desire, the attachment." Sitting meditation teaches us how to see that tangent before we go off on it. It basically comes down to the instruction, "label it thinking." To train in this on the cushion, where it's relatively easy and pleasant to do, is how we can prepare ourselves to stay when we get all worked up.

Then we can train in seeing shenpa wherever we are. Say something to another person and maybe you'll feel that tensing. Rather than get caught in a story line about how right you are or how wrong you are, take it as an opportunity to be present with the hooked quality. Use it as an opportunity to stay with the tightness without acting upon it. Let that training be your base.

You can also practice recognizing shenpa out in nature. Practice sitting still and catching the moment when you close down. Or practice in a crowd, watching one person at a time. When you're silent, what hooks you is mental dialogue. You talk to yourself about badness or goodness: me-bad or they-bad, this-right or that-wrong. Just to see this is a practice. You'll be intrigued by how you'll involuntarily shut down and get hooked, one way or another. Just keep labeling those thoughts and come back to the immediacy of the feeling. That's how not to follow the chain reaction.

Once we're aware of shenpa, we begin to notice it in other people. We see them shutting down. We see that they've been hooked and that nothing is going to get through to them now. At that moment we have prajna. That basic intelligence comes through when we're not caught up in escaping from our own unease. With prajna we can see what's happening with others; we can see when they've been hooked. Then we can give the situation some space. One way to do that is by opening up the space on the spot, through meditation. Be quiet and place your mind on your breath. Hold your mind in place with great openness and curiosity toward the other person. Asking a question is another way of creating space around that sticky feeling. So is postponing your discussion to another time.

At Gampo Abbey, we're very fortunate that everybody is excited about working with shenpa. So many words I've tried using become ammunition that people use against themselves. But we feel some kind of gladness about working with shenpa, perhaps because the word is unfamiliar. We can acknowledge what's happening with clear seeing, without aiming it at ourselves. Since no one particularly likes to have his shenpa pointed out, people at the abbey make deals like, "When you see me getting hooked, just pull your earlobe, and if I see you getting hooked, I'll do the same. Or if you see it in yourself, and I'm not picking up on it, at least give some little sign that maybe this isn't the time to continue this discussion." This is how we help each other cultivate prajna, clear seeing.

We could think of this whole process in terms of four R's: recognizing the shenpa, refraining from scratching, relaxing into the underlying urge to scratch, and then resolving to continue to interrupt our habitual patterns like this for the rest of our lives. What do you do when you don't do the habitual thing? You're left with your urge. That's how you become more in touch with the craving and the wanting to move away. You learn to relax with it. Then you resolve to keep practicing this way.

Working with shenpa softens us up. Once we see how we get hooked and how we get swept along by the momentum, there's no way to be arrogant. The trick is to keep seeing. Don't let the softening and humility turn into self-denigration. That's just another hook. Because we've been strengthening the whole habituated situation for a long, long time, we can't expect to undo it overnight. It's not a one-shot deal. It takes lovingkindness to recognize; it takes practice to refrain; it takes willingness to relax; it takes determination to keep training this way. It helps to remember that we may experience two billion kinds of itches and seven quadrillion types of scratching, but there is really only one root shenpa—ego-clinging. We experience it as tightening and self-absorption. It has degrees of intensity. The branch shenpas are all our different styles of scratching that itch.

I recently saw a cartoon of three fish swimming around a hook. One fish is saying to the other, "The secret is non-attachment." That's a shenpa cartoon: the secret is—don't bite that hook. If we can catch ourselves at that place where the urge to bite is strong, we can at least get a bigger perspective on what's happening. As we practice this way, we gain confidence in our own wisdom. It begins to guide us toward the fundamental aspect of our being—spaciousness, warmth, and spontaneity.

Empty Your Cup

Dennis Genpo Merzel

Is your teacup full? Is your head full to the brim with concepts, thoughts, and opinions? Then it's time to empty it, because Zen teacher Dennis Genpo Merzel says that it's only our ideas that block us from realizing our true Self and fulfilling our potential as human beings.

For some of us, it can take years to clarify why we are practicing Zen and what the real issue is. I have been sitting for more than thirty years—just a short time as this practice goes—but it has been long enough for me to see that the problem we encounter at the beginning is still a problem after practicing for more than a quarter century. Always, the problem is our ideas. Our ideas and concepts are endless, and yet we can become very attached to them. We would rather die than let go of some of our favorites.

Maybe you've heard the tale of the American professor who went to Japan to meet with a Zen master. When at last he was received into the teacher's quarters, the professor announced, "I've come to see you because I would really like to practice here and attain enlightenment." The teacher didn't say anything. He simply went on serving tea. He poured the professor's cup full and just kept pouring. The professor cried, "Wait, wait, stop! My cup is full!" The master replied, "Then empty your cup." This is the first teaching in Zen. It is also the last.

In the Yiddish, Dutch, and Polish languages, the word for *cup* also means "head." So "empty your cup" can also mean "empty your head"—and this is the point of the story. How can we empty our mind so that it becomes like an empty cup, open and receptive? If we want to accomplish the Way, this is a very important question.

Recently I read a book by a Theravadin master who works with both Asian and Western students. Based on his experience, he believes that attachment to ideas is the most difficult issue for students, regardless of where they come from. Helping students give up their attachment to ideas is probably one of the most challenging tasks we teachers encounter. The most difficult ideas to drop are usually the ones that seem most profound, the ones that we feel righteous about. These ideas might not be working for us anymore, but we cherish them anyway. They might be causing suffering for others or ourselves, but we will find something else to blame. We will do almost anything to avoid letting go of our precious ideas, even though they have become our prison.

My mother was quite ill for several years before she died, and sometimes she struggled with confusion. One night she phoned me in a panic and said, "I've lost myself! I can't find myself!" Against my better judgment, I congratulated her and said, "There is no self, Mom! What did you really lose?" She told me not to be so cute. And she was right, I shouldn't make light of it. The self is our heaviest burden and the burden that we are most afraid to lose.

Some of my juiciest, best, and most tender moments of sitting occur just before I give a talk. I let go of my thoughts and just sit, taking in the presence of the group and seeing what comes up as a topic. When we sit in zazen and really let go of the self, we experience what Dogen Zenji described as "dropped off body and mind"—clear awareness, not filtered or colored by the notions and concerns of the self. Freedom from the tyranny of the small self is something each of us can accomplish through practice. Only our ideas block us from realizing our true Self and fulfilling our potential as human beings.

Everyone resists dropping their ideas, and we can practice for many years without ever realizing our true Self. We fear letting go of the very ideas that limit us. We may see that an idea is confining and restricting and yet still cling to it. We can help ourselves by asking, "What do I really need to give up in order to accomplish the Way?" One thought that might occur to you is something we've all heard: to accomplish the Way, we have to give our life to the Dharma. But what does that mean? Just what is being given up, and to whom? And really, who wants your life? To anyone else, it would be excess baggage.

When we sit with the question "What do I need to lose in order to accomplish the Way?" we can come up with all kinds of interesting answers. We need to watch out, though, because the mind is very cunning. We can be stupid in every other aspect of our life, but when it comes to deceiving ourselves, the mind has no equal. Our mind can generate a laundry list of ideas about what it would take, but if we examine them, we will see that they are only excuses. We don't need to give up our families or our jobs, our lifestyle or our culture, to accomplish the Buddha Way. We only have to let go of the self.

The real question is, what stops us from letting go of the self? If the self is just a bunch of ideas, why do we find it so hard to drop? Again, we can come up with all kinds of reasons and excuses. "I'm too old. I can't sit like the young people." Or maybe, "I can't do it because I'm a man. Women have a better chance. They aren't as stubborn." We may laugh, but a lot of us men think like that. I've heard some women complain that men have it easier because men are more confident. We can think that we're too young, that we haven't practiced long enough, that we don't have the time, or that our lives are just too complicated. We are all experts at finding excuses about why we can't let go of the self. But the truth is, nothing really blocks any of us from dropping off body and mind and letting go of the self.

We create our own barriers to realizing our true Self. Bassui called it halfhearted effort. Rinzai called it lack of faith. It's hard to admit that maybe we don't want it badly enough or that we don't have enough faith to stick with our practice. No one likes to face those possibilities. Still, we need to ask ourselves just how far we want to go with our practice. To really accomplish the Way takes a lot of time and energy, and that means taking time away from other parts of our lives. We're only deceiving ourselves when we put the blame somewhere else. We have to take responsibility for ourselves and our practice. The implications are serious and far-reaching. It boils down to taking responsibility for our lives.

Whether we realize it or not, every moment of every day, we are creating our future, our destiny, our karma. What we have created is waiting for us in the next moment. We come to this practice because we want to become more conscious, and that means waking up—seeing how we are creating our karma every moment and taking responsibility for it. A wonderful and profound shift takes place when we do that: we develop deep appreciation for our lives. Our eyes open up to the amazing truth that everything is the Dharma, and every moment is the teaching. *This is it!* Nirvana is not in the future, and paradise is not somewhere else. Right here, this very moment, *is* the time and place. As my son, Tai, often says, "It doesn't get any better than this!"

If right here and now is it, how can we truly appreciate that? The secret is to travel light: we need to keep dropping our ego, our ideas, and our concepts. We also need to keep facing our fear. We don't need to get rid of fear; we only need to learn how to work with it. The best way to work with fear is to let it be.

When we sit with our fear and really look at it, we can see it for what it is: just another concept. At first, we might worry that our fear will overwhelm us; but if we continue to sit with it, we will see that fear really has no substance. Then, as fear begins to lose its power over us, we can begin to see the irony of it all: the concept of fear is used by the ego to protect another concept—our most valuable concept—the idea of self.

You and I need to empty our own cups; no one can do it for us. It only takes a moment to drop the self, but it must be a moment of complete, wholehearted effort. We have to face our fear and be willing to let go. In order to muster the drive and commitment to do it, we first have to become tired of the burden of self, really hungry for liberation. The key to accomplishing the Way and realizing our true Self rests in our own hands.

Annie Mirror Heart 

Maura O'Halloran

In 1979, a young Irish American woman named Maura O'Halloran left her waitressing job in Boston to study Zen in Japan. She was one of those rare people whom you know—without needing to be told—accomplished something real in their Buddhist practice. Her story is made only more poignant by her death at the age of just twenty-seven. Before she died, Maura O'Halloran started to write a novel, a lightly fictionalized account of her travels. In this, its only chapter, she tells the story of her difficult first months in the monastery.

It was dusk when she arrived. She walked from the station through the village to the outskirts where the temple lay. She didn't know anyone where she was headed, and not a word of the language. With each step closer, the urge to turn and run became greater.

The temple steps were steep and she had to stoop to pass through the entrance. This humbling posture robbed her of her remaining confidence. The temple was silent, self-contained, awesome. She stood just inside the gate and clutched her small bundle of possessions, her one familiar token in an unknown world. She began to shiver in the evening chill. A dim light flickered on, and she marched quickly toward it. She stumbled and her bundle rolled from her arms. She tried not to cry.

She reached the light and entered a dim room where a little monk was flinging papers about, shuffling and muttering in excited Japanese.

"I'm Annie Shaw," she said. "I'm expected."

The monk's black, pajama-like robes flapped around him as he searched under the desk and on top of shelves. "Ah!" he shouted, and banged a paper on the desk before her. On it, penned in a childish scrawl, was, "Please come this way." He peered at it, straining to pronounce it: "Pleezu kumu deesu waiyu."

Then he was off, waving the paper before her nose like a carrot before a donkey, and making gestures that to a Westerner looked like "go away," but obviously meant "follow me." Stumbling through the narrow, dark maze, she felt like Alice chasing the Mad Hatter. The little monk, whose name was Hogen, was still shuffling and mumbling, "Pleezu kumu deesu waiyu." After pulling and straining at a door swollen in its tracks, he slid it open to reveal her room.

Hogen looked proud. He had cleaned the room himself, Annie learned later, in anticipation of the lady foreigner. He had scoured the temple to find a spare desk with legs aligned and had chosen the prettiest cushion cover he could find. It was floral, with huge magenta roses.

With a majestic sweep of his arm, he ushered her into her new abode. "Oh my God," she thought. "It hasn't got a window and I won't be able to stretch my legs out across it." She wanted to collapse into an armchair or onto a bed, but there was only a hideous magenta cushion and a Spartan plywood desk. The dinner bell sounded, and before the full horror of the room engulfed her, Hogen whisked her back into the black of the temple labyrinth.

He led her to a large, bare room, furnished only with eight identical benches. Two monks were watching her shyly. "How are yoo?" "You berry welcome," they said, and tittered. With the sound of clappers, they grabbed their *oryoki* sets [stacked and cloth-wrapped eating bowls]. Hogen gave her a similar parcel and indicated that she should imitate him.

The monks sat and unwrapped their sets in inhuman quiet. Two bowls, a tiny side plate, a pair of chopsticks and a cloth square were all wrapped in another square like an Oriental version of the mess kit she used in the Girl Scouts. Hogen demonstrated how to place the bowls so that contact with the bare wood of the bench made no noise. The formalities involved in just passing one's bowls for rice and soup seemed insurmountable—the order fixed, the bowls specified: three fingers, the right hand, wipe before passing, on to the palm, *gassho* [hand gesture with palms placed together], soup on the right, rice on the left, chopsticks point towards you, make an offering, seven grains of rice. Wait for the clackers. And they were off.

She was incredulous. They were guzzling their food with the frenzy of savages, yet making not a sound except for a stray chopstick accidentally grazing a tooth. She had expected them to eat as if seeking to become one with each grain, to chew the universe and swallow the cosmos.

She chewed her rice thoroughly, even meditatively, she told herself. Looking to Hogen for reassurance she picked up her side plate with a little mound of brown slime on it. Greasy, oozy, it tasted lethal. She had been faring reasonably well with her chopsticks up to that point, but the viscous mess slid round her plate, resisting every attempt to be scooped or speared.

Now from the corner of her eye she could see them passing hot water, pouring, filling their bowls. Hogen was urging her to finish, yet still the slime escaped her, dripping and plopping through the sticks. Try the rice. That was gluier and by holding the bowl near her chin, she could shovel it in efficiently. Now they were wrapping the bowls. At least her rice was nearly gone. She tried to stand when they sprang to their feet, holding their neatly wrapped bowls, but Hogen pushed her back down. She felt like a dunce in the corner. They were wiping the benches.

"Good evening," said a voice in a recognizable tongue. "Why don't you just pick it up and knock it back?" And now she really could have cried. "I'm Shonen, Go Roshi's son. You must be Annie."

Patiently, he showed her how to eat every grain of rice, how to wash the oryoki set by pouring the water from bowl to bowl, how she should drink the water in order to waste nothing. Finally came the elaborate bowing and the folding involved in rewrapping the wretched things.

Shonen invited her to his room for green tea and dried rice cakes, and she was grateful for the gesture. His room was tiny, scarcely bigger than her own hole, but bursting with books, manuscripts, and reams of practice calligraphy strewn in an arc around the desk. From the corners of the bookcases iron nails protruded at unexpected angles, displaying wrinkled robes drooping in baggy folds.

He struck a match, then lit a stick of incense and a cigarette. Casually he stuck the incense in a brass bowl in front of a plastic Buddha, and drew on his cigarette. From outside came a voice. He bolted upright and quenched the cigarette. But it was only Hogen, who gently slid the door open, peeped inside, and grinned. Shonen threw the cigarette at him. With a loud laugh Hogen thanked him and lit it himself.

They began to chatter animatedly in Japanese. She heard her name mentioned often but was content just to lean against the bookshelf and observe. They looked comical. Two round, bald heads nodding, living a fourteenth-century existence enveloped in clouds of smoke from king-sized tobacco sticks. The monks reminded her of schoolboys puffing in the bathroom. They became giggly as they discussed her. This blue-eyed woman was to become a monk in a mountain temple of remote northern Japan. Unbelievable!

It was only seven o'clock, but to Annie it felt like midnight. She groped her way back to her cell, where she dragged out the damp-smelling futons and piled on a heavy wad of assorted bedding. Already fully dressed, she added a woolly hat and scarf and hauled the bulky spreads over her body. She wondered if she could even turn over under the weight. She stared at the void where the ceiling must be, and in her stomach she felt a hole as black as the void above her.

Did she have any idea what she was undertaking here? Yet gazing into that void, she felt that somehow her whole life had been leading up to this moment. It was no accident that she had stumbled upon a reference to this remote monastery. It was something that sooner or later she had to do. She must try. She must really throw herself into this. Still, she thought, what wouldn't she give right at this moment to be seated in front of an open fire with a whiskey in her hand?

Morning came quickly, insistent and cold. Bells were ringing. Sleepy, she tried to dismiss them, but Hogen was at the door, reading from a scrap of paper that said, "I show you get dressed." He was making squealing noises and was obviously in a hurry. When she still couldn't understand, he started dragging her clothes off. Her first reflex was to belt him but she reasoned that he'd hardly threaten her virtue at five o'clock in the morning in a bustling monastery. She was further reassured by the sounds of washing and toothbrushing just outside.

Hogen pulled a parcel in from the corridor and shook out a kimono, gesturing that she should put it on. He showed her how the right side slipped under the left, then how to loop it up with various strings, and make sure not to let the lapels bag. This, he emphasized, was most important, but it seemed to her just another ridiculous triviality. Still, she chuckled at the idea of a man dressing her so platonically, even maternally. As he patted the lapels flat on her chest it was apparently without consciousness that this was a woman's chest. Could there really be some corner on the earth where she might be free of her sex?

The first few days seemed eternal and she doubted each day whether she could survive until the next. The year she had promised herself seemed unthinkable. While everything was new, there was still a depressing absence of stimulation. Nothing really happened. She was cold and bored and ravenously hungry. There were no heaters and it was December. She could never finish her meals on time so she took only minute portions.

Today she was up at five to splash her face in the icy water of an outdoor basin, then wash by the light of the moon. Next came the frenetic morning exercises, everyone roaring the count together. By half past six she found herself outdoors, sweeping the grounds. She stared at the raw red of her toes, like so many frozen sausages around the thongs of her sandals. Perched on those wooden platforms and in dawn's grey light, she could have been a geisha stepping down from her carriage after a night's work, not a *gaijin* [foreigner] with a bamboo twig stabbing listlessly at fallen leaves. She wanted out.

"That's all wrong." She was startled to hear a curt Japanese accent. "Sweep like this." The monk demonstrated jerky little side whips with all the motion in the twig, the handle almost rigid.

"There is a Zen way to sweep?" she muttered to herself. "I wonder if there is a Zen way to knock your arrogant block off."

A Zen way to sweep—this was truly humiliating. Upstairs she had tried to dust the meditation hall, and the first swipe of the duster had ripped a hole in the shoji screen. Then she had swept against the grain of the *tatami* [straw-mat floor covering], instead of up and down. She seemed to do everything wrong.

On her fifth day they told her she would have her ceremony soon. Up to that time she had only seen Go Roshi at meals. He looked at his food; he ate his food. He bowed to them; they bowed to him. He went to his room, where she could hear a television blaring.

What kind of man was he? She knew something of his story. He and his twin brother had been the oldest in a large farming family. His brother was destined to take over the farm and Roshi to become a priest. When he was about eleven years old, his twin was accidentally shot. It was no one's fault, but Roshi was then expected to inherit the farm and fulfill his filial duties. He protested that he still wanted to be a priest. They refused to let him go. He chopped off his finger to show his earnestness. They still refused. So he ran away from home, a terrible disgrace. He took to the roads, not yet a teenager, wandering and chanting all the while [the Buddhist mantra] *Namu myoho renge kyo.* He roamed around the country questioning various Zen masters on the meaning of life and death. Finally he went to Daiko Roshi, who said, "When apples are ripe and falling from their branches, what will you do?" "Gather them," he said. Daiko gave him a basket and showed him to the orchard. He remained for thirty-five years.

The clock struck eight as he walked in. The monks sat in two rows. The lights were off and the shoji was open, allowing harsh winter sunshine to stream across the passage and onto the benches. It lit Go Roshi's face. He was speaking animatedly, and as he laughed, his heavily repaired teeth glinted golden. She thought of him at twelve years old, alone, on pilgrimage. It made this venture into Zen seem all the less probable for an ordinary person like herself. The little finger of his left hand was a stub.

He mentioned her name several times during his talk. No one translated. He stopped speaking, stared at her, laughed, and addressed her in English. She was flabbergasted. She thought he knew no English. "Your ceremony will be in a few days. Are you ready?"

"What ceremony?" she asked.

"You become priest ceremony," he said.

She knew this would come sooner or later but she had thought it would be later. "Well, I mean, don't I have to know something? Believe things?"

"No, the less you know and believe the better."

"But does it mean I can never leave?"

"No, leave when you please."

"But, I mean, what do I promise?"

"I only ask that you request permission for outings."

This was mystifying. A priest with no beliefs or commitments? What was a priest, anyway?

"Well," she said, "I suppose I'm ready then."

Go Roshi clapped his hands in childish glee and dragged a huge cardboard box from behind the shoji. He unwrapped it slowly, with the precision of someone dismantling a bomb. He wound up the string and tucked it in his sleeve. Then he presented her with her robes and told her to go out and try them on.

To her it felt like Christmas and playing dress-up, all rolled into one. Barefoot, swathed in the long, silk kimono, she floated back and forth the length of the corridor. Hogen transformed himself into a photographer, focusing and clicking his imaginary camera to record the latest in temple fashions. The silent, empty corridors echoed with their laughter.

Then Go Roshi went away for a few days and she felt miserable again. The lack of communication felt like a darkness around her, as if her entire world had sunk in on her. The monks tried to talk to her, consulting their dictionaries. They said they felt comfortable with her, then conferred for the right words to tell her they were glad she had come to Shodoji. She felt a real affection for them, yet they seemed so totally foreign and unreachable. They treated her kindly, but could they possibly conceive of who she was and the world from which she came?

On the day scheduled for the ceremony, Shonen came to her room and told her to wear the white kimono. "But your hair . . ." he said. "No one has shaved your head yet." Her thick, dark hair had always been a source of pride for her. "Shave your head, O.K.?" Shonen said. "Hurry up, O.K.?"

"Yes, fine," she said. "It's a nuisance anyway."

"Ah so," Shonen said. "You not usual woman." That made her laugh and she found that she felt quite cheerful about it.

Shonen began with the clippers. Her long locks looked so forlorn, strewn on the wood. Now her head felt light. She touched it, naked and bristling. Shonen gathered the locks up, still in a hurry. She could only stare at herself in the mirror. So much for bravado. Shonen paused for a long stare. "It suits you," he said. "But you are not usual woman."

He doesn't know that she doesn't even feel like a woman anymore.

"Please, fast, fast," he said. "You now become a priest. In ceremony, repeat after me Japanese words."

"But Shonen-san," she said, "What do they mean? I must know what I'm saying. This is so important."

"No, Miss Annie, words are not important. You cannot really make promise, for you are not free. Do ceremony now and you begin life, where promise will naturally become itself. Come. Come. Never mind. Words are only words."

"Well, why the hell do the ceremony?" she thought. She could feel herself beginning to get angry. The Buddha is not a god, but the place teems with statues and altars to him. Why all the formalities and petty regulations, if one is supposed to become free? So much foolish ritual and bowing. She was getting cross. She rubbed her bald head. A small voice inside advised that she'd get nowhere by endless questioning and rejecting. The way to understand this thing is not by analysis but by immersion. But she knew that immersion sometimes results in drowning.

The meditation hall smelled of straw mats and incense. She breathed it deeply and felt calmed. She decided to avert her eyes from the gaudy altar and the huge vases of fake flowers. She could see no beauty in the statues. They were looming, grotesque, with their rows of candles and offerings. It felt like a pagan mockery of the Catholic churches of her childhood. She felt she had stumbled once again into the religious world she had left behind.

Shonen was signaling her to prostrate herself before the images. Somehow she managed. The ceremony seemed a blur. She remembered repeating in a whisper Shonen's cues. Roshi was waving something that looked like a horse's tail in her face and chanting. Everyone joined in, voices loud, the drum pounding, primitive. Their huge voices were booming with wild energy and it unnerved her. Roshi gave her a paper with elaborate *kanji* [the characters used in Japanese writing] and intricate folding. The horsetail was waving again.

The shouting finally ended. She felt faint. Now she was a Buddhist priest, although no one would tell her what that meant. They went downstairs for tea. Her new priestly name meant "Mirror Heart." Everyone said this was a good name, but they continued to call her Annie.

A monk named Mochian was smiling. "One moment pleez." He rooted through the sleeves of his robes and thrust a bar of chocolate into her hands. "*Omedeto gozaimasu.*" He bowed his head to the floor. Shonen translated this as "Congratulations," then continued, "You will make excellent priest. I very happy you do us the favor become this temple priest. We grateful. Thank you. You give pure energy."

This was embarrassing. She felt like a hypocrite.

The ceremony over, it was time for work again. She went up to the third floor and climbed over the huge Buddha, dusting and polishing him. She wore five layers of undershirts and sweaters but still felt chilled to her bones. The Buddha was not smiling, only enormous and awesome. She shuddered at the prospect of wringing the rag in icy water to wash the altars and floors.

Cleaning before breakfast was even worse. For this she began at one end of the corridor with a wet rag, hands on the cloth, hips high in the air, and ran down the passage with her weight on the wet cloth. It was effective but she was running in the smear of the water, which instantly began to ice. Her feet froze and stuck as she ran. Each step felt like the sensation of ripping a Band-Aid from a raw cut. She asked herself if she could possibly put up with any more of this. Still, the thought kept throbbing in her mind: "I'm now a Buddhist priest."

In her meditations during *zazen* she counted her breaths from one to ten. When she lost count because her mind became distracted she returned to one. She had yet to get as far as ten. Her record was six breaths. "It's my own mind," she thought, "yet I can't even quiet it to count as far as ten." She recalled the complex calculus problems her mind had fathomed at university, the theories it had probed. The mind held facts from when she was young, from hundreds of years ago, from events she'd never experienced and places she hadn't been. It could hold them more vividly than the present, apply them, relate them, sift them, and arrive at new conclusions. This wonderful mind. But she couldn't count ten breaths. For one mere minute she could not still her mind. It flew off on a thousand fantasies. Why did the mind abandon its task to replay tired conversations, or wonder if the black stuff at breakfast was seaweed, or if her mother's favorite tulips were white or yellow? Her mind seemed to be mocking her.

She sat straight and stared at the sliding screen before her. One breath, two. Was that a cat she heard? She remembered that she liked cats.

"This most intimate possession," she thought, "belonging only to me, is not mine at all. Which is the mind—this incessant prattler, or the one struggling to shut it up, to drown it with numbers? But that's not right either. Shonen said it can't be forced. But if it won't stop spontaneously and it can't be forced, it seems to be a deadlock. Yet I think that's too rational an approach. Well, damn it, I am a rational being."

The next morning Annie went to her first *dokusan* [formal interview with the Zen teacher]. She stood at the door to Go Roshi's room, Shonen behind her to translate. Roshi wasn't looking at her, but into space, or perhaps, she should say, through space. His gaze did not seem to have an object but rather to slice. It was at once penetrating and vacant. His robes were patched purple silk, and across his knees he held a stick. She'd heard of masters beating their students and even a story of one getting his leg broken in dokusan. Here before her was the same dear man who had laughed with her and made her feel at home, but now he was frightening. He might do anything.

But her first dokusan was an anticlimax. Roshi made the same innocent small talk anyone might make. When she went again the next day, she expected to be calm. Yet standing at the door, she felt sick. Behind Roshi loomed the immense statue of his teacher.

The lighting was from the base of the statue, giving it sinister shadows. Behind her stood his son, ready to translate for them.

This time he did not smile. A small hoarse voice, hers, spoke her *koan.* Why did she feel dwarfed by these presences? He's only human and a very kindly one. Her temples were throbbing. Having said her koan, she waited. He paused an uncomfortably long time and cleared his throat. "You must work now on *muji* koan. Become one with muji. Never let go of muji. Throw away your head. Stop reading. Don't concern yourself with the meaning of muji. Become muji. Let it fill you like a great piston pounding up and down in your belly until you feel that you'll explode." She wanted to ask what muji was, but had no voice.

"But if I don't know what it is, how can I lose myself in it?" she asked.

"Never leave it," Go Roshi said. "Practice this koan when you clean, when you eat, when you go to the toilet. You never know when or where *satori* [the experience of enlightenment] may strike you." He rang the little brass bell to dismiss her.

Outside the door she pounced on Shonen. "What is muji?"

"Nothing," he said.

"What?"

"I'll explain later. Now it's time for sutra service."

With gongs and drums pounding, the monks' voices chanted the sutras. Her mind pounded. Did he mean that she should become muji? Become nothing? Her body was quite solid and material. It was a contradiction in terms.

After breakfast Shonen called her into his room. Now it seemed to her to have a cozy homeliness about it. The altar needed dusting and fresh flowers. A Bank of Tokyo calendar was peeling off the wall. His long robes still hung at odd angles about the room. He was smiling and peeling an apple. "It's puzzling, isn't it?" he said. "Here, take this Nagano-ken apple. Most delicious. I must tell you first that your koan originated with a famous monk named Joshu. One day a young monk asked Joshu, 'Does a dog have buddhanature?' Joshu answered, 'Mu.' Mu is a negative answer. It means 'no, nothing, nothingness.' But in Buddhism everything has buddhanature, so how can Joshu say 'mu'? You live in a world of things—the phenomenal world, where everything appears separate. I am here, you are there, apple is there. There is no connection. At the same time, there is essential world. There is no thing. No separate thing."

"I don't understand," she said.

"Everything is atoms, yes? Atoms are particles. Now scientists discover these act both like wave and particle."

This rang a vague bell for Annie.

"We think particle has decided place, size, time. How can it be both? How infinite and finite? This is impossible. Impossible to our minds because our minds can only think in our concepts. Our concepts come through our language from our experience. Our senses say apple and Shonen and Annie are separate. This is practical. This is functional. This works, so we say it is truth. Science of Newton worked, so everyone said it was true. But it is not whole truth. In everyday world we not experience whole reality. So no understanding and we become very attached to finite things. For twenty-five hundred years Buddhism has taught this world what modern science now realizes. How? No special tools, computer, science buildings. Through zazen many people experience for themselves this reality.

"You can understand, Miss Annie. You need no scientific training, only patience to sit and sit. Many people have *kensho* early, sometimes after only a few weeks, but then must train a long time so understanding goes into cells."

She asked Shonen to explain what kensho was. "Kensho is first time you see essential world. First time you see yourself. For some people this is very deep and at once understanding everything. Most people this is shallow, the beginning. You work on muji koan until kensho, then train with other koans."

"Shonen, when did you have kensho?"

"Not yet, Miss Annie. I try very hard but still muji is my koan. Many young priests come and have kensho quickly, but I am patient. Last month my father give *sesshin* [a Zen retreat] and a man, fifty-one years doing muji koan, have kensho. My father crying. This man, so pure heart, so beautiful kensho."

She felt discouraged. She munched her apple. "But you understand so well, Shonen."

"That my problem. I'm like scientists. My father say, 'You understand with head. Now with your belly.' "

The monthly *zenkai* began. For this event, people from the area assembled for one day and two nights of extra meditation, dokusan, and talks by Roshi. Hogen instructed her in the appropriate clothing to wear. He liked to fuss over her, a real mother hen. Now he made sure her collars all overlapped properly, straightened and tugged everything into place, then stepped back a moment to admire.

She went to dokusan again. Go Roshi said she was to come alone. They struggled in his primitive English. He asked, "What do you make of muji?"

"Your son explained to me many things about muji and Buddhism and enlightenment, but frankly I can't make anything of it. I repeat 'nothingness' whenever I can remember to, but don't see what it's all about." She wondered, but didn't add, how such monotonous reiteration could lead to any enlightenment at all.

"My son doesn't know a thing about Buddhism," Roshi said. She was astonished. "Your approach is incorrect," he said. "You must use the Japanese syllable *mu.* Never mind the meaning, only concentrate, pour your entire being into it. When you scrub the floors,"—he startled her by jumping up and pretending to wash the floor—"that is muji. When you wash your face,"—miming again, he splashed water, then jumped back in mock horror—"it's freezing, brr, brr. That's muji. 'Oh, today I'm exhausted,' "—he flipped on his cushion and snored outrageously—"that's muji. Do you understand?"

"I don't know," she said.

"Good," he said. "That's best. Don't-know mind is best. Hold on to don't-know mind and fight with all your might." He shook the little handbell. She was dismissed.

"Hold on to don't-know mind," he had said. Yet apparently that's not the same "don't know" as Shonen's. Roshi said his son didn't know a thing about Buddhism. That was puzzling, too. Shonen was obviously very learned in Buddhist matters. The whole business baffled her. Why can't it all be straightforward and logical?

She went back into the meditation hall. She loved its smell. Tonight for zenkai they were using little oil burners. The tatami felt warm, almost alive beneath her feet. The hall was filled to capacity. She was pleased with the sight. It was more encouraging than the usual handful of monks huddled half-freezing in the semi-gloom. The people gave her energy, and Roshi's words were fuel.

She stared at the shoji screen before her. "Mu, mu, mu." The patterns of the shoji began to dance in an odd way. Her eyes were unfocused though concentrated. The effort made the shoji seem to shine. Her breath came slower and slower. Mu, mu. She felt as if she were at the bottom of a clear pool. Sounds were muffled, words and sentences floating on the surface. She was at the very bottom, looking up a great, slow distance at the light. Mu, mu, mu. It came from the pit of her belly. A tangible peace was settling through her body, a vast stillness, a hollow, booming mu.

After zazen they had chanting. Usually she found it loud, even unpleasant, but this time she was very moved. She watched Hogen's pudgy little face. He was chanting with his whole heart. Although the incense, the words, and the costumes were still completely foreign to her, her eyes slid fondly across each ardent face. She felt she might cry.

Afterwards they had tea. Forty-five people knelt in lines behind their benches and one by one stood up to give a short self-introduction. Shonen translated for her. Someone asked if it was true that the foreign lady would really do *takuhatsu*. Shonen asked her.

"Tell me again what takuhatsu is," she whispered. "I've forgotten."

"Miss Annie," he whispered back, "you must learn this word. Takuhatsu is begging."

She was indignant. "Of course I'll go." Did he think because she was a woman or a foreigner that she wouldn't? But she began to wonder just what this begging could involve that her decision to do it produced such obvious awe in the assembly.

A handsome, elderly man signaled her to follow him, and they went with Shonen and two other men—a plumber and a skinny, awkward computer programmer—to a small bare room she hadn't seen before. Inevitably, they started smoking. They smiled and said their names, which she immediately forgot.

The elderly man made pleasant, inconsequential conversation about her family and her journey. She warmed to him at once. He spoke softly but firmly. When he flicked his ash, he'd rest a moment, watch it and resume what he was saying. It gave an unhurried flow, almost melodic, to his manner. He exhaled a long, steady stream of smoke. "Miss Annie," he said, "do you know you are Buddha?"

"I beg your pardon?" she said.

"You are Buddha," he said.

"Do you mean some kind of reincarnation?" she said.

"No, I do not," he said.

"Well, Buddha died some twenty-five hundred years ago, didn't he?" She recalled Shonen mentioning that figure.

"No," he said, "the Buddha is alive and before my very eyes. Miss Annie, you are Buddha."

She was flattered but a bit embarrassed. "No, really," she said. "I can't even sit cross-legged properly."

"Plain Miss Annie even with weak legs is Buddha," he said. "You must know that. You must realize that in your every moment and every movement, you and Buddha are not different. You have nothing to seek. You are living Buddha. You have no need to search but you do not know that. You must take my word for it, but you will search in vain, search frustrated until you realize beyond any doubts or questions that you are Buddha completely and that you have never been anything but that."

Then he and the plumber told how they had reached enlightenment. The computer kid had not yet experienced kensho. They told other enlightenment stories, remembering this or that character, laughing. They spoke of the monk who was carrying a basin of hot water with great concentration. He bumped into a pole and came to an awakening. There was the one who was drinking his soup, saw a potato, and his world fell apart. He cried out in the silence of the meal. Another one stared at the sky all night, but believing it was only half an hour, met the dawn with tears. When Roshi came out of his room to wash, the monk was prostrating himself outside the door. He'd been there for an hour, weeping in gratitude. Many stories were not so dramatic. Most people were doing sesshin and got kensho in Roshi's room.

She went to her room extremely excited. Becoming enlightened needn't be a matter of decades in a mountain cave. It could be hers soon. He'd said that she'd never been anything but Buddha. The idea was intoxicating. The elderly man's voice was so authoritative, his manner compelling. That night when she fell asleep her dreams were full of mu.

The next day Roshi suggested that she should buy thicker underwear before takuhatsu. He gave a monk named Bodhin money and asked him to accompany her to the village. She didn't particularly like Bodhin; he was the one who had corrected her leaf-sweeping. He was constantly picking on the new young monks, harshly pointing out their mistakes, making fools of them before the others. It seemed cruel when there were so many minute details to remember, none of which were taught systematically. Anyway, she and Bodhin were to go to the village together.

This was the first time she had left the monastery since she arrived. It crossed her mind to make a dash for it and escape now while she had the opportunity. She knew other monks had "leaped over the wall." Could she just disappear too?

It was a country village but bustling with life. The shops displayed their wares out front in colorful stalls. Everyone seemed to know everyone and in spite of the bitter weather chatted comfortably. Occasionally they bowed to Bodhin and Annie. Bodhin reverently returned the greetings. From the lampposts on every street hung bright, plastic and tin decorations in the shape of colored snowflakes. In the afternoon sunlight they looked festive. Bodhin said that decorations always hung there, different ones depending on the season. She liked them. They were garish but gave every day an air of holiday. Some people stared at her curiously. One shopkeeper asked Bodhin if she was a boy or a girl.

Then they went into a shop where "Jingle Bells" was playing, and her heart missed a beat. The air had the crisp tingle of Christmas, but this was Japan, far from her father's hot punch and her mother's plum pudding. The next day would be Christmas Eve. She knew she must be strong. Mu, mu. The word had no appeal, couldn't distract her.

With twilight came the first snowflakes and gradually lights flickered on throughout the village. They walked back to the monastery slowly, silently.

They returned just in time for dinner. After the final clapper sounded, Annie was startled to see Mochian—the monk who had given her the bar of chocolate the day she became a priest—enter the room carrying a tray of soft drinks and a single bottle of champagne. The champagne was meant to be her Christmas celebration. Together the monks began singing "I'm Dreaming of a White Christmas." They all huddled around low benches, looking excited and blowing puffs of icy breath. Mochian opened the bottle. It was only the size of a beer bottle—just a sweet and swift sip for everyone. The tiny taste was merely tantalizing. She would have loved more.

Then the entertainment began. Mochian stood up slowly, breathed deeply, and, from the pit of his belly, poured forth his song. There was deep melancholy in it, as if the mountains were mourning beside a churning sea. It became wild, tempestuous. He seemed to sing with an emotion that was hardly human. When he had heaved the last strains from deep in his gut, the other monks all clapped uproariously, almost relieved that his suffering was over. Mochian smiled, knelt down at his place and poured the last drop of his champagne into Annie's empty cup. Her eyes were watering and she could scarcely tear them away from him long enough to ask Shonen, "What on earth was that about?"

"Frogs in a rice paddy at dawn," he said.

"What? It can't be! Are they all committing mass suicide or something?"

He looked at her, puzzled. "No, Miss Annie, no mass, no suicide, just frogs. I think Mochian-san likes frogs."

Hogen was next. He gently crooned "Silent Night." His face was cherubic. "Pleez, Miss Annie, not homeshikuness." But to her surprise she felt at home—a strange home, certainly, but with the peace of a real home. When it was her turn, she sang "God Rest Ye Merry, Gentlemen." She guessed they might be familiar with it, and, sure enough, they beamed in recognition. In this little Buddhist temple in the snowy mountains of Japan, the Christmas spirit was more genuine than any she had experienced in a long time. Not once until she lay on her futon did homesickness overwhelm her. Then her peace and pleasure crumpled. It was, after all, Christmas Eve.

When she woke in the morning her quilt was frozen from her condensed breath. For a moment she had no idea where she was. She didn't want to know. She reversed the quilt and hugged her knees to her chin. It was five minutes to five, pitch black and bitter cold. Go on, she thought, have yourself a merry little Christmas.

No one in the monastery seemed to realize that Christmas is the most important day of the year for Westerners. At Shodoji it was a day like any other, with work as usual. She was prepared to brood but before she could summon a full-fledged depression, Wakuan bustled in, interrupting her languid dusting of Kannon-sama. "Miss Annie, vely solly, have work for you. Come thees way, pleez."

He led her to a storeroom filled with bundles of dried beans still on their stalks. "Vely solly, now everyone vely busy. Everyone make *daihannya.*" This was true. They had spent the past week folding sheets of paper in intricate fan-like patterns, writing on them, then binding them with red paper bands. These daihannyas were amulets sent each New Year to the temple's supporters. She had admired their fine, precise concentration in the folding, then the bold sweeping strokes of calligraphy. They worked all day and late at night after she retired.

"These beans we need by New Year. Will you pleez do? Take off all skins." He might as well have asked her to turn the beans into gold. How on earth could she shell them all in a week? "Vely solly." Sure, happy Christmas to you too, she thought. All of a sudden the dusting didn't look so bad anymore. He showed her the bags and bowls and even gave her a cushion.

Then he slid the door shut. She heard his feet pattering off on the bare planks and then silence. The depression that had been threatening all day hit unbidden. In the feeble light she stared at those mounds of gnarled bean stalks. She screamed and hurled herself on them, weeping and weeping from her guts. All she'd held in, all the "Be strong's" and "It's okay, you can do it's" were ripped away in the roaring torrent of her tears. She cried and cried and cried. No one even heard. The gong sounded for lunch. It was Christmas dinner—stringy noodles in hot water and soy sauce soup.

She went to her room and tried to rest but could only think of the beans, so she went back downstairs. There was a musty smell in the room. She began by stripping the beans still in their shells from the stalks and throwing them into boxes. Six o'clock rang for the evening meal. They ate silently as usual. She returned to her prison. Outside it was murky but in that dank windowless cell it was just the same as it had been at ten in the morning. She worked until her body was limp. She dragged herself back to her room at midnight, five hours after her usual bedtime. Her hands were filthy, but she didn't wash them or her face or teeth. She took off her outer robe and fell into her futon.

Again it was five a.m. After breakfast it was straight down to the beans. After lunch—the beans. For dinner they had beans. She thought she'd puke but instead returned to the beans. Four hours' sleep, still no bath. The others were working similar hours with the daihannyas but it didn't seem to take the same toll. None of them had the huge dark circles that sagged below her eyes. They were still human, chatting and joking among themselves. She grew more and more resentful. Why was she stuck with this job? The others were laboring just as hard—but beans, dirty beans, in that dark hole, alone? Her fingers, unused to the friction, were blistering. She tried keeping her mind on her koan, "mu, mu" over and over again, tried to focus there. At times it was soothing, more usually infuriating.

It was the fourth day of the beans. She was progressing but couldn't possibly be finished in time. During those four days she'd barely exchanged a word with anyone. She hated the others for working hard with such equanimity. That night she looked at the pile, contemplating "accidentally" setting fire to it. Instead she decided to give herself a bit of a treat, have an early night and quit at ten thirty.

At 10:07 she heard a scuffling sound outside the door. Rats? No, it was Mochian, carrying a tin tray. "Miss Annie sleepy?" The question was such a grossly inadequate estimation of her condition that she had to laugh. The laugh was too loud, too long; it was a laugh of semi-hysteria, but a great relief. Mochian cocked his head to the side and looked a little puzzled, but smiled pleasantly and offered her a steaming mug of hot chocolate. It was frothy and sweet. She drank it very slowly without really looking at him or talking, but each sip felt like a long sigh. As she finished she became aware that he had been staring at her. He knelt patiently with the battered aluminum tray, waiting for her to finish. He took her empty cup and scampered away. About five minutes later he reappeared, this time with a mug of coffee, a cucumber sandwich and a plate of bean paste cakes. Again, from his knees he humbly offered them to her. He knew so little English and yet understood so well that she needed him. This time she wolfed the food down. The bread was dirty from her filthy fingers. As she gorged on the bean paste cakes, Mochian started stripping beans. Soon he was working with the same rapt concentration she had seen when he removed chaff from the rice. He seemed unaware of her or anything else.

She got back to work too, energized. He showed no signs of tiring. She was beginning to feel irritated again. If she didn't keep at it as long as he, she'd feel guilty, but she really wanted to sleep. She tried to tell him, okay, you can stop now. He just smiled and nodded. Finally at 12:10 she could stand it no longer and said good night. He smiled and nodded and said, "Good night."

The next morning at five he was busy as usual in the kitchen. After breakfast she returned to her dungeon. He had managed two and a half boxes of beans. How could he? He mustn't have slept at all. The fifth night he brought her refreshments and disappeared. Shortly afterwards she went to bed. In the morning three more boxes had been mysteriously shelled. Her resentment melted into shame.

On the sixth night he brought her coffee and miso. He began to work. She was determined to keep up with him. As the hour grew later the cold became more intense. He wrapped her in a bright green blanket. She was bleary-eyed but now her heart was in it. Like the disciples at Gethsemane, however, the flesh was weak. She dozed on a box of beans and awakened at four o'clock with a pain in her neck, draped over the bean box and chilled to the bone. Mochian may not even have noticed. He was still working with the same speed and concentration. Finally, completing the task in time looked feasible. On the seventh day at 4:15 they finished. There was a momentous quality about the event. She should have been elated, but she only wanted to collapse, take a bath and put the whole week out of her mind.

The following day was New Year's Eve, a day that means as much in Japan as Christmas does in the West. For many Japanese it is the occasion for making an annual pilgrimage to a temple, either Buddhist or Shinto. This is usually followed, at least for the men, by a heavy drinking session. Shonen warned her that she should catch a nap after the evening meal. She needed no persuasion. At 11:30 he woke her and told her to put on her ceremonial robes. They went down to the main doorway. Already people were beginning to gather, mostly country people with children whose eyes sparkled with excitement. Some little ones were drooping with sleep, strapped to a bent mother's back. The doors were wide open, as always.

The visitors helped themselves to big bowls of sweet black beans. These looked sickeningly familiar. The temple bell, housed at the top of a stone tower under a wooden roof, would begin to ring at midnight. Half a dozen people could easily have stood inside this bell. It was rung by means of a thick wooden beam suspended by chains and rammed into its side. At midnight it boomed into the darkness, across the snow-covered village, echoing off the mountains. Slowly, it sounded again, then again, one hundred and eight times.

Inu was the bell ringer. She could just imagine how cold his bare head must be. The other monks were inside, but with the door open they weren't much warmer. They did the required chants and took turns making prostrations. Then they trailed around the temple offering incense before a multitude of small altars she'd never noticed before. These were tucked away on little shelves in corners—a smiling bodhisattva, a menacing guardian deity, each with a couple of flowers, a candle and an incense holder. The rituals were becoming familiar to her but it was the breakfast that surprised her.

Sake the first thing in the morning, before even a bowl of rice! The meal was a feast. In front of each monk were five little plates of mysterious Japanese delicacies. She recognized carrots and fish but nothing else. Even the staples, rice and soup, were special. The rice was pink, mixed with aduki beans and topped with sesame. The clear soup had carrot flowerets floating prettily in it, as well as ornamental mushrooms, pink whirligig circles. In the middle was a white gluey lump called *omoehi*, a kind of rice cake associated with prosperity, celebration, and a Happy New Year.

Here the first and only chapter of Maura O'Halloran's "novel" breaks off. She stayed on at the temple and in her third year received dharma transmission, recognizing her realization and authorizing her to teach Zen. But three months later she was killed in a bus accident in Thailand on her way home. At the monastery, a statue was built to honor her and she was given the posthumous name "Great Enlightened Lady." In 1994 her journals and letters were published in a marvelous book called Pure Heart, Enlightened Mind.

Trying to Speak: A Personal History of Stage Fright

David Guy

It's not much talked about in any religion, but fear is one of the most important spiritual issues. From a Buddhist point of view, once we believe we have a self it's fear for that self that makes us do all the things that cause pain for ourselves and others. Fear is the engine of samsara. David Guy offers us some lessons on facing our deepest fears. His is public speaking. Substitute your favorite.

My first bout of stage fright, the one that inaugurated my real problems, occurred when I was sixteen years old and in English class at a boy's private school, beginning to realize I wanted to be a writer. Our English teacher that year was a tall, vaguely handsome British man, a graduate of Cambridge, who had been a shot putter and discus thrower on the British Olympic team. He was popular around school as a soccer and track coach, an inspiring figure in general.

But as an English teacher he was a disaster. Frequently unprepared, he would sit on the edge of his desk in silence for minutes after the class bell rang, wincing at his own cigarette smoke while trying to conjure from the depths of memory whatever work we had read for the day. When this effort failed him, as it often did, his only recourse was to have us read aloud from our weekly compositions. It was an experience that I dreaded, for good reason. I was just beginning to find my voice, starting to see writing as my life's work. I was experimenting with techniques that were beyond what I could handle. And I was surrounded by classmates who didn't care for writing at all, had the usual adolescent scorn for pretension, were merciless with sarcasm. They were, in other words, sixteen-year-old boys, and I was desperate to avoid their reckoning. For an entire semester, I had managed to avoid being called upon. And then, on a dismal, rainy afternoon near the end of the semester, motioning to me with a wave of his cigarette, our teacher asked me to begin.

I couldn't speak. I couldn't choke out a single word.

I'd been met by a paralyzing wave of stage fright, larger than I'd ever experienced. My face began to flush. My palms began to sweat. My heart beat with such quickness that I couldn't catch my breath; my chest wouldn't expand. The harder I tried, the more it closed in on me: the panicky feeling fed on itself.

"Are you all right?" our teacher asked. "Are you ill?" The class itself was silent, expectant. Minutes seemed to go by in which the only sound in the room was the scrape of shoes on the wooden floorboards.

"I'm not ill," I finally managed to say. In a halting voice I told him that I could not read my piece aloud; I was too self-conscious.

It was one of the more humiliating moments of my life, and it came at a time when my self-confidence was in short supply. That was the year my father died. And in that year, when I was carrying the knowledge of his illness around like a great weight, nothing seemed to go right. I couldn't make the football team. I couldn't do the work in chemistry or math. I couldn't get a date with the girl I cared for. Now I couldn't speak.

I had lost faith. Not some specifically religious faith, though that was happening, too. I had lost faith in the world as an essentially benign place where things would work out. They weren't going to work out. My father was going to die.

The poet and social critic Paul Goodman once said that faith is the knowledge that the ground will be there when you take a step. A faithful person strides boldly and purposefully into the world, knowing there is a world for him. When we lose faith, we grow tentative. We don't believe there is a world for us.

I would guess that in many crises of stage fright—also writer's block, another instance of losing one's voice—some similar deep trauma is behind them, at least the first time. We fail, and then we lose faith, and the most basic activity—speaking—becomes the problem.

After that English class, I took great pains to avoid all occasions of public speaking. Later that year I was nominated for student council president, and I declined because I knew I would have to make a speech. Several years later, in Reynolds Price's writing class at Duke University, I went through agonies when I had to read my stories aloud. And when I finally published a novel, at the age of thirty-two, I was terrified at the thought of reading from it in public. The first offer I got, I turned down.

It was at this point that I took a class in dealing with stage fright. In a room full of equally mortified people, we each stood up, wide-eyed with fear, and gave speeches under our teacher's watchful gaze. I read from my newly published novel.

Our teacher was a superb speaker herself, a drama instructor who had worked with young actors for years. She walked us, step by step, through the physiology of stage fright.

We begin by sensing a fluttery nervousness somewhere, probably down in our belly, and we tighten up so as not to feel it. That tightening is often so automatic that we fail to notice it occurring. It moves up the body until it reaches the diaphragm, which it prevents from expanding. With our lungs constricted, we physically can't catch our breath. Since oxygen isn't circulating, our heart begins to pound, and a panic reaction sets in: the face and body flush, the hands and feet sweat. Unable to breathe, we tighten more, which in turn induces further panic. All this happens in a matter of seconds.

Confronted with this phenomenon, I would instinctively try to relax. But *trying* to relax is a contradiction in terms, and it made me shut down even more, sapping my energy. "I'm sure you know, David," the teacher said, "that you stand up to speak and your voice goes to gravel." I knew no such thing—I was too nervous to hear myself—but she had a tape to prove it. She taught me not to calm down, but to take that nervous energy and use it, to belt out my readings. "You'll never get too loud, or exaggerate too much. The more you ham it up, the better."

With her guidance, I learned how to speak loudly and forcefully before an audience. I managed, with some effort, to breathe. But as useful as her instructions were, I still felt terror every time I moved to speak in front of others. The fear—of failure, of public humiliation—remained, and I ran from it instinctively.

It was not until years after my public speaking class, this time in a Buddhist context, that I was finally really able to look at my fear and to understand it, to *be with* it. Buddhism, which expresses much faith in experiencing what is happening, taught me that the way to change your karma is not to respond—run when you're afraid, hit someone when you're angry—but to feel the feeling without responding. Then it is not passed on. It does no harm.

It is that experience of deep feeling that teaches us about stage fright and, more generally, about fear.

When my wife and I returned to North Carolina nine years ago from a stay in Cambridge, Massachusetts, where we had both studied Vipassana meditation, I knew I wanted to find a place to practice. After about a year, I saw an advertisement in our local weekly for a Zen center in Chapel Hill. I was hesitant, at first, about practicing in a new tradition, but my concerns were quickly allayed. Of all the forms of Buddhism, Soto Zen is probably the closest to Vipassana. There are surface differences: in Zen we sit facing the wall, keep our eyes open slightly, hold our hands in a *mudra* [formal hand gesture]. There is somewhat more of an emphasis on the body in Zen, more concern with correct posture. But our basic practice, like that of Vipassana, is to keep letting go of thoughts and to come back to bodily feelings.

At the Zen center there is a brief service of bowing and chanting at the end of sittings. This seemed strange at first: I had never done a floor bow before, nor much chanting. But I came to appreciate the bows as expressing a devotion I already felt, and saw the chanting as a physical practice like walking meditation.

At every service, a person called the *kokyo* announces the name of each chant and, following the group recitation, sings elaborate dedications. After I had sat faithfully for several years at the Zen center, Taitaku Pat Phelan, the resident teacher, approached me and asked if I might like to try being the kokyo. In theory, I did—I had come to love the chants—but I was wary.

For one thing, being kokyo is very much a performance—many of the kokyos had beautiful voices. For another, when the time comes to perform, you have to do it without hesitation. There is a clunk on the bell, and you sing. When I would give a talk or reading, if I was hit by a wave of stage fright, I paused. There was no pausing for the kokyo.

I was terrible the first few times. I had strong attacks of stage fright, couldn't get my breath. My voice cracked and wobbled. I had never shown myself up that way in front of this group. In any other context the solution would have been to find a replacement. But the world of Zen is often ass backwards. You see a problem and wade right into it. "If this is deeply humiliating," Pat said, "if it really makes you feel miserable, you shouldn't do it."

I didn't feel that bad. I was, after all, surrounded by friends.

"Then this is an ideal situation for practicing with your problem. You can see it clearly. Don't try to change the feeling. Just observe it. See it as something interesting."

She was right. In the crucible of my stage fright, I was afforded a superb opportunity to look at fear. These were laboratory conditions. While stage fright certainly doesn't seem small when it comes up, it is nonetheless a limited fear, and a predictable one. You can observe it without being overwhelmed by it.

I learned some things about fear in this situation I never could have otherwise. They have become my guidelines for dealing with it.

Feel fear when it arises, not when you would like it to arise. I was sitting two periods of zazen just before I had to perform. My tendency in that situation was to think those periods were for my practice. I didn't want to waste time worrying about performing.

But we have no control over what comes up in our body and mind, and no "subject" for zazen is better than any other. To brush something aside because it arises at an inconvenient moment is to not value our life as it unfolds. And from a practical standpoint, fear will come up until it is heard. It will grow as strong as it needs to. If it is an hour before the occasion and fear comes up—or two hours, two days—feel it then. Feel it any chance you get.

The obsessive thinking that accompanies fear is useless. On occasions when I was kokyo, the thoughts were especially absurd: Drop the chant book and run from the room. Hand the book to the woman beside me and ask her to do it. Walk up to the priest—in the middle of service—and tell her I can't go on. That kind of thinking never ends. It is an expression of fear, and its purpose is to distract you from the anxiety of the situation. But the only way to deal with fear is to allow yourself to feel it, to experience it in all of its discomfort. There is no other solution.

Fear is most workable in its physical manifestation. There may, indeed, be a meditation master who is so adept at watching his mind that he can observe even the rapid-fire thinking that takes place during fear, but I am certainly not that person, and most meditators I know find it difficult to watch the mind at all. The best advice in this situation is that of Zen in general: Let go of thoughts and bring your attention back to bodily sensations. As many times as you get caught in thought, come back to the body. That is the practice.

Fear demands to be felt, and it can be felt most readily in the body, as a powerful sensation. The experience may be uncomfortable, but as you watch fear manifest in the body, the truth of the Buddha's words is revealed: It does arise because of conditions. It is not a wall of emotion, but a constantly changing process. And it finally ends. It has its say and departs.

In time, sitting and watching fear, we see its true emptiness. There are various sensations in the body, some strong, some weak, some painful, some pleasurable. Thoughts also come and go. We take a segment of that experience and call it "fear." But we're the ones who label it. We create "fear." In the body and mind it is just more thoughts and feelings.

The more deeply you can feel fear, the easier it will be to handle. The words that Zen teacher Ed Brown once spoke at a *sesshin*, a seven-day practice period, still ring true to me: We feel anger up in the chest, sadness in the mid-abdomen, and fear in the deep abdomen. Fear is the deepest feeling in the body and the most basic human feeling. To feel into fear is to look deeply into ourselves.

The sensations of stage fright—the pressure at the diaphragm, for instance—are actually a tightening so as not to feel fear. This tightening begins at the sphincter ("tight-assed" is not just an expression) and proceeds up the torso until, so to speak, it has us by the throat. It can tighten the whole body. It moves very quickly.

The earlier, and further down, you catch this process, the better. If you can feel that tightness at the diaphragm—with full awareness, without trying to change it or put an end to it—it isn't as disabling. If you can feel the tightness at the sphincter, it won't move up into the torso. And if you can feel the sensation of fear before there is any tightening at all, you will see that it exists as a ball of energy in the pit of the stomach. It might be uncomfortable, but if you can stay with it, you will see it for what it is: just energy. The moment you become aware of it, it is *your* energy. You can use it.

We can never get cocky with fear. As soon as we have it licked, a wave comes along that shows us who is boss. I might go for days at the zendo with no stage fright at all. Then suddenly I'm like that sixteen-year-old kid in English class.

Nevertheless, *the experience of learning to meet fear builds upon itself.* It is a skill, and the more we do it, the better we get. Seeing its true symptoms, its beginning as physical energy, takes away some of its mystique. We see not necessarily that we can handle it all the time, but that it is a phenomenon of life, like any other.

So fear is not defeated, but doesn't have to be defeating. We are never finished with it—nevertheless, we don't have to dread its return. Being free of fear is not a matter of never feeling it, but of not being flattened when we do. We can feel it and know it is a natural phenomenon, also an impermanent one, which will have its say and be gone.

Radical Acceptance

Tara Brach

Feelings of unworthiness and self-blame can kill our joy in life, says psychologist and Insight Meditation teacher Tara Brach. The Buddhist teachings are not based on any idea of original or inherent sin. Rather, we are seen as basically good—compassionate and awake—and so the path is one of self-acceptance and trust in our own true nature.

When I was in college, I went off to the mountains for a weekend of hiking with an older, wiser friend of twenty-two. After we set up our tent, we sat by a stream, watching the water swirl around rocks and talking about our lives. At one point she described how she was learning to be "her own best friend." A huge wave of sadness came over me, and I broke down sobbing. I was the farthest thing from my own best friend. I was continually harassed by an inner judge who was merciless, relentless, nit-picking, driving, often invisible but always on the job. I knew I would never treat a friend the way I treated myself, without mercy or kindness.

My guiding assumption was, "Something is fundamentally wrong with me," and I struggled to control and fix what felt like a basically flawed self. I drove myself in academics, was a fervent political activist, and devoted myself to a very full social life. I avoided pain (and created more) with an addiction to food and a preoccupation with achievement. My pursuit of pleasure was sometimes wholesome—in nature, with friends—but it also included an impulsive kind of thrill-seeking through recreational drugs, sex, and other adventures. In the eyes of the world, I was highly functional. Internally, I was anxious, driven, and often depressed. I didn't feel at peace with any part of my life.

Feeling not okay went hand in hand with deep loneliness. In my early teens I sometimes imagined that I was living inside a transparent orb that separated me from the people and life around me. When I felt good about myself and at ease with others, the bubble thinned until it was like an invisible wisp of gas. When I felt bad about myself the walls got so thick it seemed others must be able to see them. Imprisoned within, I felt hollow and achingly alone. The fantasy faded somewhat as I got older, but I lived with the fear of letting someone down or being rejected myself.

With my college friend it was different—I trusted her enough to be completely open. Over the next two days of hiking on high mountain ridges, sometimes talking with her, sometimes sitting in silence, I began to realize that beneath all my mood swings, depression, loneliness, and addictive behavior lurked that feeling of deep personal deficiency. I was getting my first clear glimpse into a core of suffering that I would revisit again and again in my life. While I felt exposed and raw, I intuitively knew that by facing this pain I was entering a path of healing.

As we drove down from the mountains that Sunday night, my heart was lighter but still aching. I longed to be kinder to myself. I longed to befriend my inner experience and to feel more intimacy and ease with the people in my life.

When some years later these longings drew me to the Buddhist path, I found there the teachings and practices that enabled me to directly face my feelings of unworthiness and insecurity. They gave me a way of seeing clearly what I was experiencing and showed me how to relate to my life with compassion. The teachings of the Buddha also helped undo my painful and mistaken notion that I was alone in my suffering, that it was a personal problem and somehow my fault.

Over the past twenty years, as a psychologist and Buddhist teacher, I've worked with thousands of clients and students who have revealed how painfully burdened they feel by a sense of not being good enough. Whether our conversation takes place in the middle of a ten-day meditation retreat or during a weekly therapy session, the suffering—the fear of being flawed and unworthy—is basically the same.

For so many of us, feelings of deficiency are right around the corner. It doesn't take much—just hearing of someone else's accomplishments, being criticized, getting into an argument, making a mistake at work—to make us feel that we are not okay.

As a friend of mine put it, "Feeling that something is wrong with me is the invisible and toxic gas I am always breathing." When we experience our lives through this lens of personal insufficiency, we are imprisoned in what I call the trance of unworthiness. Trapped in this trance, we are unable to perceive the truth of who we really are.

A meditation student at a retreat I was teaching told me about an experience that brought home to her the tragedy of living in trance. Marilyn had spent many hours sitting at the bedside of her dying mother—reading to her, meditating next to her late at night, holding her hand, and telling her over and over that she loved her. Most of the time Marilyn's mother remained unconscious, her breath labored and erratic. One morning before dawn, she suddenly opened her eyes and looked clearly and intently at her daughter. "You know," she whispered softly, "all my life I thought something was wrong with me." Shaking her head slightly, as if to say, "What a waste," she closed her eyes and drifted back into a coma. Several hours later she passed away.

We don't have to wait until we are on our deathbed to realize what a waste of our precious lives it is to carry the belief that something is wrong with us. Yet because our habits of feeling insufficient are so strong, awakening from the trance involves not only inner resolve, but also an active training of the heart and mind. Through Buddhist awareness practices, we free ourselves from the suffering of trance by learning to recognize what is true in the present moment, and by embracing whatever we see with an open heart. This cultivation of mindfulness and compassion is what I call Radical Acceptance.

Radical Acceptance reverses our habit of living at war with experiences that are unfamiliar, frightening, or intense. It is the necessary antidote to years of neglecting ourselves, years of judging and treating ourselves harshly, years of rejecting this moment's experience. Radical Acceptance is the willingness to experience ourselves and our life as it is. A moment of Radical Acceptance is a moment of genuine freedom.

The twentieth-century Indian meditation master Sri Nisargadatta encouraged us to wholeheartedly enter this path of freedom: ". . . all I plead with you is this: make love of yourself *perfect*." For Marilyn, the final words of her dying mother awakened her to this possibility. As she put it, "It was her parting gift. I realized I didn't have to lose my life in that same way that she did. Out of love—for my mother, for life—I resolved to hold myself with more acceptance and kindness." We can each choose the same.

When we practice Radical Acceptance, we begin with the fears and wounds of our own life and discover that our heart of compassion widens endlessly. In holding ourselves with compassion, we become free to love this living world. This is the blessing of Radical Acceptance: As we free ourselves from the suffering of "something is wrong with me," we trust and express the fullness of who we are.

Forgiveness Meditation

Ezra Bayda

Forgiveness, says Ezra Bayda, is an essential spiritual practice, one that benefits us as much as those we forgive. Easy to say, of course, but he offers us a step-by-step meditation that can help us really forgive. It begins with one of Buddhism's essential truths: that when someone causes us pain, it is because of their own suffering.

What does it mean to forgive? Is there someone you don't want to forgive?

Forgiveness is often tainted with the idea that there should be some form of magnanimous acceptance of others even though they did us wrong. This understanding of forgiveness is not what a forgiveness practice is about. Forgiveness is about practicing with and healing resentment, the resentment that blocks our desire to live from our True Nature. Forgiveness is about loosening our hold on the one thing we most want to hold onto—the suffering of resentment.

In forgiveness practice, we work to see through our own emotional reactions. We practice noticing what stands in the way of real forgiveness. Genuine forgiveness entails experiencing our own pain and then the pain of the person to be forgiven. This experience can help dissolve the illusion of separation between ourselves and others.

Think of someone you feel anger, bitterness, or resentment toward: your mate, your parents (living or dead), one of your children, your teacher, your boss, a friend—anyone about whom there is active agitation in your heart. To make your understanding of forgiveness practice more experiential, keep this person in mind as you read this article.

When you bring this person to mind, how does it feel? Holding on to resentment often has the feeling of an unsettled account: "So-and-so has hurt me; therefore, they somehow owe me." As we cling to the hard, bitter feeling that someone owes us, we also may feel the need to pay this person back. As resentment festers, the attitude of "I'll show them!" takes over and hardens us. We shore up our hardened heart with the sense of false power and righteousness that arises with resentment.

If someone were to ask a spiritual teacher, "What should I do with all this resentment I feel against my friend?" the teacher might respond, "It's not good to hold on to resentment. Why don't you just let it go?" But can we just let it go? Even when we know how much resentment hurts us, we often don't have that option. If we could just let it go, we wouldn't be stuck in the throes of resentment. Letting go is not a real practice. It's a fantasy practice based on an ideal of how we'd like things to be.

Genuine forgiveness has three stages. The first is simply acknowledging how unwilling we are to forgive the other. We let ourselves experience the degree to which we prefer to hold on to our resentment, anger, and bitterness, even when we see how it closes us to living a genuine life. We see how we resist our inherent openness by choosing to stay stuck in our hardness. By bringing nonjudgmental awareness to how we resist forgiveness, we see clearly, not in order to feel guilty—which would be the result if we were living from the ideal that we *shouldn't* be resentful—but to enable us to experience resistance for what it is. We have to experience in our body how our unwillingness to forgive feels. We have to see our self-centered judgments clearly as thoughts, rather than accepting them as objective truths. Staying with the *physical experience* of resistance allows a sense of spaciousness to gradually develop, within which the tight fist of our resentment can be loosened. We can't move on to the second stage of forgiveness until we've entered into and experienced—in both our bodies and minds—the depth of our unwillingness to forgive.

The second stage is bringing awareness to the emotional reactivity toward the person we resent: to experience it without judgment, to see it with an open mind. As we visualize the person we resent, we notice what emotional reactions arise. We ask, "What *is* this?" Is it anger, resentment, bitterness, fear, grief? Whatever arises, we just experience it within our body. If we get lost in thoughts, memories, or justifications, we keep coming back to what we feel in the body. Where is the tightness, the contraction? What's the texture of the feeling? We stay with the awareness of our physical-emotional reactions as long as it takes to reside in them. That means relaxing into them, as painful as they are. At some point we no longer need to push them away.

Let's say we've been criticized repeatedly by someone. Instead of sulking or lashing back in reactivity, we remember the practice path. First we feel the anger and resentment rising. Next we listen to and label our thoughts: "Why do you always have to put me down?" "You're such a negative person." "No one should have to put up with this." Then we move from thinking and blaming into locating the resentment in our body. We feel the tightness in the mouth, the heaviness in the shoulders, the ache in the heart, the rigidity of the muscles. Staying with the physical experience, striving to avoid getting hooked into thoughts of self-justification and blame, we ask, "*What is this?*" We come back again and again to the physical reality of the moment. At this point we're not even entertaining thoughts of forgiveness; we're just bringing awareness to our suffering without trying to push it away. Once we can rest like this in our bodily experience, we're ready for the third stage.

The third stage of a forgiveness practice is to say words of forgiveness. It's important to realize that saying these words has nothing to do with condoning the actions of another. It's about forgiving the person, not what they did. It means seeing that the action came from the person's own pain. And the way we do this isn't by looking for the other's pain, but by attending to our own. Once we've attended to our own, we're more open to truly seeing the other's. At this point, saying words of forgiveness helps us open into the heart. Trying to open to the other's pain before passing through the first two stages of forgiveness practice—clearly seeing our resistance and resting in our experience of it—won't work; then we're just adding cosmetic mental constructs over our suppressed feelings.

Only after we've experienced how our own emotional reactivity stands in the way of real forgiveness can we truly understand that the other was just mechanically acting, in the only way a person can, out of beliefs and conditioning. We can then say the words:

> I forgive you.
> I forgive you for whatever you may have done
> from which I experienced pain.
> I forgive you because I know
> that what you did came from your own pain.

In speaking of a poem he had written, the Vietnamese monk and Zen meditation teacher Thich Nhat Hanh recalled a letter about a twelve-year-old girl, one of thousands of Vietnamese boat people, who had thrown herself into the ocean after being raped by a sea pirate. This letter ignited so much rage in him that he wanted to get a gun and kill the pirate. At the same time he realized how easy it was to think only of the victim, not of the rapist. In no way was he condoning the sea pirate's act; he was pointing to the fact that when our hearts are closed, we're all capable of thinking, feeling, and doing horrible things. He called the poem "Please Call Me by My True Names," as a reminder that we must acknowledge *all* of our names, not just the ones we like to identify with. This is how we can access those closed-hearted parts of ourselves that we otherwise rarely encounter. In so doing, we can come closer to genuine compassion and forgiveness.

A few years ago I watched a TV documentary about the decision to drop the atomic bomb during World War II. My understanding had been that the decision was made to avoid losing over one hundred thousand men in a land invasion of Japan. Whether or not I agreed with this rationale, at least it had some merit. But the film pointed out that Japan had tried to surrender shortly before the bomb was dropped, approaching Russia as a third party to broker peace with the Allies. President Truman and his advisers decided not to negotiate, refusing even to hear the terms of surrender before they dropped the bomb. Dropping the bomb wasn't just about ending the war and saving American lives; it was also about showing Russia who carried the biggest stick. At that point in the program, I had such a strong reaction that I had to turn the television off. I felt tremendous self-righteous indignation against the people I had once believed were at least acting from some positive moral position.

In practicing with the rage—experiencing my own anger without the blaming thoughts—I remembered what Thich Nhat Hanh had said about his poem. I realized, experientially, that I was not so different from President Truman or his advisers. Nor was I different from those who dropped the bomb, or from the millions of people who cheered when they heard the news that a bomb was dropped on Japan. This was a sobering moment for me, considering that countless people were killed, and the suffering that was caused still reverberates. Whether or not the documentary had the facts straight, my self-righteous belief-based rage was as solid as a rock. In looking at my anger and opening to what had appeared to be so abhorrent, I saw that the fear-based, narrowly patriotic stance that had resulted in the death of so many wasn't really foreign to me at all. In fact, that conditioned trait was equally present in me.

This realization came from experiencing and seeing through my own anger. This is an important point. It's easy to comprehend intellectually that others are acting from their own protectedness and pain, and that we share with them certain traits that we prefer not to see in ourselves. But such conceptual understanding doesn't really touch our lives. It can never lead to the compassionate and genuine forgiveness that's possible once we've practiced with our own closed-heartedness and seen through it.

In practicing forgiveness, it is possible to move from living in our own isolated pain—which usually manifests as anger and resentment—to experiencing the universal pain that we all share. This suffering is what we realize experientially when we're able to see that we're not essentially different from those we've been quick to judge. Experiencing the truth of suffering frees us to move into the universal heart: the essential fact of our basic connectedness. In this place, the illusions that lead us to think we are separate and protected selves naturally dissolve. We no longer view the world through the lens of "us" versus "them." We no longer perceive the other as an enemy. We no longer seek revenge for what we regard as wrongdoing. We no longer demand recompense.

To enter into the process of forgiveness at this level, where the illusion of separation between self and other begins to dissolve, is a profoundly transformative practice. It's also challenging, partly because we don't want to do it, and partly because entering into our own pain is never easy. It is rare that the transformation of resentment occurs in just one or two sittings. If the resentment is deep, it may take months. Timing is also an important element. Sometimes the pain is too raw; we have to wait until the feelings are less intense.

It's sometimes said that you can't forgive others until you forgive yourself. While that sounds good, the formula is just a little too pat. It's a partial truth that misses the heart of the matter. What is this "self" that we must first forgive? There is no one solid self. This illusion of the self is the essence of the self-centered dream. Real forgiveness is our True Nature; it's not about one "self" forgiving another "self." This *experiential* understanding becomes apparent when we no longer believe in the illusion of the self. So instead of formulating notions of forgiving ourselves before or after forgiving others, we simply direct our healing awareness toward what is. We focus on wherever we feel resentment and whomever we can't forgive.

Even though it's some of the most important work we can do, forgiveness is one of the practices we least want to work with. The forgiveness meditation that follows is meant to be practiced over time, with patience. As we return to it regularly, warmth and compassion may gradually replace the hardness and bitterness of resentment. Remembering the words traditionally posted at the entrance of Zen temples can be helpful:

> Let us be respectfully reminded:
> Life and death are of supreme importance.
> Time swiftly passes by and with it our only chance.
> Each of us must aspire to awaken.
> Be aware: Do not squander your life.

These words point to the folly of our upside-down way of thinking, of the magnitude of our constant decisions to let emotional reactions like resentment close us down. As we feel the pain of our hardness, and as the consequences of our unwillingness to open really hit us, perhaps we'll be more motivated to begin the essential work of forgiveness.

How to Do Forgiveness Meditation

When anger and resentment have calcified the heart, practicing forgiveness as a specific meditation can be very useful. This guided meditation directs awareness to areas that might otherwise go unaddressed. Its primary purpose is to help us see through the emotional reactions that stand in the way of real forgiveness. Essentially, it's about clarifying and healing our resentment. Real forgiveness requires first experiencing our own pain and then the pain of the person to be forgiven; from this understanding, the apparent barriers between ourselves and others can dissolve. The meditation has three parts.

In the first part, we see how unwilling we are to forgive the other person. We experience the degree to which we prefer holding on to our resentment.

In the second part, we bring into awareness all of the emotional reactivity we feel toward the person. The point is to *experience* it without judgment, to see it with "What is this?" mind. Only by clearing ourselves emotionally can we proceed to the third part.

In the third part, we "forgive" the other person. This is not the same as condoning their actions. It means that, through practicing with our own resentment, we come to see that the other person was simply acting from their own pain.

One of the most important aspects of this meditation is to bring awareness of the other person into the heartspace, the area in the center of the chest. Doing this may feel foreign and uncomfortable at first; this is a natural consequence of habit and resistance. Bringing awareness into the heart area makes it less likely that we'll spin off into simply thinking about our feelings. Rather, it allows us to experience them in a way that is both genuine and transformative.

Here are the instructions:

Sit or lie in a comfortable position, staying as still as possible. Take two or three deep breaths, then just breathe naturally.

Bring into awareness the particular person toward whom you feel resentment.

Feel for a moment what arises with even the thought of forgiveness. How much longer do you wish to keep your heart closed to this person, and consequently to life as a whole? If you had just a few days to live, would you want to continue feeling resentful and bitter?

Now remember the situation that sparked your resentful feelings. Feel whatever arises. Don't try to do anything; just experience the feeling in your body. Experience the degree to which you do not want to forgive this person. Experience the degree of unwillingness to even bring this person into your meditation. Acknowledge your unwillingness, and bring a nonjudgmental awareness to the sensations of resistance. How does it feel, in your body, to push the person away?

Allowing the resistance to just be, let the container of awareness widen around it. Now bring to awareness sensory phenomena from outside the body: hear the sounds, feel the air temperature. Feel how the texture of the resistance changes as a sense of spaciousness surrounds it.

Begin breathing into the heart area. Feel the texture of the heart.

Now try to bring awareness of this person closer to your being. Breathing into the heartspace, bring their presence, via the inbreath, into the heart. On the outbreath, just breathe out—not trying to do anything special. Without self-judgment, experience all of the arising emotions. Is there anger, resentment, bitterness? Is there fear or grief? Asking "What *is* this?" notice whatever arises and experience it in the body. When you get lost in thoughts, memories, or justifications, come back via the breath into the heartspace, to the sensations in your body. Where do you feel tight, contracted, stiff? Where is the pain, the rigidity, the nervous quivering? How does it actually feel? Asking "What *is* this?"—feel it. Stay with the awareness of your bodily emotional reactions. Stay with them as long as is necessary to be able to reside in them, painful as they may be, without having to push them away. Stay here. Breathe. Hear the sounds outside. Hear the sounds in the room. Feel the air around you. Breathe. Reside here.

Return to your visualization of the person you wish to forgive. Draw this person's presence, via the inbreath, even deeper into the heartspace. As you feel the inbreath, say the person's name. Then say these words:

> I forgive you.
> I forgive you for whatever you may have done,

whether intentional or unintentional,
from which I experienced pain.

Whether it was from something you did
or from something you said, I forgive you.

I forgive you,
because I know that what you did
came from your own pain.

Repeat these words until you feel the barrier between you and the other person begin to dissolve.

If you still don't feel the sense of forgiveness, if some measure of hardness around the heart remains, just continue to breathe into the heartspace for a while, at least acknowledging the possibility of forgiveness at some future time. As you practice this meditation regularly, the process of forgiveness will gradually loosen the tight grip of resentment.

Having practiced this meditation a few times, it might be helpful to record it on tape, reading slowly and allowing two- or three-minute pauses to experience the arising feelings. Feel free to change the words to any that might resonate more naturally.

Listening Deeply for Peace

Thich Nhat Hanh

One of the most powerful ways to improve how we relate to other people is to understand their suffering—the pain it causes them, how it drives them, why it makes them hurt other people in turn. This is as true for nations as it is for individuals, says Thich Nhat Hanh, the Vietnamese Zen teacher and activist. Peace will only become a reality, he says, when world leaders learn to listen deeply to the suffering—their own and their enemy's—that is the root of all conflict.

A traditional Vietnamese Zen garden is very different from a Japanese Zen garden. Our Zen gardens, called *hon non bo*, are wild and exuberant, more playful than the formal Japanese gardens with their restrained patterns. Vietnamese Zen gardens are seriously unserious. For us, the whole world is contained in this peaceful place. All activities of life unfold in true peace in the garden: in one part, children will be playing, and in another part, some elderly men will be having a chess game; couples are walking; families are having picnics; animals are free to wander around. Beautiful trees are growing next to abundant grasses and flowers. There is water, and there are rock formations. All ecologies are represented in this one microecology without discrimination. It is a miniature, peaceful world. It is a beautiful living metaphor for what a new global ethic could bring.

War is not a necessary condition of life. The root of war, as with all conflicts, is ignorance, ignorance of the inherent goodness—the buddhanature—in every human being. The potential for ignorance lives in all of us; it gives rise to misunderstanding, which can lead to violent thoughts and behavior. Although ignorance and violence may not have manifested in your life, when conditions are sufficient, they can. This is why we all have to be very careful not to water these seeds and not to allow them to develop roots and grow into arrows.

The Roots of War

When one country attacks another, it is out of great fear and a kind of collective ignorance. For instance, the French fought to keep Vietnam as their colony because they thought that if they possessed Vietnam, they would be happy. So they sent many young men to Vietnam to kill and to be killed. We know, when we look deeply, that happiness does not come from possessing something or someone; it comes from kindness and compassion, from helping to ease suffering.

If the American people had sat down and practiced looking deeply, they would have seen that the Vietnam War was entirely unnecessary, that their own lives could not be improved through the suffering of another country or the suffering of their own young men. The United States senselessly wasted many lives in this war when it could have supported both North and South Vietnam in their different models of development, helping the Communists and the non-Communists alike to rebuild their societies. This would have been much wiser than supporting one side and fighting the other. If France and the United States had yielded autonomy to Vietnam, Laos, Cambodia, and Thailand, helping these countries to develop instead of waging war, all sides would have profited from such a friendly relationship. After a long period of suffering, these countries are finally moving in this direction, but this could have happened much earlier without the terrible loss of life.

All violence is injustice. We should not inflict that injustice on ourselves or on other people. Historians and teachers as well as politicians should look deeply at the suffering caused by wars, not just at the justifications that governments give for them. We have to teach our children the truth about war so they learn from our experiences and understand that violence and war are not the right way, that they are not the right actions to take. We have to show our children that people on both sides of war—the French and American soldiers in Vietnam, as well as the Vietnamese people—were victims of the ignorance and violence rooted in their societies and governments. Remember, there were no winners.

As long as we allow hatred to grow in us, we continue to make ourselves and others suffer. As we look deeply at the wars in our recent history, we have to transform our hatred and misunderstanding into compassion. We have to recognize that those who have made us suffer are also victims. Many who had a father, brother, or friend killed in the Vietnam War have been able to transcend their suffering and to reconcile with the other side, Vietnamese and American. They have done this for their own sake and for the sake of their children.

How can we as individuals influence the collective consciousness of our nations and move in the direction of peace? We do this by uprooting the roots of violence and war within ourselves. To prevent war, we cultivate nonviolence. We practice mindfulness in our daily life so that we can recognize and transform the poisons within us and our nation. When we practice nonviolence in our daily life, we see the positive effects on our families, society, and government.

Peace Is Possible

In the summer of 2001 in our community in Plum Village, France, about eighteen hundred people came and practiced with us.

Among them were a few dozen Palestinians and Israelis. We sponsored these people, hoping they could have the opportunity to practice walking meditation together, to share a meal together, to listen to the teachings of mindfulness practice, and to learn the act of deep listening and gentle, loving speech. The Israelis and Palestinians spent two weeks with us and participated in all activities.

At the end of their stay, the whole community gathered together and our visitors stood up and gave a report. After only two weeks of practice, they had transformed very deeply. They had become a community of brothers and sisters, Palestinians and Israelis. They said to us, "Dear community, dear Thich Nhat Hanh, when we first came to Plum Village we couldn't believe it. Plum Village did not look real to us because it is so peaceful. In Plum Village, we did not feel the kind of anger, tension, and fear that we feel constantly in the Middle East. People look at each other with kind eyes, they speak to each other lovingly. There is peace, there is communication, and there is brotherhood and sisterhood." One member of the delegation said, "We spent two weeks in paradise." Another person wrote to me after he returned home and said, "This is the first time that I have believed that peace is possible in the Middle East."

What did we do to make the third truth—that well-being and peace are possible—real to them? Honestly, we did not do much. We just embraced these friends from the Middle East as brothers and sisters. They learned to walk mindfully with us, to breathe in and out mindfully with us, to stop and be there in the present moment with us, and to get in touch with what is pleasant, nourishing, and healing around them and within themselves. The practice is very simple, but supported by a practicing *sangha*, they were able to succeed more quickly than on their own and to touch the peace and happiness within each of them.

Together we all followed the basic practice: to do everything mindfully. We established ourselves in the here and now in order to touch life deeply. We practiced mindfulness while we breathed and walked and talked and brushed our teeth and chopped vegetables for meals and washed dishes. That is the basic daily practice that our friends learned. We in the sangha offered our support, sitting with our visitors and practicing listening with compassion with them.

We trained them to speak in such a way that the other side could hear and understand and accept. They spoke in a calm way, not condemning anyone, not judging anyone. They told the other side of all the suffering that had happened to them and their children, to their societies. They all had the chance to speak of their fear, anger, hatred, and despair. Many felt for the first time that they were listened to and that they were being understood, which relieved a lot of suffering within them. We listened deeply, opening our hearts with the intention to help them express and heal themselves.

Two weeks of the practice of deep listening and using loving speech brought a lot of joy to our visitors and to all of us in Plum Village. We were reminded, hearing these stories, that during the Vietnam War, we Vietnamese, too, had suffered terribly. Yet our practice allowed us then and allows us still to see that our world is beautiful, with all the wonders of life available every day. This is why we know that our friends from the Middle East, too, can practice in the middle of war around them.

There were moments during the war when we wished so hard that there would be a cease-fire for just twenty-four hours. We thought that if we had only twenty-four hours of peace, we would have been able to breathe in and out and smile to the flowers and the blue sky. But we did manage to breathe in and out and smile, even then, because even the flowers had the courage to bloom in the middle of war. Yet still, we wanted twenty-four hours of peace during the war. We wanted the bombs to stop falling on us.

During the war in Vietnam, young people came to me and asked, "Do you think there will be an end to the war?" I could not answer them right away. I practiced mindful breathing, in and out.

After a long time I looked at them and said, "My dear friends, the Buddha said everything is impermanent, including war."

Before going back to the Middle East, our friends promised us that they would continue the practice. They told us that on the local level they would organize weekly meetings so they could continue to walk together, sit and breathe together, share a meal together, and listen to each other. Every month they have had an event to do this. They practice true peace even in the midst of war.

True Peace Negotiations

When you come to any negotiation, whether at work or in a meeting with other parents, teachers, or neighbors, you have hope for peace. When your representatives go to a negotiation table, they hope for peace. But if you and they do not master the art of deep listening and loving speech, it is very difficult to move toward peace in any situation or to get concrete results. If we have not transformed our inner block of suffering, hatred, and fear, it will prevent us from communicating, understanding, and making peace.

I beg the nations and governments who would like to bring peace to the Middle East and other countries to pay attention to this fact. We need our governments to organize peace negotiations so that they will be fruitful. A very important factor for success is creating a setting where true communication can be practiced, where deep listening and gentle, loving speech can occur. It may take one month or two just for people to learn how to listen to each other, to talk so that the other side can hear and understand. It is important not to be in a hurry to reach a conclusion or an agreement about what to do for peace to be possible. One month or two is nothing compared with years of pain and suffering. But if we have a great determination, then five days may be enough to restore communication between people. Two weeks were enough for our Palestinian friends and our Israeli friends to begin to understand and to accept each other as brothers and sisters, to begin to practice and create peace. Two weeks were enough for them to have hope.

Too often in the past, peace conferences have been environments where people came and fought each other, not with weapons but with their fear. When we are carried away by our fear and prejudices, we cannot listen to others. We cannot just bring two sides together around a table to discuss peace when they are still filled with anger, hatred, and hurt. If you cannot recognize your fear and anger, if you do not know how to calm yourself, how can you sit at a peace table with your enemy? Facing your enemy across a table, you will only continue to fight. Unable to understand yourself, you will only continue to fight. Unable to understand yourself, you will be unable to understand the other person.

The secret of creating peace is that when you listen to another person you have only one purpose: to offer him an opportunity to empty his heart. If you are able to keep that awareness and compassion alive in you, then you can sit for one hour and listen even if the other person's speech contains a lot of wrong perceptions, condemnations, and bitterness. You can continue to listen because you are already protected by the nectar of compassion in your own heart. If you do not practice mindful breathing in order to keep that compassion alive, however, you can lose your own peace. Irritation and anger will come up, and the other person will notice and will not be able to continue. Keeping your awareness keeps you safe.

Peace conferences must create environments that can help people calm down and see that they are suffering and that the other side is suffering also. Many leaders have tried to sponsor talks and discussion, but theirs was not the way of practice. They did not practice to transform anger and fear into deep listening and loving speech. When leaders do practice, there will be a chance for true reconciliation. After the practices of deep listening and kind and loving speech have dissolved bitterness, fear, and prejudice, people can begin to communicate with each other. Then reaching peace will be much easier. Peace will become a reality.

Deep Listening with Other Countries

If America invests all her heart and mind into this practice, then other people will also be able to tell her about their suffering. If America goes back to herself and restores the spirit of her forefathers, America will be truly great. She will then be in a position to help other countries establish similar forums, to invite other groups and countries to express themselves.

The setting must be one of safety and love. Countries from around the world can come together not as enemies that bomb and destroy each other but as wise people sponsoring sessions of deep listening. All nations could come and help with the practice; people from different cultures and civilizations would have the opportunity to speak to one another as fellow human beings who inhabit the same planet. In addition, people who are not just politically minded but humanists who understand the suffering of others could be invited—people who know how to sit and listen calmly, with compassion. These people would know how to create an atmosphere of peace without fear so that others can have the chance, the inspiration, and the desire to speak. We must be patient. The process of learning about each other's suffering will take time.

If such an international forum were broadcast around the world, everyone could participate and have the chance to learn about the causes of suffering. The first and second noble truths of the Buddha, the awareness of suffering and the awareness of the causes of suffering, could be practiced together by billions of people.

The first and second noble truths will lead us to the third and fourth noble truths; namely, the awareness that there is a path out of suffering and that that path consists of certain concrete steps, such as right understanding, right thinking, right speech, and right action.

Creating Peace

The antidote to violence and hatred is compassion. There is no other medicine. Unfortunately, compassion is not available in drugstores. You have to generate the nectar of compassion in your heart. The teaching of the Buddha gives us the means to generate the energy of compassion. If we are too busy, if we are carried away every day by our projects, our uncertainty, our craving, how can we have the time to stop and look deeply into the situation—our own situation, the situation of our beloved one, the situation of our family and of our community, and the situation of our nation and of the other nations? Looking deeply, we find out that not only do we suffer but also the other person suffers deeply. Not only our group suffers but the other group also suffers. Once awareness is born, we know that punishment, violence, and war are not the answer.

The one who wants to punish is inhabited by violence. The one who endures the suffering of the other person is also inhabited by the energy of violence. Violence cannot be ended with violence. The Buddha said that responding to hatred with hatred can only increase hatred a thousandfold. Only by responding to hatred with compassion can we disintegrate hatred.

The future is a notion. The future is made of only one substance, the present. If you are taking good care of the present moment, why do you have to worry about the future? By taking care of the present, you are doing everything you can to assure a good future. Is there anything else you can do? Live the present moment in such a way that peace and joy may be possible here and now—that love and understanding may be possible. Dwelling happily and peacefully in the present moment is the best thing we can do to ensure peace and happiness in the future.

We have to practice looking deeply as a nation if we want to get out of this difficult situation of war and terrorism. Our practice will help the other nations to practice. I am sure that America is very capable of punishing. The United States can send bombs; the whole world knows she is very capable of doing so. But America is great when she acts with lucidity and compassion. I urge that when we are suffering, when we are overcome by shock, we should not do anything, we should not say anything. We should go home to ourselves and practice mindful breathing and mindful walking to allow ourselves to calm down and to allow lucidity to come, so we can understand the real roots of our suffering and the suffering of the world. Only with that understanding can compassion arise. America can be a great nation if she knows how to act with compassion instead of punishment. We can offer peace. We can offer the relief of transformation and healing.

It is my deep wish that the American people and the people of other countries become spiritual allies and practice compassion together. Without a spiritual dimension and practice, we cannot really improve the situation of the world. We can come together as a family in order to look deeply into our own situation and the situation of the world.

Practicing peace is possible with every step, with every breath. It is possible for us to practice together and bring hope and compassion into our daily lives and into the lives of our families, our community, our nation, and the world.

Prayer Flags and Refugees

Pico Iyer

One of the most magical places in this world is the small Himalayan town of Dharamsala, India. It's the home of the Dalai Lama and of the Tibetan government-in-exile, and a destination for spiritual seekers from around the world. Son of an Indian diplomat who knew the Dalai Lama, Pico Iyer has been coming here since he was a teenager, and he knows that behind all the color is the tragedy of a people in exile.

I drove between avenues of trees, villagers working in the lush fields around me, camels, lipsticked girls with large bowls on their heads, signs along the road saying, in India's inimitable fashion, "Thanks for inconvenience." Up above, suddenly, in the radiant spring sunshine, a few hours out of Jammu Airport, I could see snowcaps, shockingly clear against the high blue skies, and speaking for the even higher peaks of the Himalayas just behind them.

My rickety Indian-made Ambassador lurched over mountain streams, on single-lane bridges that looked ready to collapse, and then, as we began to climb the pine-covered slopes, flashes of rhododendron visible through the trees, I began to see more and more people dressed in claret robes. We passed through Dharamsala proper, the nondescript Indian town that sits at the bottom of the

Kangra Valley, and then began to ascend a winding mountain road, past monuments to soldiers, army cantonments, and an old Anglican church where Lord Elgin lay buried amidst the overgrown crosses. Finally, we bumped into the scrappy line of stalls, run-down guesthouses, and spinning prayer-wheels that the world thinks of as Dharamsala.

At first sight, it's hard to believe that this unprepossessing place, thick with the scent of refuse, and filled with pierced and beaded seekers drifting among potholes, is one of the great pilgrimage sites of the modern world, sought out by screenwriters, philosophers, and movie-stars. But then you begin to walk around and see the golden turrets of a Tibetan Buddhist temple tucked among the trees, and note the hill on which sits the modest yellow house of exiled Tibet's spiritual and political leader, the 14th Dalai Lama. You make out paths leading up through the bear- and leopard-filled mountains to the snowline. You hear chanting through the dark from a nunnery, and drumming from down in the valley where the spiritual leader of Mongolia is staying. And you see, as the sun rises over the snowcaps, scores of weathered Tibetans walking and walking around the central temple, muttering prayers and spinning prayer-wheels, as if to speak of all that exiled Tibet has managed to achieve, since its land was invaded by China in 1950 and fully taken over in 1959, and all that it has yet to gain.

"It's okay," said the Dalai Lama, breaking into a high chirrup of infectious laughter when I asked him about his adopted home this spring (seconds before, he had been speaking about how Tibet itself seems on the brink of oblivion). "Now we have been in India forty-four years, in Dharamsala forty-three years, maybe thirty years from now everything will be fine."

When first the Tibetan leader arrived here, with his devoted community, sight unseen, in 1960, he remembers the excitement of waking up to snowcaps and seeing wildflowers everywhere; his new home allowed him to tinker with his garden and to take long hikes into the hills, leaving his bodyguards breathless behind him. Every summer, though, he notes, with characteristic honesty, the withering monsoons for which Dharamsala is notorious would destroy all the flowers he had so carefully tended, making him homesick, for a moment, for the high dry air of the Tibetan plateau.

As with much that he says, the friendly anecdote is a parable of sorts, and a kind of metaphor: Dharamsala is the place from which "by far the most serious" government-in-exile in the world (in *The Economist*'s words) has organized its more than eighty schools across India, the 190 nunneries and monasteries it has built since 1960, and the fifty settlements and communities that shelter hundreds of thousands of exiled Tibetans. In one corner of the hills is a Tibetan Children's Village, where two thousand kids learn their culture's language and history as they could never do at home (many of them are in fact sent out from Tibet over the Himalayas in order to get a Tibetan education here); in another, the Tibetan Institute of Performing Arts preserves Tibet's dance and opera traditions. Down one winding road sits a library containing Tibet's archives, and down in the valley is a sumptuous cultural institute, the Norbulingka, where apprentices make scrolls and statues and wood carvings in a garden of walkways and flowers alarmingly reminiscent of Shangri-La. And yet, for all that, after almost half a century in exile, the Tibetans are no closer to a vanishing home that is on the brink of extinction now.

I go to Dharamsala—and have been going for almost thirty years—in order to savor its silent spaces, but also to witness the paradoxes of exile, and the mingled heroism and frustration of trying to build a new home that, at some level, its makers hope will one day make itself redundant, as a *mandala* does. If you want mountain views, I tell my friends, you're better off in Darjeeling, and if you wish to see Tibetan culture live as it might have done centuries ago, fly up to Ladakh; if you want to savor the wistfulness of a former British hill station, you may be better served in Simla, and as a center of the East-meets-West dance, nowhere is more colorful and comfortable than Kathmandu. Yet Dharamsala is the place where all the themes converge, in a sort of dizzying mandala in which a myriad of cultures circle around one another, not sure of whether they're in search of enlightenment or something else. When I called up the Dalai Lama's younger brother this spring, I was put on hold to the tune of "It's a Small, Small World."

When first you arrive in McLeod Ganj—the unpaved little heart of Upper Dharamsala (the Tibetan area that sits six miles by road above the Indian town of Dharamsala)—you may feel as if you've fallen into a bad trip, in every sense of the word, and a place as unmelodious and mongrel as its name. Languid blonde girls in harem pants and shaven-headed boys who haven't washed in days saunter past the Peace restaurant, en route to the Faith gift shop, talking of dharma bummers and showing off a style that might best be called "McLeod Grunge." Adds for "Dream Yoga" and "Zen Shiatsu" and every kind of mishmashed transformation flutter from outside "Esoteric Boutiques" and "Buddhist Book Stores." Tibetan blades with silky hair down to their waists and slow smiles move around the dreadlocks and the incense, seeing how they can turn their exoticism to advantage.

Yet Dharamsala is, if nothing else, a lesson in impermanence and illusion, the Buddhist truths. Nearly everyone here is in flight—the Tibetans from China, the foreigners from home—and yet many a story you hear is one of suffering and surprise. That high-cheeked Tibetan stud in the black leather jacket, standing outside the "only Internet café where all profits go directly to the Tibetan cause," traveled fifty-nine days through the snow to get here, he will tell you, and if you ask him whether he has any contact with his family back home in Tibet, his eyes mist over and a silence falls. And that flamboyant character in ponytail and sandals turns out to be a volunteer who's left a job at an ad agency to teach English to the nuns who've escaped imprisonment and torture to come here. Both parties are looking for salvation of a kind—a new life—but both seem to sense that it will very likely go unfound.

The first time I came to McLeod Ganj, in 1974, I drove straight up to the Dalai Lama's house (Luckily for me, my father had met the Tibetan leader soon after he came into exile, in 1960, and so I had more access than many might), and as we sat in his airy living-room, summer clouds floating through, it was easy to feel as if we were truly apart from the world, in the clouds, out of time. Even in 1988, when I came to celebrate the Tibetan New Year here—long-horns sounding from the roof of Thekchen Choeling Temple in the predawn chill—there was only one semi-comfortable hotel in which to stay, and its dining room was empty save for me and a lonely French Buddhist nun. But after the Dalai Lama won the Nobel Prize in 1989, and as more and more people started going to Tibet, or finding Tibet in their neighborhoods, suddenly Dharamsala—the living heart of Tibetan color and wisdom and hope, and home to its open-hearted embodiment—became disproportionately well-known. Multistory Indian hotels began appearing on once-virgin ridges and now a little directory lists eighty-one guesthouses alone charging less than $7 a night.

"The thing that separates here from Manali, Dheradun, and Simla," says Tenzin Geyche, the private secretary to the Dalai Lama who's been working with the Tibetan leader since 1964, "is that it's so international"; in some seasons, the Dalai Lama's other private secretary, Tenzin Takhla adds, the population here is 50 percent Israeli (there is even a rabbi among the German bakeries and wood-fire pizza joints of Dharamkot nearby). And since Kashmir became something of a war zone, more and more Indians look in on Dharamsala when they want a holiday in the hills. Nothing remains unchanged. "Some people say that when we came to Dharamsala, many of the Indians here were vegetarians," the Dalai Lama told me on my recent visit, exuding his characteristic delight in challenging himself and his assumptions. "But now, more and more are eating meat. So, that means"—his eyes crease up at the irony of it all—"that we Tibetans are teaching them bad habits!"

More seriously, there is always a potential for unrest as the eleven thousand or so Indians of Upper Dharamsala watch the eleven thousand or so Tibetans receiving all the attention and support of the world at large: even a tiny guesthouse here sells itself as an "Exile Government Undertaking." A few years ago, a Tibetan boy stabbed an Indian, and small riots broke out in the area, the windows of Tibetan stores were shattered, and even the government-in-exile's secretariat, a long walk away, was attacked. "A lot of the people who come out now, they don't even remember the old Tibet," says one of the men who was in the Dalai Lama's party when he fled Tibet. "All they think about is the Almighty Dollar."

For most foreigners, though, Dharamsala remains an often idyllic place of secluded temples and sunlit valleys, where a state oracle offers government advice in a trance and the heir apparent to Tibetan hopes, the 17th Karmapa, still a teenager, stays after his flight from China (the very word "Dharamsala," appropriately enough, refers to the shelter for pilgrims attached to a temple). One bright spring morning I scrambled down a mud path, just across from my cozy guesthouse (itself across from the Dalai Lama's house and his private monastery), and found myself alone on a rough shepherd's path through the trees, white butterflies twirling around me, and black-and-white crested birds singing from the trees. In the distance I could just make out the shining rooftop of a Buddhist temple, and as I pulled open a creaky gate ("Please keep close the gate," said a sign), I found myself, as in a fairy tale, at a small stone bridge leading to a sleepy monastery. Small monks were sitting on a patch of grass, playing a board game in the light. Prayer flags fluttered against the high cloudless blue. A few steps down, some foreigners who were staying (for $3 a night) inside the Tse Chok Ling Temple sat above commanding views across the valley.

Those views are one reason why the British settled upon the area in 1849, first setting up an army cantonment here, and then a whole community for escape from the heat of the plains. A Forest Officer and a Deputy Commissioner were soon ensconced in British cottages here, and an army church built amidst the Himalayan cedars, or deodars; if Lord Elgin had not died in 1863, it is said, Dharamsala would have become the summer capital of British India. The community was reduced to rubble by an earthquake in

1905, and then again by Partition in 1947, but in both cases it soon rose again.

"It was so remote," the Dalai Lama's younger brother, Tenzin Choegyal, recalls of Dharamsala when he arrived here in 1960. "You couldn't get many things from the market." The Dalai Lama moved into a small house that is now, aptly, a mountaineering institute, and his junior tutor into a place that is now a meditation center, both of them enjoying the fact, no doubt, that centuries ago the Kangra Valley was famous for its Buddhist temples. Soon the calendar became as full of Tibetan customs as the countryside all round. When I arrived in Dharamsala this spring I saw explosions of red in every corner of the town—in Internet cafés, in little video dens, in Japanese restaurants—as up to three thousand nuns and monks from around the Tibetan world gathered for the annual spring teachings, or "Great Prayer Festival," that customarily follows the Tibetan New Year (in late February or early March). As soon as the Dalai Lama concluded his two weeks of public lectures, the *Shotun*, or Yogurt, Festival took over the Tibetan Institute of Performing Arts, and for ten days black-masked dancers and comical singers entertained crowds of delighted locals. Both prayer halls of the central temple were filled from dawn to nightfall with monks praying (at the Dalai Lama's request) for world peace, and when the imprisoned 11th Panchen Lama's fourteenth birthday arrived, Tibetans carrying candles appeared all around the temple and banners were strung across the main street.

Something was always happening at the main temple, which now contains its own stylish museum, Italian café, and shop selling "Quality Curative Incense." And as if in honor of the Buddhist teaching, the place was never the same from day to day. Sometimes groups of uniformed schoolchildren were crouched over drawings in a public competition held outside the main hall; sometimes the monks led a special prayer around a bonfire. Occasionally special auspicious food was handed out to anyone who wanted it, and sometimes there were esoteric dances and ceremonial mandalas. And almost every day, in the quiet afternoons or after dark, I watched young monks perform classic Tibetan debating, one of them sitting on the ground, aspiring to look unmoved while the other fired questions at him and lunged towards him with a lightning clap of hands.

One day a whisper ran through town that the Dalai Lama was offering a public audience, and an unending line of Western nomads formed around the security office where passports were checked and passes handed out. Then, as the sun came out, the Tibetan leader stood outside his audience room and a circle of silent votaries, first foreign and then Tibetan, lined up around his driveway for a quick blessing or a shake of his hand. After even the briefest of encounters, boys in swelling pantaloons and hoop-earringed girls issued forth with huge smiles, or tears in their eyes.

And around this constant flux the whole zany carnival of Indian daily life was always in full swing. One little restaurant inscrutably serenaded diners with a Muzaked version of "Here Comes the Bride," while the buses outside said "I love my India" on their sides, or "Oh! God save me." In many a dark, bare-walled opening, some resourceful kid had set up a DVD player and a flat-screen Sony, and projected five brand-new Hollywood releases a day ("This is the property of Miramax Studios. It is to be used for screening purposes only," flashing across the screen every five minutes). One overeager Indian hotel, anxious to offer best wishes for the Tibetan New Year, *Losar*, had even strung a banner above Temple Road, leading to the Dalai Lama's house, announcing, in huge letters, "HAPPY LOSER."

The other component adding the final coup de grace to the whole cross-cultural swirl is the arrival of luminaries from everywhere—Martin Scorsese, JFK, Jr., Harrison Ford—to learn what they can from the Dalai Lama. Goldie Hawn is often seen on the debris-stricken streets and Steven Seagal clomps around town in full Tibetan gear. The McLlo restaurant, a loud place next to the central bus stand, features a picture of Pierce Brosnan tucking into its fare, a hand held to his heart (or is it his stomach?). And when you use a public toilet, you see that it was donated by Richard

Gere, who has selflessly devoted time and money to the Tibetan cause for more than twenty years now, and actually set up a waste-management program to try to clean up the area's congenital mess.

And yet for all the brightness and sunshine of the Tibetan flowers and prayer flags and smiles—for all the magnolia against the snowcaps, next to golden wind chimes, in the ravishing Norbulingka Institute—there remains a strain of poignancy to the borrowed Elysium that reminds one of the archetypal traveler's truth that what is liberation for the visitor is often a painful imprisonment for the local. From my guesthouse I could hear a solemn gong through the trees and see monks playing tag on the whitewashed terraces of their monastery; yet on the road leading to it there were always Indian beggars and women waving receipts from hospitals to show the money they needed. One bright afternoon I drove up to Naddi, an Alpine village where green fields run up to a stunning line of snowcaps, the only sound a rushing stream far below; just two miles away, though, at the Children's Village the bright crèche was full of orphans, and the little girls who sang me a delightful version of "Jack and Jill" were very likely children who would never see their parents again.

I fell into conversation one day with a Tibetan woman and heard how she was an orphan herself, discovered by chance along the streets of Kathmandu by the Dalai Lama's sister. Now she had two children of her own, at the Children's Village, but the $2 cab fare and a leg ailment meant that she almost never got to see them.

Another bright Sunday morning, I stepped into a bookshop—McLeod Ganj shops are generally open on Sundays and closed on Mondays because, some say, the soldiers in British times wanted to shop on their one day off—and came upon a version of "This Land Is Your Land," sung with Tibetan lyrics, by the bookstore owner, who had stolen into his homeland in 1980 and been moved to write about what he had seen and felt. Even the tire covers on the jeeps in the Namgyal Monastery say, "Time is running out," followed by a line of gravestones. "Now we are finished," said a resistance fighter, mournfully. "Though I hope I am wrong. The Chinese are playing for time and we are playing into their hands." The Dalai Lama's decision that the most the world could hope for was a "saved" and not a "freed" Tibet still disappoints this one-time guerrilla. "Without freedom," he says, eyes penetrating and clear, "there is no hope."

The same day I walked into the sepulchral gloom of Nowrojee General Merchants, the Indian shop that has been supplying the area with its necessities since 1860, and found the last of the Nowrojees, as he sees himself, seventy-five years old, sitting in the dark, amidst dusty British ads for "Lux Toilet Soap" and "Andrews Liver Salt." His father, he said, had taken over the shop in 1904, and his elder brother, now deceased, had looked after it for sixty-two years. But he did not expect a sixth generation to take over because "Now nobody wants to live here."

"Dharamsala was so beautiful then, so peaceful," he said, recalling how all the family's sixteen employees had slept in the shop and went out each morning to pay calls on every bungalow. "I used to walk down to college, from six thousand feet to three thousand feet, four miles down, four miles up, every day. Everything was open: the nature, the fields. Now sanitation is not there, administration is not there. You cannot believe that this was once the biggest enterprise in northern India."

The old man can still remember when "we offered the land to His Holiness and the Tibetans. Then, an economic revival was there. But now"—a smile, with very few teeth in evidence—"now there has been too much revival. A flower blossoms and then it fades. Overcrowding, so much noise. I used to dream of growing old here, of dying here."

Not far away, in the Church of St. John in the Wilderness, founded by the British in 1852, a scratchy cassette is playing a version of "Onward Christian Soldiers" while birds sing in the rafters and the cheerful south Indian priest puts on a cassock above sneakers and jeans to deliver an Easter Sunday service. A ragtag group of worshipers has gathered in the draughty space to sing "Morning Has Broken" from a folder containing two photocopied pages (and concluding with "Have a Nice Day"). The plaques all around, put up by "Brother Officers of the Gurkha Rifles," recall men killed in Mesopotamia, Palestine, Baluchistan, and even one Thomas William Knowles, murdered by a bear on 25th October 1883, aged fifty ("In the midst of life we are in death").

The point of travel for me is to journey into complication, even contradiction; to confront the questions that I never have to think about at home, and am not sure can ever be easily answered. Dharamsala, alive with the sound of monks practicing dialectical reasoning, takes one as deeply into the dialogue of realism and hope as anywhere I know. The foreigners who stay here are often strikingly serious and compassionate, and spend months learning Tibetan or helping those in need; the place is bright with mystical paintings and prayer-flags and glorious mountain sunshine; the long walk around the Dalai Lama's house is always vivid with old Tibetans praying for the health of their leader and their home. And yet all of it remembers a culture that seems very far away. "As a human being, I am hopeful," says a Tibetan very close to the Dalai Lama. "But as a Tibetan . . . I don't know."

The Dalai Lama has worked as hard as anyone alive to make optimism and realism seem compatible. "If you look at things locally in Tibet," he told me this spring, "of course there is not much hope. But"—the famous gift for pragmatism takes over—"if some day there are six million Tibetans in Tibet and ten million Chinese and they are Buddhist, maybe, something okay." We don't know the future, he might be saying, but we have to act as if it will end tomorrow. He, his vibrant temples, the stirring institutions kept alive by the Tibetans around him, speak for hope; the stories that come out of Tibet, and the broken offices of McLeod Ganj, sometimes speak for something else. The visitor to Dharamsala tries to make sense of his competing feelings, and to make out the sound of the prayers above the klaxons on the road.

Proof of Our Goodness

Robert Thurman

The greatest leaders are moral beacons who confirm that our deepest hopes can become reality, that human nature is capable of great goodness. Like Mahatma Gandhi and Martin Luther King, Jr., His Holiness the Dalai Lama makes his spiritual life an example for all through political expression. Here is Robert Thurman, the dean of American Tibetology and a close associate of His Holiness, on what the Dalai Lama means to the world today.

Lately when I have attended His Holiness the Dalai Lama as he gives Buddhist teachings to large assemblies, I have had an odd sensation: it feels as if I have entered a time warp, and am actually witnessing Shakyamuni Buddha himself in all his glory as a teacher. As the *Noble Vimalakirti Sutra* describes him, "Dominating all the multitudes, just as Sumeru, the king of mountains, looms high over the oceans, the Lord Buddha shone, radiated and glittered as he sat upon his magnificent lion-throne."

Over many years I had attended His Holiness's teachings and found them informative and inspiring, but I had always felt that it was the Dalai Lama I knew sitting there before me. Buddha was often mentioned as a remote founding figure, far back in ancient history. Sure, this new sense I have is just subjective, my going "dotty," like a typical devotee. Maybe so. But it also gives me a clue about what the Dalai Lama has come to mean for the world.

I think the Dalai Lama has grown so close to Shakyamuni Buddha that their manifestations have become indistinguishable; the Dalai Lama has become living proof of the Mahayana vision of Buddha's inexhaustible compassionate presence. I think people sense that fact, each one according to his or her level of insight, as constrained by preconceptions, experience, and understanding.

This does not mean that the Dalai Lama is a "God-king" or a "living God," as is sometimes written in the press. For Buddha is not "God," who, if He did exist as conceived by Western monotheists, would be absolutely unimaginable, forever trans-human. Buddha, though also ultimately inconceivable, on the relative level is a being who was thoroughly human at one time, like you or me, and then through many lives evolved into something more than human and more than any God. He is a wise and compassionate, omnipresent but not omnipotent, universal awareness and powerful energy called "Realized One" (*Tathagata*), "Blissful One" (*Sugata*), "Teacher of Humans and Gods" (*Devamanushyanam Shasta*) and many other names. He/she is everywhere embodied/disembodied as reality, manifesting as seeming individuals in sensitive response to the needs of beings. Any particular manifestation of Buddha is thus a kind of living doorway to each individual's own happiness, a mirror, to that individual, of the reality that must be understood for that individual to realize his or her own wisdom, freedom from suffering, immortality, and supreme happiness.

It is natural that this might all seem merely hypothetical and unrealistic, the high-flown, challengingly optimistic philosophy (or Buddhology) of the Mahayana Buddhist sutras. It becomes concrete only in the live encounter with such a Buddha-manifestation. It takes a living personification of the Buddha-qualities to make our own freedom and enlightenment seem really possible, a live exemplar of the Buddha-happiness to make our own mouths water for the taste of our own real happiness. This is the real meaning of the Dalai Lama's presence. It is felt by all who meet him, through whatever medium, consciously or unconsciously.

It is not merely that the Dalai Lama represents "Buddhism," thought to be a distinct religious system. He is much more than a nominal leader of an organization. He does not seek to convert anyone to "Buddhism." "Buddhism" is not a world organization, competing with other organized world religions, seeking strength in numbers. It is an age-old movement seeking to educate the heart and mind of any being for freedom and happiness, no matter what their ideology. It is a teaching of the reality of selflessness and relationality. The Dalai Lama is a simple monk, an adept mind scientist, a thorough scholar, a spiritual teacher, a diplomat, a Nobel Peace Prize Laureate, an apostle of nonviolence, an advocate of intelligence and universal responsibility, and the living exemplar of what he calls "our common human religion of kindness."

We live in an era of extreme contrasts: technology informs us more than ever and yet makes us feel weaker and more frightened than ever. The art of caring for the sick seems more sophisticated than ever, and yet the food-chain is poisoned, the environment polluted, and good advice on how to live well is harder than ever to find. Pluralism on all levels seems more essential than ever, yet the cruelty of fanatics rages more violently than ever. Knowledge and technology have infinite potential to transform our world, potentially for the better, yet all around us devastation proceeds inexorably.

In this climate of manifold desperations, both quiet and shrill, the Dalai Lama seems to emerge from another civilization, to descend from a higher altitude, as if from another dimension, a living example of calm in emergency, patience in injury, cheerful intelligence in confusion, and dauntless optimism in the face of apparent doom. Inspired by Jesus, Gandhi, and Martin Luther King, Jr., he carries on that tradition under the extreme duress of the half-century-long agony of Tibet.

Especially since the emergency call of 9/11, the world seems headed into a tailspin. Instead of a post-cold-war century free of war, endless war is declared from several sides. Instead of increasing prosperity and joyful, optimistic sharing, the gulf between rich and poor grows cataclysmic, and the world economy seems heading for collapse. Instead of a scientifically sound era of healthy living, new plagues rear their terrifying heads. Hopelessness and fear send everyone rushing for an exit, diving into an isolated personal shelter. The West's Four Horsemen of the Apocalypse are riding wild upon the range.

In the midst of this, the Dalai Lama remains undaunted, even cheerful. He doesn't give up the responsibility for his own people, a nation of six million very close to succumbing to systematic genocide with no one in official power to protect them. He doesn't revile the harmful leaders as "evil"; he calls for dialogue and reconciliation, still, after more than fifty years of violence and oppression. He insists on the message that intelligence and kindness together can solve any situation. He sees that all is possible, even the good, the true, and the beautiful, and people therefore feel a huge weight lifted from them when they meet him. Though he is a simple monk, what the Zen people call a "true man of no rank," without any powerful organization, recognized nation, institutionalized religion, or rich industry or foundation, he still stands out as a natural leader of the plain people, a living symbol of nonviolence. He looms head and shoulders over the crowd of political leaders who tend to parade themselves as masters of violence.

What does the Dalai Lama mean? He is a living prince of peace, a teacher of intelligence, an inspirer of goodness of heart, a reincarnation of the Buddha of universal compassion. He comes to join us in our world today, offering us hope and help in our stressed-out lives and calling upon us to take up our own wild joy of universal responsibility.

A Mind Like Sky

Jack Kornfield

The renowned Insight Meditation teacher Jack Kornfield takes us on a meditation journey. We begin with precise awareness, then we expand our attention ever outward until it is as vast, open, and brilliant as the sky itself. That space, he says, is our true home.

Meditation comes alive through a growing capacity to release our habitual entanglement in the stories and plans, conflicts and worries that make up the small sense of self, and to rest in awareness. In meditation we do this simply by acknowledging the moment-to-moment changing conditions—the pleasure and pain, the praise and blame, the litany of ideas and expectations that arise. Without identifying with them, we can rest in the awareness itself, beyond conditions, and experience what my teacher Ajahn Chah called *jai pongsai*, our natural lightness of heart. Developing this capacity to rest in awareness nourishes *samadhi* ("concentration")—which stabilizes and clarifies the mind—and *prajna* ("wisdom"), which sees things as they are.

We can employ this awareness or "wise attention" from the very start. When we first sit down to meditate, the best strategy is to simply notice whatever state of our body and mind is present. To establish the foundation of mindfulness, the Buddha instructs his followers "to observe whether the body and mind are distracted or steady, angry or peaceful, excited or worried, contracted or released, bound or free." Observing what is so, we can take a few deep breaths and relax, making space for whatever situation we find.

From this ground of acceptance we can learn to use the transformative power of attention in a flexible and malleable way. Wise attention—mindfulness—can function like a zoom lens. Often it is most helpful to steady our practice with close-up attention. In this, we bring a careful attention and a very close focus to our breath or a sensation, or to the precise movement of feeling or thought. Over time we can eventually become so absorbed that subject and object disappear. We become the breath, we become the tingling in our foot, we become the sadness or joy. In this we sense ourselves being born and dying with each breath, each experience. Entanglement in our ordinary sense of self dissolves; our troubles and fears drop away. Our entire experience of the world shows itself to be impermanent, ungraspable, and selfless. Wisdom is born.

But sometimes in meditation such close focus of attention can create an unnecessary sense of tightness and struggle. So we must find a more open way to pay attention. Or perhaps when we are mindfully walking down the street we realize it is not helpful to focus only on our breath or our feet. We will miss the traffic signals, the morning light and the faces of the passersby. So we open the lens of awareness to a middle range. When we do this as we sit, instead of focusing on the breath alone, we can feel the energy of our whole body. As we walk we can feel the rhythm of our whole movement and the circumstances through which we move. From this perspective it is almost as if awareness sits on our shoulder and respectfully acknowledges a breath, a pain in our legs, a thought about dinner, a feeling of sadness, a shop window we pass.

Here wise attention has a gracious witnessing quality, acknowledging each event—whether boredom or jealousy, plans or excitement, gain or loss, pleasure or pain—with a slight bow. Moment by moment we release the illusion of getting "somewhere" and rest in the timeless present, witnessing with easy awareness all that passes by. As we let go, our innate freedom and wisdom manifest. Nothing to have, nothing to be. Ajahn Chah called this "resting in the One Who Knows."

Yet at times this middle level of attention does not serve our practice best. We may find ourselves caught in the grip of some repetitive thought pattern or painful situation, or lost in great physical or emotional suffering. Perhaps there is chaos and noise around us. We sit and our heart is tight, our body and mind are neither relaxed nor gracious, and even the witnessing can seem tedious, forced, effortful.

In this circumstance we can open the lens of attention to its widest angle and let our awareness become like space or the sky. As the Buddha instructs in the Majjhima Nikaya, "Develop a mind that is vast like space, where experiences both pleasant and unpleasant can appear and disappear without conflict, struggle or harm. Rest in a mind like vast sky."

From this broad perspective, when we sit or walk in meditation, we open our attention like space, letting experiences arise without any boundaries, without inside or outside. Instead of the ordinary orientation where our mind is felt to be inside our head, we can let go and experience the mind's awareness as open, boundless, and vast. We allow awareness to experience consciousness that is not entangled in the particular conditions of sight, sound, and feelings, but consciousness that is independent of changing conditions—the unconditioned. Ajahn Jumnien, a Thai forest elder, speaks of this form of practice as *maha vipassana*, resting in pure awareness itself, timeless and unborn. For the meditator, this is not an ideal or a distant experience. It is always immediate, ever present, liberating; it becomes the resting place of the wise heart.

Fully absorbed, graciously witnessing, or open and spacious—which of these lenses is the best way to practice awareness? Is there an optimal way to pay attention? The answer is, "All of the above." Awareness is infinitely malleable, and it is important not to fixate on any one form as best. Mistakenly, some traditions teach that losing the self and dissolving into a breath or absorbing into an experience is the optimal form of attention. Other traditions erroneously believe that resting in the widest angle, the open consciousness of space, is the highest teaching. Still others say that the middle ground—an ordinary, free and relaxed awareness of whatever arises here and now—"nothing special"—is the highest attainment. Yet in its true nature awareness cannot be limited. Consciousness itself is both large and small, particular and universal. At different times our practice will require that we embrace all these perspectives.

Every form of genuine awareness is liberating. Each moment we release entanglement and identification is selfless and free. But remember too that every practice of awareness can create a shadow when we mistakenly cling to it. A misuse of space can easily lead us to become spaced-out and unfocused. A misuse of absorption can lead to denial—the ignoring of other experiences—and a misuse of ordinary awareness can create a false sense of "self" as a witness. These shadows are subtle veils of meditative clinging. See them for what they are and let them go. And learn to work with all the lenses of awareness to serve your wise attention.

The more you experience the power of wise attention, the more your trust in the ground of awareness itself will grow. You will learn to relax and let go. In any moment of being caught, awareness will step in, a presence without judging or resisting. Close-in or vast, near or far, awareness illuminates the ungraspable nature of the universe. It returns the heart and mind to its birthright, naturally luminous and free.

To amplify and deepen an understanding of how to practice with awareness as space, the following instructions can be helpful. One of the most accessible ways to open to spacious awareness is through the ear door, listening to the sounds of the universe around us. Because the river of sound comes and goes so naturally, and is so obviously out of our control, listening brings the mind to a naturally balanced state of openness and attention. I learned this particular practice of sound as a gateway to space from my colleague Joseph Goldstein more than twenty-five years ago, and have used it ever since. Awareness of sound in space can be an excellent way to begin practice because it initiates the sitting period with the flavor of wakeful ease and spacious letting go. Or it can be used after a period of focused attention.

Whenever you begin, sit comfortably and at ease. Let your body be at rest and your breathing be natural. Close your eyes. Take several full breaths and let each release gently. Allow yourself to be still.

Now shift awareness away from the breath. Begin to listen to the play of sounds around you. Notice those that are loud and soft, far and near. Just listen. Notice how all sounds arise and vanish, leaving no trace. Listen for a time in a relaxed, open way.

As you listen, let yourself sense or imagine that your mind is not limited to your head. Sense that your mind is expanding to be like the sky—open, clear, vast like space. There is no inside or outside. Let the awareness of your mind extend in every direction like the sky.

Now the sounds you hear will arise and pass away in the open space of your own mind. Relax in this openness and just listen. Let the sounds that come and go, whether far or near, be like clouds in the vast sky of your own awareness. The play of sounds moves through the sky, appearing and disappearing without resistance.

As you rest in this open awareness, notice how thoughts and images also arise and vanish like sounds. Let the thoughts and images come and go without struggle or resistance. Pleasant and unpleasant thoughts, pictures, words, and feelings move unrestricted in the space of mind. Problems, possibilities, joys, and sorrows come and go like clouds in the clear sky of mind.

After a time, let this spacious awareness notice the body. Become aware of how the sensations of breath and body float and change in the same open sky of awareness. The breath breathes itself; it moves like a breeze. The body is not solid. It is felt as areas of hardness and softness, pressure and tingling, warm and cool sensation, all floating in the space of the mind's awareness.

Let the breath move like a breeze. Rest in this openness. Let sensations float and change. Allow all thoughts and images, feelings and sounds to come and go like clouds in the clear, open space of awareness.

Finally, pay attention to the awareness itself. Notice how the open space of awareness is naturally clear, transparent, timeless, and without conflict—allowing all things, but not limited by them.

As one is reminded in the texts, "O Nobly Born, remember the pure open sky of your own true nature. Return to it. Trust it. It is home."

May the blessings of these practices awaken your own inner wisdom and inspire your compassion. And through the blessing of your heart may the world find peace.

Buddhism Is Not Self-Help

Tsoknyi Rinpoche

People in the West practice Buddhist meditation for many different reasons, from relaxation and better relationships to personal liberation or even a better game of golf. It's our motivation that determines the scope of our spiritual practice, says Tsoknyi Rinpoche, who asks that we practice not for ourselves but to achieve enlightenment for the sake of all sentient beings.

Whether our dharma practice will progress in the right direction depends on our attitude, our intention. Motivation is extremely important: it is what everything stands or falls with, and this is true not only in spiritual practice but in whatever we set out to do. Therefore, in Buddhist practice it is of utmost importance to continually correct and improve our attitude.

The attitude we need to cultivate is one that is suffused with *bodhichitta* [awakened mind-heart]. This enlightened attitude has two aspects. The first aspect is the urge to purify our negativity: "I want to rid myself of all shortcomings, all ego-oriented emotions such as attachment, aggression, stupidity, and all the rest." The second aspect is the sincere desire to benefit all beings: "Having freed myself of all negative emotions, I will benefit all sentient beings. I will bring every sentient being to the state of complete enlightenment."

The compassionate attitude of bodhichitta should encompass oneself as well as all others. We have every reason to feel compassionate towards ourselves. In the ordinary state of mind we are helplessly overtaken by selfish emotions; we lack the freedom to remain unaffected when these emotions occupy our mind. Swept away by feelings of attachment, anger, closed-mindedness, and so forth, we lose control, and we suffer a great deal in this process. In such a state, we are unable to help ourselves, let alone others. We need to relate to our own suffering here with compassion in a balanced way, applying compassion toward ourselves just as we would do with others. In order to help others, we must first help ourselves, so that we can become capable of expanding our efforts further. But we shouldn't get stuck in just helping ourselves. Our compassion must embrace all other beings as well, so that having freed ourselves of negative emotions we are moved by compassion to help all sentient beings.

At this point in our practice, it's okay if our attempts to experience the attitude of bodhichitta are a little bit artificial. Because we haven't necessarily thought in this way before, we need to deliberately shift or adjust our intention to a new style. This kind of tampering with our own attitude is actually necessary. We may not yet be perfect bodhisattvas, but we should act as if we already are. We should put on the air of being a bodhisattva, just as if we're putting on a mask that makes us look as if we are somebody else. The true, authentic bodhichitta only arises as a natural expression of having realized the view. Before experiencing this spontaneously and fully, however, we need to consciously try to move in that direction. Even though our efforts may feel a little artificial at this point, it is perfectly okay—assuming of course that this is the good and necessary kind of artifice.

The need to improve our attitude, to correct our motivation, is not particularly difficult to understand, nor is it that difficult to actually do. Although it may be simple, this does not mean that we should belittle its importance. At this point, we should repeatedly cultivate the bodhisattva attitude. This is very important. To look down upon it as an inferior or unimportant practice seriously detracts from real progress on the spiritual path. Therefore, again and again, in all situations try your best to motivate yourself with bodhichitta.

In Tibet there is a lot of livestock: many cows, sheep, yaks. The skin from these animals needs to be cured in order to be useful; it needs to be softened by a special process. Once the hide has been cured, it becomes flexible and can be used in all sorts of ways: in religious artifacts, to bind up certain offerings on the shrine, as well as for all kinds of household purposes. But first it needs to be prepared in the right way: it needs to be softened, made flexible. If the hide is simply left as it is, it hardens and becomes totally stiff; then it is nothing but an unyielding piece of animal skin. It is the same way with a human being's attitude. We must soften our hearts, and this takes deliberate effort. We need to make ourselves gentle, peaceful, flexible, and tame, rather than being undisciplined, rigid, stubborn egocentrics.

This softening of our heart is essential for all progress, and not just in terms of spiritual practice. In all we do, we need to have an attitude that is open-minded and flexible. In the beginning this act of improving our attitude is definitely artificial. We are deliberately trying to be a bodhisattva, to have the compassionate attitude of wanting to help all sentient beings. This conscious effort is vital, because it can genuinely soften us up from deep within. If we do not cultivate this attitude, our rigidly preoccupied frame of mind makes it impossible for the true view of bodhichitta to grow. It's like trying to plant seeds in a frozen block of ice atop Mount Everest—they will never grow, they will just freeze. When, on the other hand, you have warmed up your character with bodhichitta, your heart is like fertile soil that is warm and moist. Since the readiness is there, whenever the view of self-knowing wakefulness, the true view of Dzogchen that is ultimate bodhichitta, is planted, it can grow spontaneously. In fact, absolutely nothing can hold it back from growing in such a receptive environment! That is why it is so important to steadily train in bodhichitta right from the very beginning.

The word *dharma*, in the context of this discussion, means "method." The dharma is a method to overcome the delusion in our own stream of being, in our own mind—a way to be totally free of the negative emotions that we harbor and cause to proliferate, and at the same time to realize the original wakefulness that is present in ourselves. There are ten different connotations of the word *dharma*, but in this context we are speaking of two types: the dharma of statements and the dharma of realization. The dharma of statements is what you hear during a lecture or a teaching session. Within the dharma of statements are included the words of the Buddha, the Tripitaka, as well as the commentaries on the Buddha's words made by the many learned and accomplished masters of India and Tibet.

Through hearing the explanations that constitute the dharma of statements and through applying these methods, something dawns in our experience. This insight is called the dharma of realization, and it includes recognizing our own nature of mind. In order to approach this second kind of dharma, to apply it, we need the right motivation. Again, this right motivation is the desire to free oneself of negative emotions and bring all beings to liberation. We absolutely must have that attitude, or our spiritual practice will be distorted into personal profit seeking.

Basically there are three negative emotions: attachment, aggression, and closed-mindedness. Of course these three can be further distinguished into finer and finer levels of detail, down to the 84,000 different types of negative emotions. But the main three, as well as all their subsidiary classifications, are all rooted in ignorance, in basic unknowing. These are the negative emotions we need to be free of, and their main root is ignorance.

Someone might think, "I approach dharma practice because my ego is a little bit upset. My ego is not very intelligent, not quite able to succeed. I come here to practice in order to improve my ego." That attitude is not spiritual.

Here's another attitude: "My ego works so hard. I must take care of my ego. I must relax. I come here to practice and become relaxed, so that my ego gets healthier and I can do my job." That type of attitude is okay, but merely okay; it's just one drop of a very small motivation.

We can, in fact, have a much larger perspective. As long as we harbor and perpetuate the negative emotions of attachment, anger, closed-mindedness, pride, and jealousy, they will continue to give us a hard time, and they will make it difficult for others to be with us as well. We need to be free of them. We need to have this attitude: "I must be free of these emotions."

When you leave a meditation program or retreat, I want you to go home naked. You can think that you left your negative emotions there as a donation! Honestly, that is the purpose of such a place. It is not right to go on retreat or hear teachings with the attitude, "I must go there in order to get something; I must achieve something." Instead, have this attitude: "I am practicing a spiritual path in order to lose something—to get rid of my attachment, my anger, my closed-mindedness, my conceit, my competitive jealousy."

Next, I would like to suggest that you practice in such a way that you are at ease with the whole process. Gradually expand that attitude of ease to encompass more and more. Once you've freed yourself of all these annoying emotions and become naked, it's not like you can just lean back and take it easy. That is not sufficient. You can awaken a sense of responsibility for all the other sentient beings who are exactly the way you used to be, tormented by negative emotions. You can begin helping them—first one, then two, then three, and finally all sentient beings.

Otherwise, what Gampopa said may come true: If you do not practice the dharma correctly, it could become a cause for rebirth in the lower realms. That may happen for many people. In fact, it happens more frequently among old practitioners than with beginners.

Someone may relate to dharma merely as a kind of remedy to be used when confused or upset. This of course is not the real purpose of spiritual practice. In this kind of situation, you do some practice till you have settled down, and then you set it aside and forget all about it. The next time you get upset, you do some more practice in order to feel good again. Of course, reestablishing one's equilibrium in this way is one of the minor purposes of practice, but it's not the real goal. Doing this is a way of using the dharma as if it were a type of therapy. You may of course do this, but I do not think it will get you enlightened. Feel a little bit unhappy, do some dharma, get happy. Feel a little bit upset, then feel fine, then again feel unhappy. If you just continue holding this very short-term view in mind, then there is no progress. "Last night I didn't sleep—my mind was disturbed, and the dog was barking next door. Now my mind is a little upside down, so I need to do a session to cure it. Okay, this morning I'll meditate."

Do not practice in this way. Dharma practice is not meant merely to make oneself feel better. The whole point of spiritual practice is to liberate oneself through realization and also to liberate others through compassionate capacity. To practice in order to feel better only brings one back up to that same level—one never makes any real progress. At the end of one's life, one just happens to feel good till the end of one's last session and then that's it—nothing happens beyond that. With this attitude of merely feeling good becoming the type of Buddhism that spreads in the West, we may see a huge scarcity of enlightened masters in the future. They will become an endangered species.

Please understand that the pursuit of "feeling better" is a samsaric goal. It is a totally mundane pursuit that borrows from the dharma, and uses all its special methods in order to fine-tune the ego into a fit and workable entity. The definition of a worldly aim is to try to achieve something for oneself with a goal-oriented frame of mind—"so that I feel good." We may use spiritual practice to achieve this, one good reason being that it works much better than other methods. If we're on this path, we do a little spiritual practice and pretend to be doing it sincerely. This kind of deception, hiding the ego-oriented, materialistic aim under the tablecloth, might include something like "I take refuge in the Buddha, Dharma, and Sangha, so I must be pure." Gradually, as we become more astute at spiritual practice, we may bring our materialistic aim out into the open. This is quite possible: people definitely do it. But if this is how you practice, you won't get anywhere in the end. How could one ever become liberated through selfishness?

There comes a point when we start to lose faith in the illusions of this world: our level of trust in illusions begins to weaken, and we become disappointed. Using spiritual practice to nurture our ego back into good health while still retaining trust in these illusory aims does not set us free. True freedom does not mean having a healthy faith in illusions; rather, it means going completely beyond delusion. This may not sound particularly comforting, but it is true. It may be an unpleasant piece of news, especially if we have to admit to ourselves, "I have really been fooling myself all along. Why did I do all this practice? Am I completely wrong?" What can you do to pretend this isn't true? Facing the truth is not pleasant.

The real help here lies in continually correcting and improving our motivation: understanding why we are practicing and where we are ultimately heading. Work on this and bring forth the noble motivation of bodhichitta. Then all methods and practices can be used to help you progress in that direction.

Again I must emphasize this point: if we want to approach ultimate truth, we must form a true motivation. This includes compassion for all other sentient beings who delude themselves continuously with the contents of whatever arises in their minds. Compassionate motivation says, "How sad that they believe so strongly in their thoughts, that they take them to be so real." This deluded belief in one's own thoughts is what I call the "granddad concept." First, we hold our thought as true. Next, we accept that delusion, and it becomes our granddad. You know what it's like to suffer from this delusion yourself, in your own experience. Bring to mind all other sentient beings who let themselves get caught up in their granddad delusion and, with compassion, form the wish to free them all. That's the true motivation: please generate it.

Motivation is easy to talk about yet sometimes hard to have. We always forget the simplest things, partly because we don't take them seriously. We would rather learn the more advanced, difficult stuff. And yet the simple can also be very profound. When a teaching is presented as a brain teaser and it is hard to figure out but you finally get it, then you may feel satisfied. But this feeling of temporary satisfaction is not the real benefit. To really saturate yourself, your entire being, with the dharma, you need the proper motivation. Please apply this thoroughly, all the time.

Across the Fragrant Field

Bhikkhu Nyanasobhano

Bhikkhu Nyanasobhano has been called the Buddhist Thoreau. Like the great Transcendentalist sage, this American-born monk finds spiritual lessons everywhere in nature. So let's take a walk with him and find the dhamma all around us.

The teaching of the Buddha gives us the means to live by wise purpose in the midst of haphazard nature. It may be that if we apply enough skill and energy to mundane matters of making a living and protecting our property we can prosper—as the world sees it—but we can never through material prosperity alone secure any deep peace or freedom. Growing up, approaching maturity as human beings, means, at the least, understanding the necessity to honor and to live by noble standards. When the Buddha at last attained supreme enlightenment he reflected, "One dwells in suffering if one is without reverence and deference," and he himself determined to honor the magnificent Dhamma he had discovered.

It is our human nature to seek for and to depend on ideals of purpose and conduct, but it is not enough to select just any ideal or to settle on a purpose no grander than the achievement of fame and sensual gratification. Rather we must, by listening, studying, considering, and observing, find that which promises to be of consistent, universal benefit. Once we have discovered such an ideal, we cannot treat it as a distant abstraction, revering it only in theory, but must set about living in accordance with it, showing our respect through action. Nature forever dances on in inconclusive patterns, taking no account of the happiness of any lone creature; but the Buddha teaches for the benefit of all, pointing out those pure and virtuous patterns that, through the natural working of cause and effect, culminate in perfect happiness. If we are inspired by his teaching, if we see its beauty and logic, we must see also that, however difficult it seems, it is meant for our good and can be followed in this age or any age. Then we are left to decide what we, as free beings, are going to do about it.

Our trying winters will subside like all things, but whether the summers that follow will blossom with any real gladness depends on how intently we live by Dhamma. What are these garden fragrances and these wonders of clouds but more formations that cannot be held, that entertain and depart, that give no ultimate security? We say it is summer now, an epoch of ease and recreation, but is it also a summer of wise purpose and wise action, yielding good fruit? How long shall we wait for the world to perfect itself while we sink in dreams? If we idle through our seasons we will get no relief from affliction, and time, meanwhile, will press upon us and eventually break down all our indolent comforts. If, however, our ideals are noble, and if we act with good will and faith, we will find more than momentary flowers and will not have to fear the inevitable rearrangement of the world.

Across our neighborhood today legions of tiny seeds wrapped in white fluff are blowing, adding more clouds to the clouds of summer. So shall we walk out, as we have walked before, not just to enjoy the moist breeze from the woods, but to refresh ourselves with useful knowledge? Should we not, whether in leisure or on a determined errand, establish mindfulness and see what it will show us? All around us the Dhamma is manifest, available for our examination, and when we have well absorbed doctrine and considered it at length we can make use of the thousand expressions of reality we encounter to inspire us and strengthen us.

It is summer, a season for slow walking, for long contemplation of the shade and sunlight that variously fall upon us. Everywhere in our neighborhood, it seems, crickets are singing, making a shrill, monotonous music. Let us wander about today in a free hour, out in a field where the grass is thick. We find that our anxious steps are restrained, slowed, and disciplined by the bristling stalks and stems and leaves; and our thoughts, which otherwise might wander through the clouds, are forced down to the rank earth, down to the work we have to do to make our way across the field. Where are the briars that will catch at us? How long or short a step will serve right here? This season's growth fortunately is not too thick to stop us, only dense enough to make us more careful, more deliberate, and thus more conscious of what is happening. Here the Dhamma of remembered words takes on the freshness of unmowed grass.

Are we still impatient, eager to be moving in a straight line toward some tree or rock or house—as if everything of interest and importance must exist somewhere other than here? Why should we hurry at the call of a desire? Do we step into a field only to cross it and find again more immensities beyond still uncomprehended? Here, where we stand and turn, is a universe of moths and clover, where bees glide, where crickets scamper and hide, where life and death revolve under our gaze. Out of the winter all of this intensity comes to be, and into the winter it falls again. If our human world is to be accounted superior, in what does that superiority lie? We too are mortal; we wince at thorns; but we retain the power to contemplate, to conceive of a good beyond the hour's diversion, and to bring something of that good into being by our deeds.

Why should we always be crying for the sunshine and then squandering it and crying for its return? Flowers might be more plentiful, more beautiful in another corner of the meadow, but to seek always for newer, more elaborate sensations while the fair day fades can hardly be wise. It would surely be better to find our ideal wherever we stand and to work for the arising of the good—because, even during delightful weather, *dukkha*, suffering, persists. This ideal, this Dhamma we learn and then recognize all about us, is what can confront and defeat dukkha.

We see these parks, fields, and woods as beautiful, as antidotes to our anxiety, but we ought not to search them for aesthetic pleasure alone and miss their urgent illustration of dukkha. The small, vulnerable creatures whose songs and dances we enjoy fly on toward winters without wisdom, toward summers in bondage to ignorance, while we—no less mortal, no less subject to pain—have heard something of the Dhamma and pause now in our lovely summer, considering whether we must fly likewise through cycles of dukkha. This is our real advantage: the possibility of perceiving and pursuing truth—not mere longevity or strength. Looming over the crickets and the butterflies, we reflect on our own frailties and on the Dhamma that is our priceless human inheritance. Shall we go on through our fortunate hours gazing and admiring only, never acting with confidence?

Soon after the Buddha reached full enlightenment he decided to teach the Dhamma, perceiving that there were those in the world who could understand this liberating truth if they heard it. If we hear, and if we begin to see how his words so wisely describe and explain our daily experience, we will perhaps be moved to conduct ourselves in body, speech, and mind in the way he taught. Conditions fly loose everywhere, like these million seeds swirling in the careless wind; and conditions undirected, uncontrolled, give rise to mortality and sorrow endlessly. But wholesome conditions deliberately brought together—actions done in the direction of Dhamma—give rise to greater welfare for living beings. The Buddha opened the gates to liberation, to the deathless Nibbana, by teaching this Dhamma, showing this path, and encouraging long-bewildered seekers of the good to seek it here.

This field today smells sweet; the briars are manageable; yellow butterflies race around us; and at each slow step of ours grasshoppers and other tiny creatures pop off their perches to either side. We hear all around, at different distances, the chattering of insects and birds—nothing especially enchanting, only imperfect suggestions of beauty. We walk along, considering these perceptions, noticing how they overlie one another, building a world up for a moment's contemplation. We remember the ravaging winter, think of the next one not so far away, and ponder the impermanence of this moment of sunshine. Our steps, we now know, must be more careful, strong, and sure—not precipitate or hasty but aimed deliberately at the good.

We do not, it may be, see very far in the hot air of this summer day. And we do not, it may be, perceive with unshakable certainty the truth of the Dhamma. But assuredly our senses tell us how causes flame up in every moment, how friendliness and generosity beautify the mind, how restraint of the unworthy thought makes room for what is worthy. Reflecting on this much knowledge, and looking deeper with the Buddha's guidance, we gain the faith to venture onward in the right direction. It is not a matter, after all, of finding meadows still more flowery than this one but of forsaking all self-made folly wherever we walk.

Around us countless delicate seeds are blowing—tiny clouds adrift in vast currents—and above them the greater clouds roll under sun and unseen stars and inconceivable levels of being. How we have drifted, too, through many dizzy years! But now we begin to find vital truths within these summer sensations. This body will carry us a little further, surely. These good aspirations will move us toward honorable efforts.

The sun burns down on the wide green field, and we begin to get a little too warm, so at length, being reminded anew of impermanence, we set off without haste toward our home, our duties, and other scenes of contemplation. Across the fragrant field, then under great trees, and on down the sidewalks of our neighborhood we go through unmeasured immensities of time, our feet falling steadily on the earth.

As we walk from block to block many facts and symbols rise

up before us. So many signs display the truth. We get a little tired on our way, it is true, but to whom would we complain? All living beings, like us, are sailing on the wind of their own actions. We see children trotting about on these lawns with cheerful innocence, while their parents, though weighted with their own sorrows, wave at us and call a greeting. We smile and wave back at them, and our course through time grows a little steadier. The power of our own action, most wonderfully, can remake us into what we choose. Everywhere around us, whether understood or not, causes go on rolling the seasons, and causes swell to grief or gladness for every creature.

Once in the snow we looked about longingly for a path and saw only hints in nature's solemn motions, but now in a summer that vanishes just as surely we discover we have been living all along among brilliant markers. The Buddha's teachings have reached us now; the singing of crickets has reached us; and our senses become alert to wonder. Whatever the reckless skies and earth may do, it is virtue that calls up the finest season, concentration that brings the sun on our soil, and wisdom that perfects the noblest fruit.

So You Want to Be a Buddhist?

Daniel Menaker

Finally, you may now have decided you'd like to call yourself a Buddhist, or at least pretend to be one. In some circles that's pretty cool, they say. But to pull it off you'll need to know the lingo. So Dan Menaker has prepared a helpful list of Buddhist terms you can toss off at your next trendy cocktail party. (What, and the amount, you choose to drink will depend on which school of Buddhism you've decided to pretend to espouse, so be sure to make your choice match your lifestyle.)

So you want to be a Buddhist? Who doesn't? It's easy and also fun, especially if, like me and most Americans who enjoy relaxing on the deck and talking about Buddhism, you know very little about it. I mean the kind of people who, when you get a little ticked at them for breaking the gears of the bicycle they borrowed from you yesterday, say, "Could you please try to be a little more Buddhist about this?" or when they wonder if there really is such a thing as reincarnation hope to come back as a wealthy beagler.

The first thing you have to do is renounce desire. But since you want to renounce desire, that's desire in and of itself! So renounce the desire to renounce desire and you can do whatever you please, like try to get back in good with your old girlfriend

Tawnee, plus become an ipso facto Buddhist at the same time. Sweet, no? And the real Buddhists can't object, because they are enjoined to universal kindliness and have to keep on grinning that real-Buddhist grin.

The next thing you have to do is decide on whether you're going to say "BOOdist," "BUUHdist" (rhymes with "WOODist") or "BUDDist" (rhymes with "FUDDist" and also "DUDDist"). I have to say that for my money the first sounds low-rent, kind of Casper the Ghost, and the last sounds a little floral and also could be heard as "BUTTist," so the second it is, even though in order to say it that way you have to purse your lips in a sissy manner.

O.K.—you're well on your way. The next thing you have to do is know some terminology or pretend to know it, so that you can use it when the conversational waters get heavy.

Dharma: This is a great word to use in practically any sentence of gravity because it has so many meanings (I think). It's something good, a good quality of a person or a regulation of how you act, if I'm not mistaken. When an NBA star, especially one of the very tall ones, reads to any group of fetching or marginal or, especially, reviled illiterate people, that is a possible example of dharma in action. If you're still not sure what it means, be serene, be a Buddhist about it, and that could well be dharma in action, too. Helpful hint: The "h" in "dharma" is silent—and a good thing, too.

Karma: This is the most-said amateur-Buddhist word by a long shot. You can apply it to absolutely anything that happens to a person. For instance, if you enjoy infomercials and decide to order Moving Men, those plastic discs with discs of orange foam set in them that you put furniture legs on so that you can push or pull heavy items from room to room, that becomes part of your karma, and might be one of the reasons you come back in your next life as a dray horse. "Karma" will fit an infinite number of occasions but is best used sparingly, lest it deteriorate into a synonym for "whatever." To summarize: karma is the things you choose to do but don't have any choice about, like throwing down with Tawnee and then not spending the night—it's free will and fate all rolled into one hell of a complex concept, and if you don't get it, that's part of your karma, too.

Note: Karma can be troubling to those who are tempted by more practical-seeming theories of causation. Let's say you get pneumonia, God forbid. "It's your karma," a dilettante (and for all I know a real) Buddhist might say. "It's your staphylococcus," a doctor might say. But you can't beat karma, I'm afraid, because it's one of those oceanic ideas that drowns everything else, as in "It's your karma to have your staphylococcus."

Shawarma: N/A.

Reincarnation: It gets really tricky when you add to the pneumonia example that the staphylococcus in question might be the reincarnation of Nero or Senator Joseph McCarthy. Yes, it's true, from all reports I've heard: Buddhism holds that after you die you come back as someone else or an animal or even an animalcule. But you're still you, if you and your past incarnations see what I and mine mean. If you have good compounded karma from past lives and your present life, you come back on a higher plane—like the previous incarnations who are now Derek Jeter and Diane Sawyer. If you were rotten, you might be a vole or an asp or a dung beetle.

Questions: Do you come back as yourself if your life has been a karmic wash? Or is there a tiebreaker or sudden-death overtime? Wouldn't it be awful to come back and realize you're still Trent Lott? Wouldn't it be cool to start over again with Tawnee (assuming she doesn't come back as a millipede, as she deserves to, for dumping you, even though it's true that you didn't take your socks off and then ran out on her that night)?

Meditation: You sit quietly in a certain position and breathe in a certain way and try to empty your mind, all as part of the effort to renounce desire and seek the enlightenment that will bolster your standing in the karma league. It also really helps in the effort to get your thoughts off Tawnee.

Akimcanyayata: "Atayaynacmika" spelled backward.

Nirvana:

That's right—that's the definition of nirvana (which is what you are striving to achieve as a Buddhist), as I understand it: a big fat nothing. You get so enlightened, your desire is in such giga-renunciation, that you don't have to be reincarnated anymore, at least if you don't want to be. You are obliterated, released from the cycle of pain and suffering. No more 932 combined SAT scores, no more running out of cold beer, no more hold music, no more caramelized reductions and eggplant coulis, no more big electronic highway signs that tell you how fast you're going, no more irritable bowel syndrome, no more pining for Tawnee, no more Chuck Norris reruns, no more copy-center jobs, no more silage combustion, no more air turbulence, no more periodontics, no more "funny" lists. No more post-coital escape panics.

No more coition, either. Hmmm. No more ruby-throated hummingbirds, no more whoever Alison Krauss comes back as, no more soft-serve ice cream, no more first kisses, no more boogie-boarding, no more finding a cold beer in the fridge, no more throwing down with anyone whatsoever ever, no more homecomings. No more whatever the future holds in store: teleportation holidays, mansions created from utility fog and nanotechnology swarms, invisibility. No second chance with Tawnee.

If you were a Buddhist, I guess it would be up to you, and not.

Contributors

AJAHN AMARO was born in England and trained in the Thai Forest tradition. He studied with the famed Vipassana teacher Ajahn Chah and with Ajahn Sumedho, perhaps the senior Western-born teacher in the tradition. He is now co-abbot of Abhayagiri Buddhist Monastery. The book excerpted here, *Small Boat, Great Mountain: Theravadan Reflections on the Natural Great Perfection,* can be obtained free of charge from Abhayagiri Monastery, or downloaded from www. abhyagiri.org.

EZRA BAYDA, with his teacher Charlotte Joko Beck, is at the forefront of the movement to present the essential truths of Buddhism free of traditional trappings or terminology. He lives and teaches at the San Diego Zen Center and is the author of two books: *Being Zen* and *At Home in the Muddy Water.*

MARTHA BECK has been called "the best-known life coach in America," and writes a monthly column for *O* magazine. She is the author of *Finding Your Own North Star, The Joy Diet,* and *Expecting Adam.* She lives in Phoenix, Arizona, with her family. If you go to www.marthabeck.com you'll find a photo gallery of her son Adam, the subject of her article in this book, and you'll see why she's so happy she made the choice she did.

TARA BRACH is a clinical psychologist and meditation teacher who says that every day in her practice she sees the pain people suffer because of their feelings of unworthiness. That has led her to combine the two sides of her work in a path she calls Radical Acceptance. She is the founder of the Insight Meditation Community of Washington, D.C., and a cofounder of the Washington Buddhist Peace Fellowship.

PEMA CHÖDRÖN is one of Western Buddhism's most beloved teachers. A student of Chögyam Trungpa, she took full nun's ordination in 1981, and as resident teacher at Gampo Abbey in Cape Breton, Nova Scotia, has worked to establish a Tibetan monastic tradition in the West. As a teacher, she has touched hundreds of thousands of people with her message that difficult states of mind can make us kinder and wiser, if only we have the courage not to flee them. Among her many books are the classics *The Wisdom of No Escape* and *The Places That Scare You.* Her most recent book is *Comfortable with Uncertainty.*

ANNE CUSHMAN is a contributing editor to *Tricycle: The Buddhist Review* and the coauthor of *From Here to Nirvana: The* Yoga Journal *Guide to Spiritual India.* She writes frequently on spiritually oriented travel, Buddhism, and yoga. She lives in northern California.

HOWARD CUTLER, M.D., turned a series of conversations with the Dalai Lama into *The Art of Happiness,* probably the best-selling Buddhist book ever published in English. Cutler's friendly tone and astute explanations helped introduce millions of people to the basic Buddhist teachings and to the warm heart of the Dalai Lama. That successful formula has been repeated in *The Art of Happiness at Work,* excerpted here. Cutler maintains a psychiatric practice in Phoenix.

OGYEN TRINLEY DORJE, THE 17TH KARMAPA, is leader of the Kagyü lineage, one of the four major schools of Tibetan Buddhism. Son of a nomadic family from eastern Tibet, he was recognized as the incarnation of the previous Karmapa at the age of seven and was installed at Tsurphu monastery in Tibet, the Karmapa's traditional seat. When he was fourteen his daring escape from Chinese-occupied Tibet received world-wide attention. He now lives in India, where he continues his studies under many of Tibetan Buddhism's greatest living masters.

NORMAN FISCHER is a poet, writer, and Zen teacher who thinks deeply about how Buddhism will progress in the West and how it can be integrated fully into our everyday lives. As a co-abbot of the San Francisco Zen Center, he held one of the most important positions in American Buddhism. He now leads the Everyday Zen Foundation, which he founded. He is the author of *Opening to You: Zen-Inspired Translations of the Psalms* and has published several books of poetry.

BARBARA GATES is a writer and editor who cofounded the Buddhist journal *Inquiring Mind*. Her book, *Already Home*, excerpted here, is based on years of research into the ecology and history of the Bay Area, where she lives, as well as her Buddhist practice and her experience with breast cancer.

NATALIE GOLDBERG is the author of many books, including *Long Quiet Highway*, *Thunder and Lightning*, and *Top of My Lungs*. Her classic book, *Writing Down the Bones*, introduced thousands of people to creativity as a spiritual practice. Her most recent book is *The Great Failure*. Goldberg has practiced Zen for thirty years and is ordained in Dainin Katagiri Roshi's lineage. She lives in New Mexico and teaches workshops and retreats at the Mabel Dodge Luhan House in Taos.

DANIEL GOLEMAN is a Ph.D. psychologist, a best-selling author, and probably American Buddhism's finest journalist. He has been nominated twice for the Pulitzer Prize. Goleman's book *Emotional Intelligence* introduced millions of people around the world to the very Buddhist concept that self-awareness and empathy are essential to success in life. He is a member of the Mind Life Institute, dedicated to building bridges between science and Buddhism, and has played a key role in a series of dialogues between Western scientists and the Dalai Lama.

DAVID GUY is the author of five books, including *The Autobiography of My Body* and *The Red Thread of Passion: Spirituality and the Paradox of Sex.* He teaches writing at Duke University and practices at the Chapel Hill Zen Center. The article in this anthology, "Trying to Speak," is from a larger, as-yet-unpublished work about his journey to address the death of his father, who died when he was a boy, and the fears it caused in him.

TENZIN GYATSO, THE 14TH DALAI LAMA, is the spiritual and temporal leader of the Tibetan people and the winner of the Nobel Peace Prize. Unique in the world today, he is a world statesman, national leader, spiritual teacher, and deeply learned theologian.

STEVE HAGEN is a Zen teacher who has dropped many of the traditional forms and images of Buddhism for fear that Western practitioners will be disturbed or fascinated by them. He received dharma transmission from Dainin Katagiri Roshi and is head teacher at the Diamond Field Meditation and Learning Center in Minneapolis. He is the author of *Buddhism Plain and Simple* and *Buddhism Is Not What You Think*, excerpted here.

THICH NHAT HANH is, along with the Dalai Lama, the leading proponent of a Buddhist approach to politics and social action. He is a Zen teacher, poet, and founder of the Engaged Buddhist movement. A well-known antiwar activist in his native Vietnam, he was nominated for the Nobel Peace Prize by Martin Luther King, Jr. The author of more than forty books, he resides at Buddhist practice centers in France and Vermont.

PICO IYER has written many books on the mystery and potential of living in a world of crossing cultures, including *Video Night in*

Kathmandu and *The Global Soul.* His most recent work, a series of explorations of Buddhism and the questions it raises for the world, is *Sun After Dark.*

DILGO KHYENTSE (1910–1991) was one of the most important figures in twentieth-century Tibetan Buddhism. An enormous man of equally enormous influence, he was a teacher and guide to many of the Tibetan teachers who became influential in the West. Dilgo Khyentse was of the last generation of Tibetan teachers who completed their training in Tibet before the Chinese invasion, and was a personal student of the great Mipham Rinpoche. He was considered one of the greatest Dzogchen masters of his time and taught Dzogchen to teachers of all schools of Tibetan Buddhism, including the Dalai Lama.

CHARLES JOHNSON is a novelist, scholar, and an important new voice in American Buddhism. He combines his study of Buddhism with a deep knowledge of the African American struggle for liberation, offering a powerful moral view of Buddhism in society. Johnson holds the S. Wilson and Grace M. Pollock Professorship for Excellence in English at the University of Washington in Seattle. He has been the recipient of many prestigious awards, including a Guggenheim Fellowship and a MacArthur Foundation grant. His novels include *Dreamer* and *Middle Passage,* for which he won a National Book Award.

JACK KORNFIELD is one of the West's leading Buddhist teachers. After many years studying Buddhism in Burma, Thailand, and India, he joined with Joseph Goldstein and Sharon Salzberg to found the Insight Meditation Society in Barre, Massachusetts, one of the largest Buddhist centers in America. He is also the founding teacher of the Spirit Rock Center in Woodacre, California. He holds a Ph.D. in clinical psychology and is the author of *A Path with Heart* and *After the Ecstasy, the Laundry.*

Jakusho (Bill) Kwong Roshi is a successor in the lineage of Shunryu Suzuki Roshi and has been teaching Zen in the United States and Europe for more than thirty years. He is the founder and abbot of the Sonoma Mountain Zen Center outside Santa Rosa, California. In 1995, he was given the title of *Dendo Kyoshi*, Zen teacher, by the Soto School in Japan, one of only nine Western Zen teachers to receive this honor.

Geri Larkin is the guiding teacher of the Still Point Zen Buddhist Temple in Detroit. She spent three years in the Maitreya Buddhist Seminary prior to her ordination in 1995. Her teacher was the Korean Zen master Samu Sunim. Larkin is the author of several books, including *First You Shave Your Head, Stumbling Toward Enlightenment,* and *The Still Point Dhammapada,* excerpted here. In her work as a consultant, she advises private companies and nonprofits on strategic and marketing plans.

Noah Levine may be America's most tattooed Buddhist teacher. Son of a famous Buddhist writer, he left his life of punk rock, drugs, and violence to finally embrace Buddhist practice. He is now director of the Mind Body Awareness Project, a nonprofit organization serving incarcerated youths in the Bay Area, and leads meditation retreats nationally.

Daizui MacPhillamy was the dharma heir of Jiyu-Kennett Roshi, one of the first Western female Zen masters. He was ordained by Kennett Roshi in 1973 at the age of twenty-eight and studied with her at Shasta Abbey in California until her death in 1996. He was then elected to succeed her as head of the Order of Buddhist Contemplatives, and served in that position until his death in April, 2003, of lymphatic cancer.

Michele Martin spent fifteen years in Nepal and India studying with Tibetan Buddhist teachers and working as a translator of oral and written Tibetan. She majored in Russian studies and attended university in Japan before taking up study of the Tibetan language. For the past two years she has translated for His Holiness the 17th Karmapa. She currently lives in upstate New York.

DANIEL MENAKER is the author of two collections of stories and a novel, *The Treatment.* He is editor-in-chief of Random House. As evidenced by his article here, "So You Want to Be a Buddhist?", he isn't a Buddhist but can talk a good game at a cocktail party.

SAKYONG MIPHAM is the eldest son of the renowned Tibetan teacher Chögyam Trungpa and the holder of the Shambhala Buddhist lineage he established. He was trained by many of the great Vajrayana teachers of the twentieth century and in 1995 was recognized as the incarnation of the revered Tibetan teacher Mipham the Great. He also holds the Kagyü and Nyingma lineages and is spiritual director of Shambhala, an international network of meditation and retreat centers. *Turning the Mind into an Ally*, excerpted here, is his first book. In addition to his studies and practice, he enjoys golf, running, horseback riding, and yoga.

DENNIS GENPO MERZEL ROSHI is the abbot of Kanzeon Zen Center in Utah and is president of the White Plum Lineage, established by the late Taizan Maezumi Roshi. In addition to traditional Zen practice, he has developed a technique he calls Big Mind Process, a blend of Jungian psychology and Zen that allows people to open their mind to a more universal consciousness in a relatively short period of time and without formal Zen training.

PHILLIP MOFFITT, a former editor-in-chief of *Esquire* magazine, abandoned the publishing world at age forty to devote himself full-time to spiritual practice. He teaches Buddhist meditation at retreat centers throughout the United States, at which he also teaches a form of yoga called Mindful Movement. In 1994 he formed the Life Balance Institute, which helps people align their lives with their values. Moffitt writes the "Dharma Wisdom" column for *Yoga Journal.*

MAURA O'HALLORAN spent three years studying Zen at a small monastery in Tokyo and at a remote temple in northern Japan. Three months after she received dharma transmission, recognizing her realization and authorizing her to teach Zen, she died tragically in a bus accident in Thailand. She was twenty-seven years old. Maura O'Hallaron's story—her perseverance, her humanity, and her accomplishment—has been an inspiration to Western practitioners generally, and to women practitioners especially. In addition to the story published here, many of her letters and journal entries are available in a beautiful book entitled *Pure Heart, Enlightened Mind* (Tuttle, 1994).

PHILIP NOVAK is Professor of Philosophy and Religion at Dominican University in San Rafael, California, where he has taught for more than twenty years. He is the author of *The World's Wisdom*, a companion reader to Huston Smith's *The World's Religions,* and coauthor with Smith of *Buddhism: A Concise Introduction.*

BHIKKHU NYANASOBHANO is an American-born Buddhist monk who teaches at the Buddhadharma Meditation Center in Hinsdale, Illinois. He was an actor and playwright prior to his ordination in Thailand in 1987. Because his essays combine Buddhist philosophy with evocative description of nature, he has been called "American Buddhism's Thoreau." He is the author of *Landscapes of Wonder* and *Longing for Certainty.*

LARRY ROSENBERG grew up in a family with a long rabbinical tradition. He received a Ph.D. in social psychology from the University of Chicago, but dissatisfied with his job at Harvard Medical School, he turned to Buddhism. He studied Zen for eight years before finding his spiritual home in the Thai Forest tradition. He is the founder of the Cambridge Insight Meditation Center in

Cambridge, Massachusetts, and a senior teacher at the Insight Meditation Society. Rosenberg is the author of *Breath by Breath* and *Living in the Light of Death.*

ARAM SAROYAN is a poet, novelist, biographer, memoirist, and playwright. His prose books include *Last Rites*, a book about the death of his father, the playwright and short story writer William Saroyan; *Genesis Angels: The Saga of Lew Welch and the Beat Generation*; and *Rancho Mirage: An American Tragedy of Manners, Madness, and Murder*, a true crime Literary Guild selection. He is the recipient of two National Endowment for the Arts poetry awards—one of them for his controversial one-word poem "lighght." He is on the faculty of the Master of Professional Writing program at the University of Southern California.

HUSTON SMITH is the man who more than any other brought comparative religion to the American consciousness. He is not simply an academic or a synthesizer; the great strength of his work is that it is based in his own spiritual experience, as he has explored and practiced a variety of traditions in a search for the truths at the heart of all religion. Smith was the focus of a five-part PBS television series by Bill Moyers that introduced millions of viewers to his thought. Among his books is the classic *The World's Religions*, first published in 1958 and revised in 1991.

KIMBERLEY SNOW worked her way through graduate school as a chef, and after completing her Ph.D., taught English at the University of California, Santa Barbara, where she helped found the Women's Studies Program. In 1991, as described in her memoir, *In Buddha's Kitchen*, excerpted here, she moved to a Tibetan Buddhist community in northern California, where she spent the next six years studying Dzogchen with Chagdud Tulku, working in the kitchen, and editing dharma books. Today she lives in Santa Barbara with her husband, the poet Barry Spacks, and teaches workshops on writing and women's spirituality. She still goes for retreats to the Tibetan center and usually ends up working in the kitchen.

ROBERT THURMAN is the godfather of American Buddhism, a man of scholarship, spiritual conviction, energy, and accomplishment. At the age of twenty-four he became the first Westerner ordained as a Tibetan Buddhist monk. Deciding that Buddhist monkhood was not a viable career in the West, he disrobed, began a university career, and had a family (the actress Uma Thurman is his daughter). Thurman is professor of Indo-Tibetan Buddhist Studies at Columbia University and president of Tibet House U.S. He is a close friend of the Dalai Lama and a leader in the fight for Tibetan freedom. He is the author of scholarly works as well as books bringing a Buddhist perspective to contemporary life, including *Infinite Life: Seven Virtues for Living Well* and *Inner Revolution: Life, Liberty, and the Pursuit of Real Happiness.*

TRALEG KYABGON was enthroned at the age of two as the supreme head of Tra'gu monastery in Tibet. Following the Chinese invasion of Tibet he was taken to safety in India, where he continued the rigorous training of a *tulku,* or incarnate teacher. He is president of Kagyü E-Vam Buddhist Institute in Melbourne, Australia, and the author of *The Essence of Buddhism: An Introduction to Its Philosophy and Practice.* He has recently established the E-Vam Buddhist Institute, a retreat and conference facility in New York's Hudson Valley.

BONNIE MYOTAI TREACE is the first successor of John Daido Loori Roshi. She is vice-abbess of Zen Mountain Monastery in upstate New York and abbess of the Zen Center of New York City. Her background in English literature gives her teachings a strong literary and poetic component. She is active in women's and environmental issues, and after the World Trade Center attacks served as a chaplain aiding victims' families.

TSOKNYI RINPOCHE is a young Dzogchen teacher who has had a powerful effect on American Buddhism by introducing Dzogchen practice to practitioners of other traditions. Son of the great Dzogchen master Tulku Urgyen, he is the head of Ngesdön Ösel Ling monastery in Nepal. He is the author of two books: *Carefree Dignity* and *Fearless Simplicity*.

BRAD WARNER played in hardcore punk bands in the early eighties in his hometown of Wadsworth, Ohio, recording five albums under the band name Dimentia 13. He began to meditate at Kent State University, and then went to Japan to do special effects for low-budget monster movies and study Zen. He still works in film and television in Tokyo and also lectures and leads Zen meditation retreats. Warner has a Web site called "Shut Up and Sit," featuring a photo of himself in a monster costume.

DIANA WINSTON spent ten years in monasteries and retreat centers in the U.S. and Asia, including a year as a nun in a Burmese monastery. She has been teaching meditation to young people since 1993, and in 1995 she founded the Buddhist Alliance for Social Engagement, America's first urban Buddhist Peace Corps. She is a member of the Think Sangha, a think tank dedicated to writing and research on Buddhist social issues.

Credits

Buddhism: A Concise Introduction by Huston Smith and Philip Novak. Copyright © 2003 by Huston Smith and Philip Novak. Reprinted by permission of HarperCollins Publishers Inc.

"This is It" by Aram Saroyan. First published in the September, 2003 Shambhala Sun. Copyright © 2003 by Aram Saroyan. Used by permission of Aram Saroyan.

Already Home: A Topography of Spirit and Place by Barbara Gates. Copyright © 2003 by Barbara Gates. Reprinted by arrangement with Shambhala Publications, Inc., www.shambhala.com

"Butterfly Kiss for the Buddha" by Anne Cushman. First published in the Summer, 2003 issue of Tricycle: The Buddhist Review. Copyright © 2003 by Anne Cushman.

No Beginning, No End: The Ultimate Heart of Zen by Jakusho Kwong, edited by Peter Levitt. Copyright © 2003 by Jakusho Kwong. Used by permission of Harmony Books, a division of Random House, Inc.

Buddhism Is Not What You Think: Finding Freedom Beyond Beliefs by Steve Hagen. Copyright © 2003 by Steve Hagen. Reprinted by permission of HarperCollins Publishers Inc.

Hardcore Zen: Punk Rock, Monster Movies, and the Truth about Reality by Brad Warner. Copyright © 2003 by Brad Warner. Reprinted with permission from Wisdom Publications, 199 Elm Street, Somerville, MA 02144 USA. www.hardcorezen.com.

Wide Awake: A Buddhist Guide for Teens by Diana Winston. Copyright © 2003 by Diana Winston. Used by permission of Perigee Books, an imprint of Penguin Group (USA) Inc.

Turning the Mind into an Ally by Sakyong Mipham. Copyright © 2003 by Sakyong Mipham. Used by permission of Riverhead Books, an imprint of Penguin Group (USA) Inc.

Destructive Emotions: How Can We Overcome Them? A Scientific Dialogue with the Dalai Lama by Daniel Goleman, narrator. Copyright © 2003 by The Mind and Life Institute. Used by permission of Bantam Books, a division of Random House, Inc.

"The Test of Truth" by Larry Rosenberg. First published in the Fall, 2003 issue of *Tricycle: The Buddhist Review*. Copyright © 2003 by Larry Rosenberg.

Buddhism from Within: An Intuitive Introduction to Buddhism by Rev. Daizui MacPhillamy. Copyright © 2003 by Order of Buddhist Contemplatives. Used by permission of Shasta Abbey Press, Mt. Shasta, CA.

Music in the Sky: The Life, Art, and Teachings of the 17th Gyalwa Karmapa, Ogyen Trinley Dorje by Michele Martin. Copyright © 2003 by Michele Martin. Used by permission of Snow Lion Publications.

"Elegy for Everything" by Martha Beck. First published in the Fall, 2003 *Tricycle: The Buddhist Review*. Copyright © 2003 by Martha Beck.

The Art of Happiness at Work by the Dalai Lama and Howard Cutler. Copyright © 2003 by His Holiness the Dalai Lama & Howard Cutler, MD. Used by permission of Riverhead Books, an imprint of Penguin Group (USA) Inc.

"The Heart's Intention" by Phillip Moffitt. From the "Dharma Wisdom" column of the September/October issue of *Yoga Journal.* Copyright © 2003 by Phillip Moffitt.

In Buddha's Kitchen by Kimberley Snow. Copyright © 2003 by Kimberley Snow. Reprinted by arrangement with Shambhala Publications, Inc., www.shambhala.com

The Still Point Dhammapada: Living the Buddha's Essential Teachings by Geri Larkin. Copyright © 2003 by Still Point Buddhist Temple. Reprinted by permission of HarperCollins Publishers Inc.

Taking Our Places: The Buddhist Path to Truly Growing Up by Norman Fischer. Copyright © 2003 by Norman Fischer. Reprinted by permission of HarperCollins Publishers Inc.

Small Boat, Great Mountain: Theravadan Reflections on the Great Natural Perfection by Ajahn Amaro. Copyright © 2003 by Ajahn Amaro. Reprinted by permission of Abhayagiri Monastery, Redwood Valley, CA.

The Hundred Verses of Advice of Padampa Sangye by Dilgo Khyentse. First publised in the Winter, 2003 *Buddhadharma: The Practitioner's Quarterly*. Copyright © 2003 by Sechen Publications

"The Great Spring" by Natalie Goldberg. First published in the January, 2003 *Shambhala Sun*. Copyright © 2003 by Natalie Goldberg.

"The Threshold" by Bonnie Myotai Treace. First published in the Summer, 2003 *Mountain Record: The Zen Practitioner's Journal.* Copyright © 2003 by Bonnie Myotai Treace.

Turning the Wheel: Essays on Buddhism and Writing by Charles Johnson. Copyright © 2003 by Charles Johnson. Reprinted with the permission of Scribner, an imprint of Simon & Schuster Adult Publishing Group.

"Depression's Truth," by Traleg Kyabgon. First published in the March, 2003 *Shambhala Sun*. Copyright © 2003 by Traleg Kyabgon.

Dharma Punx: A Memoir by Noah Levine. Copyright © 2003 by Noah Levine. Reprinted by permission of HarperCollins Publishers Inc.

"How We Get Hooked" by Pema Chödrön. First published in the March, 2003 Shambhala Sun. Copyright © 2003 by Pema Chödrön.

The Path of Being Human by Dennis Genpo Merzel. Copyright © 2003 by Dennis Genpo Merzel. Reprinted by arrangement with Shambhala Publications, Inc., www.shambhala.com

"Annie Mirror Heart" by Maura O'Halloran. First published in the September, 2003 *Shambhala Sun*. Copyright © 2003 by Ruth L. O'Halloran.

"Trying to Speak: A Personal History of Stage Fright" by David Guy. First published in the Summer, 2003 *Tricycle: The Buddhist Review*. Copyright © 2003 by David Guy.

Radical Acceptance: Embracing Your Life with the Heart of a Buddha by Tara Brach, Ph.D. Copyright © 2003 by Tara Brach. Used by permission of Bantam Books, a division of Random House, Inc.

At Home in the Muddy Water by Ezra Bayda. Copyright © 2003 by Ezra Bayda. Reprinted by arrangement with Shambhala Publications, Inc., www.shambhala.com

Creating True Peace: Ending Violence in Yourself, Your Family, Your Community and the World by Thich Nhat Hanh. Copyright © 2003 by Thich Nhat Hanh. Reprinted with the permission of The Free Press, a Division of Simon & Schuster Adult Publishing Group.

"Prayer Flags and Refugees" by Pico Iyer. First published in the November, 2003 issue of *Condé Nast Traveler*. Copyright © 2003 by Pico Iyer.

"Proof of Our Goodness" by Robert Thurman. First published in the September, 2003 *Shambhala Sun*. Copyright © 2003 by Robert Thurman.

"A Mind Like Sky" by Jack Kornfield. First published in the May, 2003 *Shambhala Sun*. Copyright © 2003 by Jack Kornfield.

Fearless Simplicity: The Dzogchen Way of Living Freely in a Complex World by Tsoknyi Rinpoche. Compiled and translated by Erik Pema Kunsang and Marcia Binder Schmidt and edited with Kerry Moran. Copyright © 2003 by Tsoknyi Rinpoche and Rangjung Yeshe Publications. Used by permission of Rangjung Yeshe Publications.

Longing for Certainty: Reflections on the Buddhist Life by Bhikkhu Nyanasobhano. Copyright © 2003 Bhikkhu Nyanasobhano. Reprinted with permission of Wisdom Publications, 199 Elm Street, Somerville, MA 02144 U.S.A., www.wisdompubs.org

"So You Want to be a Buddhist?" by Daniel Menaker. First published in the January, 2003 issue of the *Shambhala Sun*. Copyright © 2003 by Dan Menaker.

About the Editor

Melvin McLeod is editor-in-chief of the award-winning *Shambhala Sun,* North America's oldest and most widely read Buddhist magazine. The *Shambhala Sun* offers accessible, authentic Buddhist teachings and examines all aspects of modern life from a contemplative perspective. He is also editor-in-chief of *Buddhadharma: The Practitioner's Quarterly,* an in-depth, practice-oriented journal for Buddhists of all traditions. A former correspondent for the Canadian Broadcasting Corporation, he is a student of the late Chögyam Trungpa Rinpoche.